UNIVERSITY OF NORTH CAROLINA
STUDIES IN THE ROMANCE LANGUAGES AND LITERATURES

Number 84

THE ARTIFICIAL PARADISES
IN FRENCH LITERATURE

THE ARTIFICIAL PARADISES
IN FRENCH LITERATURE

I. THE INFLUENCE OF OPIUM AND HASHISH ON THE LITERATURE OF FRENCH ROMANTICISM AND *LES FLEURS DU MAL*

BY

EMANUEL J. MICKEL JR.

CHAPEL HILL

THE UNIVERSITY OF NORTH CAROLINA PRESS

DEPÓSITO LEGAL: V. 2.647 - 1969

ARTES GRÁFICAS SOLER, S. A. — JÁVEA, 30 — VALENCIA (8) — 1969

To Kathleen

ACKNOWLEDGMENTS

It is with great gratitude that I take this opportunity to thank Professor Alfred G. Engstrom for his patience, interest, and many helpful corrections and suggestions. Only those who have had the pleasure of working with Professor Engstrom can appreciate his ability to awaken one to the beauty in literature and life.

I should also like to express my debt to the Interlibrary Loan Centers of the Universities of North Carolina and Nebraska for their cooperation and efficiency in locating and obtaining important bibliographic sources used in this study.

I also wish to thank the administrator of the Smith Fund and the Research Council of the University of Nebraska for grants which enabled me to purchase materials otherwise unavailable, and for a Summer Research Fellowship from the University of Nebraska, which allowed time for preparation of the final portion of the study. I am also indebted to Research and Advanced Studies of Indiana University for a generous grant in support of this project.

My greatest debt, however, is to my wife, Kathleen, who typed the first copy of this work and whose patience and understanding created an atmosphere in which concentrated study was possible.

TABLE OF CONTENTS

	Page
ACKNOWLEDGMENTS	9
INTRODUCTION	13

Chapter

I.	Medical aspects of Opium and Hashish	19
II.	Historical consideration of Opium and Hashish	34
III.	Opium and hashish in the literary society of the nineteenth century	58
IV.	Opium and Hashish in the Literature of French Romanticism	81
V.	Opium, Hashish and Baudelaire	127

BIBLIOGRAPHY	201
INDEX	209

INTRODUCTION

The present study is the initial volume of Professor Mickel's longer work in progress on the Artificial Paradises in French literature. I know of no comparable publication. Earlier studies have considered individual figures such as De Quincey or Coleridge or Poe or Baudelaire or Gautier or Balzac, or even several of these together; but no major published investigation to my knowledge has hitherto traced the complex influence of drugs upon a whole national literature. This first volume of Professor Mickel's study affords a detailed and carefully organized examination of the medical importance, preparation, and technical use of the drugs here concerned, their historical and literary background, their appearance and influence in French society and French Romantic literature and, finally, a demonstration of their significance in the imagery and interpretation of *Les Fleurs du Mal* that should be a revelation to readers of Baudelaire.

In these pages appear two remarkable flowers whose plants have for ages worked their magic upon the human mind and senses. In a way, they recall the Blue Flower of Novalis and German Romanticism, but they have a less ideal side and they have exerted a more lasting influence. One is the white and blue-purple blossom of "the Poppy" *(Papaver somniferum),* the Sleep-bearer, associated from ancient times with the gods of sleep and oblivion — the source of hallucinatory opium, long considered a panacea for human suffering and sorrow. The other is the unimpressive-appearing yellowish flower spike or raceme of the hashish plant *(Cannabis sativa),* associated over many centuries with the vision of Paradise.

Opium and hashish with their gifts of hallucination and dream came into special prominence in Western letters during the period of European Romanticism, when their use was fashionable among those interested in visionary experience and in the search for an ideal reality beyond the material world. Their fascination has continued in later times and received further literary attention, especially under the influence of Surrealist theory and practice and of esoteric and psychic probings into the mysteries of individual consciousness. The drug-cults of our own day are evidence of the continuing quest for Paradise by pharmacy, and the present volume has all the more pertinence in view of the current popularity of this restless and often dangerous experimentation.

Professor Mickel's study is divided into five chapters, of which the first concerns medical and technical matters. Here we find description of the plants from which opium and hashish are derived, the methods of their extraction, details as to the various ways in which the drugs are taken, the exotic vocabulary related to them, their hallucinative effects and the aftermath, and what is known of the physical and psychological results of their continued use.

The second chapter traces the historical and literary background of the drugs. We learn that, according to Galen, among the Egyptians Thoth used opium and that the poppy was supposedly created by Ceres to bring sleep in her sorrow when her daughter Proserpina was carried off to the Underworld by Pluto. Possible or clear references to opium are noted from the *Odyssey* and from Vergil, Ovid and Lucian (the description of the Isle of Dreams in the *True History*) —from Hippocrates, Theophrastus, Pliny, Celsus and Galen among the ancient doctors and herbalists— from Avicenna, Maimonides and Averroes — and from Chaucer, Boccaccio and Shakespeare. One might add also the notable references of Ronsard. The use of opium spread in later years when it was widely prescribed in European medicine, and by the early nineteenth century the opium trade in Europe had grown to vast proportions and the drug was exerting an increasingly significant influence upon men of letters. Hashish is harder to trace, though it was cited by Herodotus. It appears most imaginatively in Western literature in the mediaeval legend of the Old Man of the Mountain and his Assassins, whose curious history is pursued by Professor Mickel from the year 1090 to the nineteenth-century versions of Silvestre de Sacy and J. von Hammer.

Chapter Three traces rising French interest in opium and hashish to the influence of a cult for the exotic East (inspired in part by travel accounts and the translation of the *Mille et une nuits* and, later, by Napoleon's Egyptian campaign) and to the growing popularity of various esoteric philosophies that sought the Greater Reality, universal correspondences, and the like. The use of drugs is thus seen as flourishing in a world of semi-mystics, occultists, magnetists and spiritualists. Here we learn of the theories and experiments of the eminent doctor Moreau de Tours of the asylum of Bicêtre (author of *Du haschisch et de l'aliénation mentale* [1845]) and his associate Dr. Aubert-Roche, and of the famous and elusive "Club des Hachichins," so colorfully described by Théophile Gautier. The effects of hashish are depicted in considerable detail and shown to have afforded the Romantics an escape from boring reality into a realm of semi-mystical perceptions that seemed to free the imagination and to reach deep into the human spirit.

A fourth chapter concerns the influence of opium and hashish upon the French Romantic novel, brief fiction, poetry and exotic essay, as evidenced in the writings of Balzac, Flaubert (seen here in the environs of Romanticism for his conception of "La spirale"), Édouard Puycoussin, Dumas *père*, Théophile Gautier, Gérard de Nerval, and Eugène Sue. Notable in this discussion are such examples as Balzac's "Le Dôme des Invalides: Hallucination"; the chapter of Dumas' *Le Comte de Monte Cristo* called "Simbad le Marin," which is related to the motif of the Old Man of the Mountain, whose story it retells; Théophile Gautier's "La pipe d'opium," "Le hachich," "Le Club des Hachichins," and possibly "Le pied de momie" (in which the *pâte verte* of the figurine is seen by Professor Mickel as imaginatively linked with hashish); Gérard de Nerval's haunting treatment of the double in the story of the Caliph Hakem in his *Voyage en Orient;* and the chapter entitled "Opium" of Eugène Sue's novel, *Atar-Gull*.

Details from these and other writings afford evidence of the persistent influence exerted by opium and hashish upon men of letters and the imaginative literature of the Romantic period in France. Some of the descriptions of drug hallucination are especially vivid in their representation of the expansion of ordinary consciousness into a world of apparently ideal vision and are worthy of comparison with the best writings that we have on the subject. There is recurrent, moreover, a sense of longing for transcendent reality, analogous in a way, as we have implied earlier, to the ideal of Heinrich von Ofterdingen in German Romanticism; but the white and blue-purple poppy and the yellowish flower-cluster of *Cannabis sativa* are symptoms of a search that seems often to be more despairing and less innocent than that called to mind by Novalis's Blue Flower.

Finally, the chapter on "Opium, Hashish and Baudelaire" provides the longest and in some respects the most fascinating part of the book, not merely because it is concerned with one of the most significant of all volumes of French poetry, but more precisely because of the unexpected illumination it throws upon many of Baudelaire's most famous poems. In this concluding chapter Professor Mickel has related the verses of *Les Fleurs du Mal* and the prose poems of the *Petits poëmes en prose* to the texts of *Les paradis artificiels* and Baudelaire's other writings concerned with his drug experience, which is identified unequivocally, with detailed evidence, as outright drug addiction. These pages show clearly the remarkable influence of Baudelaire's familiarity with drugs upon the inspiration and composition of *Les Fleurs du Mal* —possibly even upon the title and the dedication to Théophile Gautier. Precise details in epithet, phrase and imagery are cited from numerous poems to show the startling pertinence of drug reference to their interpretation and meaning. There is also persuasive evidence of Baudelaire's frequent description under the same expression of the charms of the artificial paradises and the charms of women — both spiritually dangerous to mankind and to the poet.

These interpretations will not win complete assent from all readers; but, whether one is willing to see all the passages cited as exemplifying the proclaimed dual reference or finds them on occasion merely applying more generally the language of drug hallucination to the varied subject-matter of the poems, the chapter on "Opium, Hashish and Baudelaire" once read is not likely to be forgotten. One has only to consider the similarities recurrent in the poems and in the essays on opium and hashish to see the significance of the relationships established. All in all, the chapter affords a very impressive demonstration of its thesis, and an attentive reader returning to Baudelaire will hardly fail to see more in the poems of *Les Fleurs du Mal* than he has seen before, and to see many of them in a quite different way.

Professor Mickel's second volume will bring his investigation of the Artificial Paradises in French literature down to the present time and will of necessity be concerned, not only with opium and hashish, but also with other drugs employed in man's continuing search for Paradise by hallucination. The literature is far greater in scope than that of the earlier period. It will be of interest to see if it provides moral and psychological insights as powerful as Baudelaire's and if it shows that drugs have in more recent times exerted as great an influence upon significant literature as the present study shows them to have exerted upon the poetry of *Les Fleurs du Mal*.

ALFRED G. ENGSTROM

Chapter I

MEDICAL ASPECTS OF OPIUM AND HASHISH

A. Opium

"Poppy" is the name given to plants of several genera of the family known as *papaveraceae*. It is especially used for the type known as *papaver*, a genus which contains annual and perennial erect herbs of some ninety different species, mostly native to central and southern Europe and temperate Asia. This genus of the family has lobed or cut leaves and generally long-stalked, regular, showy flowers whose sepals and petals readily fall off as the flower opens. The numerous varieties of poppy plants bear beautiful, delicate flowers of red, purple, white, and varieties of these hues. The plant, the ovary of which develops into a short, many-seeded capsule, contains a milky juice. Although each species of the poppy is capable of yielding opium, only the *papaver somniferum*, the opium poppy, produces the drug in significant amounts.[1] The *papaver somniferum*, which stands approximately five to six feet in height, has white or blue-purple flowers and is native to Greece and the Orient. The best variety grows in the tropics where there is not an excessive rainfall, although France

---

[1] Opium is graded by its morphine content. According to Brown, any drug containing less than 9-1/2% morphine is not considered to be opium. Of opium's many alkaloids only three have wide clinical use: morphine, codeine, and papaverine. (Thorvald T. Brown, *The Enigma of Drug Addiction* [Springfield, Ill., 1961].)

and Germany have cultivated a type of the plant which yields a substantial amount of morphine. [2]

The method of extracting opium from the poppy capsule has changed very little since that described by Dioscorides in the first century A. D. The unripened capsule of the poppy is cut gently with a knife that usually has several blades. The creamy exudation seeps out of the horizontal cuts, is caught on a leaf, and allowed to dry until it becomes a chestnut brown. This chestnut colored substance has a sickening odor and a bitter, nauseous taste. The soft opium is molded into round lumps or irregular flattened cakes and is again allowed to dry before being sent to market. If the opium is to be used for smoking, the raw opium is placed in a solution of water and boiled slowly until it dissolves. The solution is then filtered through gauze to get rid of impurities and to reduce it, by evaporation, to a sirupy consistency. After further manipulation, heating, dissolving, and filtering, the mass is reduced through evaporation to a substance of thick and hard consistency. This process of repeated heating and filtering is designed to rid the opium of its bitter taste, pungent odor, and toxic elements. To improve its taste and smell, the product is allowed to age and ferment for three months or more. If the aging is done properly, the opium takes on an aroma which is unique and much appreciated by the expert smokers. [3]

Through the years opium has been consumed in various ways. At present, users prefer injection of morphine or heroin, two opium derivatives. Injection directly into a vein is preferred to a subcutaneous injection because of the greater sensation that results. In the nineteenth century, however, opium was more frequently taken in a solution called laudanum [4] or smoked by

---

[2] Some of the areas which have been famous for their opium are Persia, Turkey (Smyrna), Egypt and India. Both Brouardel and Réveil agree that most of the opium used in France during the middle of the 19th century was imported from Turkey and Egypt by the port of Marseille. Réveil states that "l'opium de l'Inde ne nous arrive pas en France, ou du moins il n'y est pas consommé ..." (P. O. Réveil, *Recherches sur l'opium* [Paris, 1856], p. 21.)

[3] The amount of morphine in the prepared opium is generally small —from five to nine percent— although it is sometimes as much as twelve percent. (I. J. Bensussan, *L'opium* [Paris, 1946].)

[4] Although the term laudanum dates from Paracelsus, it is believed that there was no opium in the preparation which he called by this name. How-

means of an opium pipe. Though Paracelsus apparently did not use opium in his laudanum preparation, it is this name which came to designate various preparations which contained the drug.

One of the most popular solutions was formulated by the English physician, Thomas Sydenham, whose laudanum is described by Bensussan as a "... breuvage calmant, jaune foncé, titré à 1% de morphine qui résulte du traitement par l'alcool aromatisé, par la cannelle et la girofle, d'un mélange d'opium et de safran." [5] Another famous formula which Brouardel describes was that of the Abbé Rousseau,[6] physician of Louis XIV:

> Le Laudanum de Rousseau ... est un vin d'opium obtenu par fermentation. 200 grammes d'opium sont dissous dans 3000 grammes d'eau; on ajoute 600 grammes de miel blanc et 40 grammes de levure, et on expose le tout à une température constante de 25 à 30° jusqu'à ce que la fermentation soit terminée; on évapore ensuite jusqu'à réduction à 600 grammes, et on ajoute 200 grammes d'alcool ... Il contient donc exactement une fois plus d'opium que le laudanum de Sydenham.[7]

The famous English Black Drop was a preparation of opium, vinegar, saffron, sugar and nutmeg. In his *Opiologia* of 1682,

---

ever, many of his other preparations contained opium, and it is still believed that he was referring to an opium solution in his famous statement, "... ladanum vocatur arcanum nostrum quod omnia ista superat ubi in propinqua mors est." It was actually Thomas Sydenham's laudanum preparation which became famous as an opium solution. Several derivations have been suggested for the name. It has been suggested that the term comes from the Latin participle, *laudandum* (something to be praised), or that it is a corrupted form deriving from the Latin verb *laudare*, or that it is from *l'anodynum* (a corruption of *anodynum*).

[5] Bensussan, p. 38.

[6] Leclerc writes of the Abbé Rousseau: "L'abbé Rousseau fut d'abord missionnaire apostolique au Caire pendant sept ans, puis capucin; se destinant aux missions de l'Abyssinie, il étudia la médecine et la pharmacie, afin de pouvoir soigner les indigènes. Il reçut l'approbation de la cour de Rome et, de Colbert, une pension et un logement au louvre pour poursuivre ses études. ... Il se retira à Bologne dans un couvent de capucins, puis passa dans l'ordre de Cluny. Il mourut en 1694, âgé de cinquante et un ans." (H. Leclerc, "Origine et histoire du laudanum," *Bulletin de Sciences Pharmacologiques*, XXV [1918], 232.)

[7] P. Brouardel, *Opium, morphine, et cocaine* (Paris, 1906), p. 11.

Wedelius gives the reason for the various ingredients found in laudanum:

> On ajoute à l'opium diverses substances pour plusieurs raisons : 1. pour augmenter son action narcotique (jusquiame, safran); 2. pour la corriger (castoreum, camphre); 3. pour donner au médicament une consistence suffisante (perles, corail); 4. pour rendre son odeur agréable (ambre, musc). [8]

Numerous other formulas which were used could be cited. The principal ingredient is always opium, and the incidental ingredients used to give the desired consistency and odor vary in each formula.

Although less common today than other means of taking the drug, opium smoking was formerly one of the most popular methods of consumption. It is not known how early the practice was introduced into France, but Dr. P. E. Botta, in a thesis published in 1829, states that he urged its use among the French as less pernicious than swallowing or chewing opium. [9] The opium pipe seems to have changed little since Botta's description. It is generally some 50 to 65 centimeters in length (extreme measurements vary from 25 to 80 centimeters) and is made of bamboo, ivory, metal, wood, or jade. The end of the pipe on which one draws is made of amber, horn, ivory, or wood. The other end has a bowl made of terra cotta, jade, porcelaine, or any material able to withstand heat. The shape of the bowl, which has a cavity in its center for cooking the opium and inhaling its smoke, may be of any shape. [10]

By means of a needle about 15 to 20 centimeters in length, the smoker takes some 10 to 20 centigrams of chandoo (opium prepared for smoking) from his opium box [11] or tube and rolls it into a ball. Then he puts this ball over the flame of a small lamp until it softens and begins to become a bubble. The smoker

---

[8] Taken from Leclerc, p. 230.
[9] P. E. Botta, *De l'usage de fumer l'opium* (Paris, 1829).
[10] The pipe has been nicknamed variously "gong," "dream stick," "joy stick," etc.
[11] Botta states that opium is kept in "de petites boîtes de corne ou d'ivoire, que les Chinois recommandent de tenir sous l'eau" (Botta, p. 8).

then places the chandoo against the bowl and inhales deeply at regular intervals. The smoke is held in the lungs as long as possible in order to obtain maximum effect from the drug. Smokers lie on their sides and prefer to smoke in groups with a group leader who is an expert at rolling and cooking the opium, and who can heat the pipe to the proper temperature.

Bérenguier describes well the typical phases of an opium experience and the morning after:

> La fumée de l'opium n'a rien de l'âcreté de celle du tabac, sa saveur est assez semblable à celle des amandes. Après quelques pipes, le fumeur éprouve un sentiment de chaleur et d'excitation nerveuse, les mains sont agitées d'un léger tremblement, les pupilles se contractent par suite de la congestion cérébrale, le pouls devient plus fréquent, il bat 90 à 100 pulsations, la respiration est un peu haletante, un peu de chaleur se fait sentir à la peau. On éprouve des démangeaisons plus ou moins vives à la figure et dans diverses parties du corps, mais particulièrement aux ailes du nez et au scrotum. Une faiblesse musculaire envahit tout le corps, elle rend l'exercice pénible et le repos nécessaire, la démarche devient chancelante; l'épigastre est le siège de sensations agréables. Puis les sens entrent dans un demi sommeil pendant lequel l'esprit du fumeur donne aux objets qui l'entourent les formes les plus agréables ... à ce moment on éprouve une soif ardente. Après trois ou quatre heures de cet état, on succombe à un sommeil profond, sans rêves. Le lendemain, au réveil, on a la bouche sèche et mauvaise, la langue blanche, un peu de constipation et de somnolence; l'appétit tarde à venir; on a de la difficulté à uriner par suite d'un peu d'atonie de la vessie et les urines sont moins abondantes.[12]

The powers of opium and its dangers to the physical body and psyche of man have long been known. In 1701 John Jones, although not fully aware of the significance of opium addiction, writes of the extreme pain and danger of death when a person who has used opium "lavishly" suddenly ceases to take the drug. In our own time, *drug addiction* has been defined as follows by the World Health Organization:

---

[12] F. Bérenguier, *De l'opium des fumeurs* (Montpellier, 1883), p. 38.

> A state of periodic and chronic intoxication detrimental to the individual and to society, produced by the repeated consumption of a drug (natural or synthetic). Its characteristics include: (1) An overpowering desire or need (compulsion) to continue taking the drug and to obtain it by any means; (2) A tendency to increase the dose;[13] (3) A psychic (psychological) and sometimes a physical dependence[14] on the effects of the drug.[15]

Parallel to addiction, but different in important respects, is what is termed *habituation*. In the state of habituation one experiences a desire but not a compulsion to continue taking the drug for the sense of well-being which it causes. Secondly, there is little or no tendency to increase the dose; and most important, only a psychic and not a physical dependence develops.[16] Addiction is the result of prolonged use of the opiates, whereas habituation occurs from repeated use of hashish, cocaine, and numerous other drugs.

Abrupt withdrawal of the drug from one who is addicted results in an abstinence syndrome where measurable physiological changes can be noted. Wikler describes the abstinence syndrome as being...

> characterized by the appearance of well-defined autonomic changes, restlessness, insomnia, anxiety and intense craving for these agents. The intensity and time course of this syndrome varies considerably with the nature and amount of the drug used as well as the duration of addiction and individual factors which are difficult to define.[17]

A mild abstinence syndrome results in a vague uneasiness, restlessness, yawning, fitful drowsiness, lacrimation and rhinorrhea.

---

[13] In technical language the necessity to increase the drug dose is called developing a tolerance to the drug.

[14] "Physical" or "physiological" dependence refers to the fact that, after a continuing use of such a drug, the abrupt withdrawal of the agent is followed by the development of an "abstinence syndrome" which is associated with measurable physiological changes, and which is promptly reduced in intensity by administration of sufficient amounts of the drug in question or its analogues. (A. Wikler, *Opiate Addiction* [Springfield, Ill., 1953], p. 4.)

[15] Brown, p. 33.

[16] Wikler, p. 4.

[17] Ibid., pp. 3-4.

A more advanced syndrome results in the above-mentioned symptoms plus "gooseflesh, tremors, muscle twitches, hot and cold flashes, nausea, vomiting, diarrhea, anorexia, weight loss, ejaculations in men and orgasms in women..." [18] The role and causes of this physical dependence are not yet fully understood. Some hold that the so-called physical dependence is a result of an extreme psychological dependence. Others believe that actual physical changes caused by the drug are responsible.

The exact nature and extent of damage to the cells of the body is still debatable, although it is generally conceded today that no permanent cell damage results from a prolonged and extensive use of the opiates. However, it is a strange mystique of opiate addiction that very few who have become addicted can ever remain cured even after treatment is taken. Whether a physical impairment yet unobserved remains or whether simply an overpowering psychological need remains in the addict's psyche, the victim rarely escapes from the temptation to renew his association with the drug. Harris Isbell urges a current view that the lingering craving for the drug even after "cure" is psychological:

> Addiction is caused by human weakness not by drugs — and is a symptom of a personality maladjustment rather than a disease in its own right. Usually, people who become addicted are either hedonistic, pleasure-seeking individuals (psychopaths) or are psychoneurotics. Emotionally normal, mature individuals practically never become addicted. [19]

The opiate may thus serve the need of the emotionally maladjusted personality by providing a means of turning his state of anxiety or recurrent depression into a blissful state of euphoria.

The poor physical condition characteristic of addicts does not stem from the toxic effects of the opiate on any bodily tissue, but rather from the effects of the drug on the addict's personality. As the frequency and amount of the dose increase, the addict loses all care for any activity, except that of obtaining his next

---

[18] Ibid., p. 36.
[19] Harris Isbell, "Meeting a Growing Menace — Drug Addiction," *The Merck Report*, LX (July, 1951), 7.

dose. Any ambition, will to activity, or care for personal hygiene becomes impossible. With the loss of appetite, lack of personal hygiene, and alternation between sieges of constipation and diarrhea which the addict suffers, there is little chance for him to remain in good health.

In the past, many reasons have been given why individuals began to use the opiates. In treatises of the nineteenth century four principal reasons stand out: 1. Many physicians were unaware of the addicting qualities of the opiates and other known addicting drugs. Thus they often prescribed these drugs liberally because of the great success obtained with them. (That many became addicted through this indiscriminate prescription of addicting drugs is demonstrated by the numerous warnings against their use in the treatises of the late nineteenth and early twentieth centuries.) 2. Since drugs could be obtained without restriction in the early nineteenth century and with relative ease even after regulatory ordinances were passed in France in 1845 and 1846, many became addicted through private use in search of relief from chronic pain. 3. Because of a lack of fear for the drug's addicting properties, it was used willingly as an escape from anxieties, tensions and the condition known as melancholy. 4. In addition, there were some who became addicted through curiosity piqued by written and verbal praise of the wonderful euphoria and mysterious transcendence into another state of reality and sensation which the drugs produced. Today the prime motive behind continued use of the drug is attributed to a weakness in the user's psychological constitution. The addict seeks the balm of euphoria as a means of escaping from the dreary, anxiety-filled reality in which he lives. He escapes into a different dimension, a new reality which is permeated with joy, frequently described as a warm feeling in the abdomen which resembles a continuous orgasm. Depending upon the individual's own constitution, this physical sensation is accompanied by a "buoyancy of spirits, increased imagination, temporarily enlarged... brain power" [20] and thoughts which ordinarily would not have come to him. No experi-

---

[20] C. E. Terry and M. Pellens, *The Opium Problem* (New York, 1928), p. 243.

ence better represents the irony of life. The eternal yearning for happiness and the conscious striving to rise both physically and spiritually above one's meagre station led the nineteenth century man to test the wonderful "panacea." He sought relief from physical pain or he sought the fabled spiritual bliss which writers had praised. Soon the drug from which he sought relief caused him greater pain than his former condition. Both physically and mentally he became so attached to the drug that he sought only its solace. Former ambitions, desires, and pleasures meant nothing. In the drug he hoped for comfort; but what he received was greater misery and degradation.

B. Hashish

Cannabis Sativa is the generic name given to the hemp plant of which *Cannabis Indica* is one of the few varieties. Robinson describes *Cannabis* as follows:

> ... from 4 to 12 feet in height; its stem is angular, branching, and covered with matted hairs; its leaves are palmate and therefore roughly resemble an open hand; its leaflets are lanceshaped, possessing margins dentated with sawlike teeth; its flowers are yellow and axillary, the male cluster being a raceme and therefore pedicelled, and the female a spike and consequently sessile or stemless... [21]

The drug which is obtained from *Cannabis Sativa* is called by various names in different languages. Some of its better known names are *hashish, marihuana,* and *bhang.* [22] The drug may be taken in several ways and is made into various preparations.

Three types of the extract, which in its different forms can be smoked, chewed, or drunk, are called *charas, bhang,* and

---

[21] Victor Robinson, *An Essay on Hasheesh* (New York, 1912), p. 19.
[22] The term *hashish* comes from the Arabic word meaning "herb" or "dry grass" and is used as if referring to "the herb." *Marihuana* is the term used in the Western hemisphere to designate the variety of plant grown in the Americas. The etymological derivation of the word is not known. Santamaría states that "La versión del María Juana, que alude al apodo de la soldadera —Juana, la mujer del Juan—, aunque sugestiva por el uso cuartelero que preferentemente tiene la droga, no convence del todo.

28 THE ARTIFICIAL PARADISES IN FRENCH LITERATURE

ganja. The resin which exudes from the flowering tops of the plant is called *charas* by the Indians. This sticky substance is collected from the plant and mixed with tobacco for smoking. *Bhang* consists of the dried leaves and small stalks of the plant. It is smoked with or without tobacco or is made into a sweetmeat with honey, sugar, and spices. It may also be powdered and made into a solution for drinking. *Ganja,* another smoking preparation, is prepared from the flowering and the fruiting heads of the female plant. A favorite method of taking the drug, enjoyed by Théophile Gautier and those who participated in sessions presided over by Dr. Moreau de Tours, is in the form of a confection known as *dawamesc:*

> On fait bouillir les feuilles et les fleurs de la plante avec de l'eau à laquelle on a ajouté une certaine quantité de beurre frais, puis le tout étant réduit, par évaporation, à la consistence d'un sirop, on passe dans un linge. On obtient ainsi le beurre chargé du principe actif et empreint d'une couleur verdâtre assez prononcée. [23]

Because of its nauseating taste and odor, the extract is generally sweetened, "aromatisé de cannelle, pistache, poivre, muscade et additionné de musc..." [24] Frequently the confection is made in the form of pills approximately the size of a nut and kept in beau-

---

Téngase en cuenta que hay una isla Hariguana, de las Bahamas." (Francisco J. Santamaría, *Diccionario de Mejicanismos* [Méjico, 1959], p. 698.)

The Greek word κάνναβισ, from which the Latin word is adopted, is of unknown origin. Hofmann and Walde both agree that it is a "Lehnwort aus einer unbekannten osteuropäischen Quelle...." (J. B. Hofmann, *Etymologisches Wörterbuch des Griechischen* [München, 1950], p. 154.)

From the Latin *Cannabis* come the French *chanve* or *chanvre,* the Old German *Hanapas,* Modern German *Hanf,* and English *hemp.*

Bhang is the Hindustani term to designate both the plant and a certain preparation from it. It derives from Sanskrit word *bhangá* meaning hemp. Henceforth I shall use the general term, hashish, to apply to the product of the hemp plant.

[23] J. Moreau, *Du haschisch et de l'aliénation mentale* (Paris, 1845), pp. 6-7.

[24] R. Meunier, *Le hachich* (Paris, 1909), p. 14. These are only a few of the many substances used to sweeten the drug's taste. *Essence de rose, jasmine,* etc. are used, plus several so-called aphrodisiacs such as ginger, clove, and even the dangerous *poudre de cantharides.*

tifully ornamented boxes or containers of porcelaine and earthenware.

Use of the water pipe to smoke hashish is an extremely old practice. The pipes are made in various shapes and unique designs, but the principle consists in allowing the vapours from the burning material to pass through water before they are inhaled. It is probable that considerable condensation allows a lesser amount of the drug to pass into the system.

The pharmacological actions of hashish are still poorly understood. The principal effects of the drug are confined almost exclusively to the central nervous system. It is still undecided whether hashish is a central stimulant or depressant, or both. Although an increase in the pulse rate and a lowering of blood pressure and respiration may be noted, only the effects upon the central nervous system have true significance. Hashish is rarely used in medicine today because of its variable potency and the unexplained variation in response to its use. The central effects of the drug combine elements of excitation and depression, in proportions depending upon the personality of the individual using it.

Like opium, hashish is taken for the extreme sense of euphoria which it produces. However, unlike opium, it is thought to cause almost no tolerance to develop and no permanent harm from prolonged usage.[25] The attachment to hashish is generally described as *habituation,* in contrast with *addiction,* which is used for the opiates. The difference between the two terms concerns the nature of developing dependence upon the drug. Opium addiction entails a physical dependence which results in great suffering if the user of the drug is prevented from obtaining his supply. Habituation to hashish, which includes no such physical suffering or abstinence illness, has been defined as "an emotional and psychological predilection associated with euphoria and the desire to avoid responsibilities."[26]

---

[25] Contrary to Western findings, doctors from the Near East report that a state of permanent debility develops from prolonged usage of the drug. This difference in findings remains unexplained. It is believed, however, that the discrepancy may result from the lack of investigative controls in the Near Eastern studies.

[26] Brown, p. 34.

As with opium or almost any drug, it is difficult to predict exactly what the reaction of a given individual will be to hashish. For the most part one can say that different personalities react in very divergent ways. For some it is a pleasant mental and physical experience. Others suffer extreme mental anguish and physical discomfort. Thus, in discussing the actions of the drug upon the human body, observers often describe apparently contradictory experiences and feelings. It is sometimes stated that the effect of hashish lasts from three to five hours, but that the influence may last twelve hours or even longer. In smoking hashish, the effects begin within a few minutes, whereas it takes from thirty minutes to an hour to notice the effects of the drug taken by ingestion.

Some of the immediate physical effects of the drug include an increased appetite and noticeable hunger, especially for sweets. There is also frequently a dryness of throat and mouth which causes considerable thirst. Among the more unpleasant symptoms are occasional nausea, vomiting, and diarrhea. The primary physical sensation of most persons affected favorably by the drug is a feeling of extreme euphoria; but that feeling itself is described in very different terms by different personalities. For some it is a warm glow which seems to generate an inner peace. Others compare it to a sexual orgasm. Still others describe the sensation as waves of physical pleasure moving through their bodies. Some even find themselves brought into a feeling of spiritual integration and harmony with the whole of life so that suddenly all of life's problems seem resolved. From this standpoint the description given by the jazz musician Mezz Mezzrow, is of unusual interest:

> All the notes came easing out of my horn like they'd already been made up, greased and stuffed into the bell, so all I had to do was blow a little and send them on their way, one right after the other, never missing, never behind time, all without an ounce of effort. The phrases seemed to have more continuity to them and I was sticking to the theme without ever going tangent. I felt I could go on playing for years without running out of ideas and energy. There wasn't any struggle; it was all made-to-order and suddenly there wasn't a sour note or a discord in the world that could bother me. I began to feel very happy and sure of myself. With my loaded horn I could take all the fist-swinging, evil things in the world and bring them

together in perfect harmony, spreading peace and joy and relaxation to all the keyed-up and punchy people everywhere. [27]

Many who have taken hashish describe the experience as beginning with a high-pitched laugh. The most consistent effect of the drug seems often to be a sense of good humor which develops. Everything is so amusing to the drugged individual that he wants only to laugh uproariously. Robinson describes just such an incident in a case which he observed. The individual fell into paroxysms of laughter and showed himself very sensitive to word sounds and to puns. He found great humor in the name Illitch Tchaikovsky because the "itch" of the first name sounded so vulgar to him. He loved to coin words such as "laughfinity" and "laughinosity," and he could scarcely stop laughing in spite of his best efforts, because the world seemed to him to be such a "blooming joke." [28]

The hashish experience often induces a feeling of duality. Some describe it as though two distinct beings were inhabiting their single body, each with distinct thoughts and suggestions. But many persons deny this type of duality and describe the sensation much in the way that Valéry described the one part of the self which watched the other part write. The person under the influence of hashish often observes his own foolish extravagancies in perfect judgment. There is one part of him which realizes that everything that he is doing is ridiculous, and yet he is unable to control the actions which the impulses of the other self govern. It is often described as though one critical self were standing aside watching the foolish self act in an incomprehensible manner. Survival of this critical attitude under the influence of hashish has encouraged individuals to conduct auto-experiments; but these have been handicapped by inaccurate self-observation and the failure of complete recall.

Along with the division of the self seems to go a confusion in the perception of time and space. Ideas, thoughts, and images flash through the mind with astounding rapidity. The person

---

[27] *The Drug Experience*, ed. David Ebin (New York, 1961), pp. 87-88.
[28] Robinson, p. 63.

who is drugged is amazed at his own fecundity of thought and often develops an attitude of personal superiority. Yet any attempt to relate what he is thinking usually ends in a confusing array of disconnected, fragmentary thoughts. The individual sometimes becomes obsessed by a single notion, like Robinson's friend who felt that he comprehended the greater plan of life, that he alone understood the "great idea." The innumerable thoughts which race through the individual's mind make him think that much time has elapsed when, in fact, the experience has lasted only a few seconds or minutes.

Accompanying these sensations often come the brilliant hallucinations of sight and sound caused by the hypersensitivity of the five senses. Vivid, fascinating hallucinations of vision and extreme sensitivity to sound occur most frequently, and interesting instances of synaesthesia have been reported.

> The thrills which ran through my nervous system became more rapid and fierce, accompanied with sensations that steeped my whole being in unutterable rapture. I was encompassed by a sea of light, through which played the pure, harmonious colors that are born of light. While endeavoring, in broken expressions, to describe my feelings to my friends who sat looking upon me incredulously —not yet having been affected by the drug— I suddenly found myself at the foot of the great Pyramid of Cheops. The tapering courses of yellow limestone gleamed like gold in the sun, and the pile rose so high that it seemed to lean for support upon the blue arch of the sky. I wished to ascend it, and the wish alone placed me immediately upon its apex, lifted thousands of feet above the wheat-fields and palm-groves of Egypt. I cast my eyes downward, and, to my astonishment, saw that it was built, not of limestone, but of huge square plugs of Cavendish tobacco! Words cannot paint the overwhelming sense of the ludicrous which I then experienced. I writhed on my chair in an agony of laughter, which was only relieved by the vision melting away like a dissolving view till, out of my confusion of indistinct images and fragments of images, another and more wonderful vision arose. [29]

---

[29] Ebin, pp. 45-47.

Although much of the hashish experience is pleasurable, many individuals have suffered terrifying, nightmarish hallucinations of impending death or fears that they have become insane.

A popular belief has placed hashish among the aphrodisiacs. It is well established that hashish causes no increased sexual potency and may even prevent successful completion of the sexual act. However, erotic visions frequently occur during the course of the hallucinations. One individual stated that, under the influence of hashish, he was sexually aroused in brushing past women in the subways of New York. Victor Robinson's hallucinations included wonderful sojourns in the Orient and the enjoyment of many women during the visions.

It should be noted that the hallucinations experienced by an individual are completely unpredictable. The unpredictability lies in the fact that the visions are exaggerations of thoughts and fantasies which the individual harbors within his psyche. The drug itself creates nothing. It simply sets free the inhibitions, gives free rein to the imagination of the user. The uninhibited imagination sets to work transforming anything which the person has encountered in his experience or has fashioned in his personality. The direction which these transformations take is again governed by the user's own psychological constitution. The world which is created by the drug can indeed be prosaic or unbelievably exciting. The mind can experience little effect at all from the drug in the way of hallucinations, or it can be transported into a vivid, real world of ecstasies or fear.

CHAPTER II

HISTORICAL CONSIDERATION OF
OPIUM AND HASHISH

The use of opium as a drug and narcotic reaches back to the earliest records of civilization. Diggings around the Swiss lakes indicate that the lake dwellers may have used opium as early as 4000 B.C.[1] Early mention is also found in *The Assyrian Herbal,* a work which deals with Mesopotamian drugs and medicinal herbs. Here Thompson translates the ideogram HUL GIL, literally "joy plant," as opium, and supports this translation by the following cuneiform passage:

> Early in the morning old women, boys and girls collect the juice by scraping it off the wounds (of the poppy capsule) with a small iron scoope, and deposit the whole in an earthen pot.[2]

This Assyrian ideogram also occurs in earlier Sumerian tablets, possibly dating from the 4th millenium before Christ.[3]

Considerable debate has arisen as to whether or not opium was used as a medicament in ancient Egypt. Archeological

---

[1] L. Lewin, *Phantastica — Narcotic and Stimulating Drugs* (New York, 1931), pp. 33-36.

[2] Glenn Sonnedecker, *Emergence of the Concept of Opiate Addiction* (Madison, Wisconsin, 1963), p. 5. Reprinted from the *Journal Mondial de Pharmacie,* No. 3, 1962, pp. 275-290, and No. 1, 1963, pp. 27-34.

[3] A relief of an Assyrian priest from the period of King Sargon II (8th century B. C.) is believed to picture the priest holding a poppy plant in his hand.

evidence suggests the possible use of opium as early as the eighteenth dynasty (ca. 1500 B.C.). A pair of ear-rings from the tomb of Queen Tausrit have been identified as pendant poppy capsules. Also representations of the Papaver Rhoeas [4] have been identified such as the actual flowers found on the mummified breast of Princess Nsykhounsu of the twenty-first dynasty (ca. 11th century B.C.). [5]

In the Ebers Papyrus (ca. 1500 B.C.) there is a medicine mentioned for stopping a child's excessive crying. [6] The prescription is of opium and the excrement of flies scraped from the walls.

It is clear from the above references that medicinal knowledge of opium was probable both in Mesopotamia and in Egypt many centuries before Christ. However, except for the ear-rings (which might connect opium with its legendary aphrodisiac qualities) and the translation of *Hul Gil* as "joy plant," there is little which indicates that opium was used for other than medical purposes. Galen (ca. 130-200 A.D.) observes that Thoth, the Ibis-headed god of letters, invention, and wisdom, and ancestor to the Greek god, Hermes Trismegistus, was a user of opium. [7]

According to some scholars, there may be a reference to poppy juice in the Old Testament. The word "rosh" (meaning "head") has been found mentioned in connection with the word "la'anah," which means wormwood or absinthe. "Rosh" has been translated in these passages as hemlock, but later scholars translate it as poppy-head. Also the term "me-rosh" (juice of the rosh), once translated as "poison water," is now translated poppy juice. [8]

Though scantily mentioned in relation to the Egyptians and the Assyrians, opium was well known to the Greeks and

---

[4] The Papaver Rhoeas is that poppy flower which can be addicting as opposed to Papaver Shepenn-dšr which cannot.

[5] References in the preceding paragraph were drawn from Sonnedecker, page 4.

[6] Jürgen Thorwald, *Science and Secrets of Early Medicine: Egypt, Mesopotamia, India, China, Mexico, Peru.* Trans. by Richard and Clara Winston. (New York, 1963).

[7] Albert Fields, "The Story of Opium," *The Merck Report*, April, 1949, p. 4.

[8] D. I. Macht, "The History of Opium and Some of Its Preparations and Alkaloids," *Journal of the American Medical Association*, 64 (February, 1915), 477.

frequently cited by them. The term itself is from the Greek word ὀπός (meaning juice), whence it passed into Arabic (af-yun) and subsequently into Chinese (o-fu-yung). [9] References to opium can be found in such varied sources as Greek Mythology, medical treatises, and literature.

According to mythology, Ceres created the poppy that she might sleep and forget the loss of her daughter to Pluto. The Greeks seem to have associated the poppy with death and sleep, in that Hypnos (sleep), Nox (the goddess of night), and Thanatos (death) were all three represented as adorned with poppies. [10]

Cybele too is represented wearing a wreath of poppies, a symbol of fertility. Fields asserts that Somnus, the god of sleep in Roman mythology, "... is represented as a bearded man leaning over the sleeper and pouring on his eyelids the poppy juice contained in a vessel or horn which he holds in his hand. At a later date, Somnus is depicted as a young genie carrying poppies and an opium horn, with poppy stalks in his hand." [11]

There are only a few references to opium in Greek and Roman literature. In general the references stress the sleep-bringing effect of the drug and the feeling of peace which accompanies it. In Homer's *Odyssey* Helen uses the famous Nepenthès, deemed by many to have been opium, as a narcotic to help Telemachus forget his grief:

> Then Helen, daughter of Zeus, took other counsel. Straightway she cast into the wine of which they were drinking a drug (Nepenthès) to quiet all pain and strife, and bring forgetfulness of every ill. Whoso should drink this down, when it is mingled in the bowl, would not in the course of that day let a tear fall down over his cheeks, no, not though his mother and father should lie there dead, or though before his face men should slay with the sword his brother or dear son, and his own eyes beheld it. [12]

---

[9] Macht, p. 477.
[10] Arthur B. Collom, "Tears of the Poppy," *Journal of the Kansas Medical Society*, 58 (1957), 614.
[11] Albert Fields, p. 5.
[12] Homer, *The Odyssey*, trans. A. T. Murray (London, 1919), p. 123.

Vergil refers to opium in the *Georgics,* Lib. I, v. 78: "Lethaeo perfusa papavera somno" and in the *Aenead,* Lib. IV, v. 486: "Spargens humida melle soporiferumque papaver." Only in Ovid's reference to opium in the *Fasti,* a poetical Roman calendar, does one sense a possible suggestion that opium brings more than sleep: "interea placidam redimita papaveri frontem nox venit et secum somnia nigra trahit." [13]

The most interesting literary passage concerning opium in ancient literature is in Lucian's *True History* when the author and his crew arrive at the Island of Dreams:

> Very soon we seemed quite close to the Isle of Dreams, though there was a certain dimness and vagueness about its outline; but it had something dreamlike in its very nature; for as we approached it receded, and seemed to get further and further off. At last we reached it and sailed into Slumber, the port, close to the ivory gates where stands the temple of the Cock. It was evening when we landed, and upon proceeding to the city we saw many strange dreams.
>
> The whole place is embowered in wood, of which the trees are poppy and mandragora, all thronged with bats; this is the only winged thing that exists there. A river, called the Somnambule, flows close by, and there are two springs at the gates, one called Wakenot, and the other Nightlong. The rampart is lofty and of many colours, in the rainbow style. The gates are not two, as Homer says, but four, of which two look onto the plain Stupor; one of them is of iron, the other of pottery, and we were told that these are used by the grim, the murderous, and the cruel. The other pair face the sea and port, and are of horn —it was by this that we had entered— and of ivory. On the right as you enter the city stands the temple of Night, which deity divides with the Cock their chief allegiance; the temple of the latter is close to the port. On the left is the palace of Sleep. He is the governor, with two lieutenants, Nightmare, son of Whimsy, and Flittergold, son of Fantasy. A well in the middle of the market-place goes by the name of Heavyhead; beside which are the temples of

---

[13] "Meantime, her calm brow wreathed with poppies, Night drew on, and in her train brought darkling dreams." (Ovid's *Fasti,* trans. Sir James G. Frazer [London, 1931] lines 661-662.)

Deceit and Truth. In the market also is the shrine in which oracles are given, the priest and prophet, by special appointment from Sleep, being Antiphon the dream-interpreter.

The dreams themselves differed widely in character and appearance. Some were well-grown, smooth-skinned, shapely, handsome fellows, others rough, short, and ugly; some apparently made of gold, others of common cheap stuff. Among them some were found with wings, and other strange variations; others again were like the mummers in a pageant, tricked out as kings or Gods or what not. Many of them we felt that we had seen in our world, and sure enough these came up and claimed us as old acquaintance; they took us under their charge, found us lodgings, entertained us with lavish kindness, and, not content with the magnificence of this present reception, promised us royalties and provinces. Some of them also took us to see our friends, doing the return trip all in the day.

For thirty days and nights we abode there — a very feast of sleep. Then on a sudden came a mighty clap of thunder; we woke; jumped up; provisioned; put off.[14]

The allegorical description of the city with its rampart "... lofty and of many colours, in the rainbow style," its "palace of Sleep" with his lieutenants, "Nightmare, son of Whimsy, and Flittergold, son of Fantasy," and the widely differing character of the dreams themselves relate to the mysterious world of dream. But the author has the "whole place embowered in wood, of which the trees are poppy and mandragora," suggesting that he was aware of the world of fancy and nightmare which drugs can produce.

Exactly when opium came to be used medicinally in Greece is unknown. It is believed by some that Hippocrates (460-357 B. C.) knew of opium and refers to it in a remedy which he recommends for leucorrhea. Nearly a century later, Theophrastus (370-286 B.C.) mentions poppy juice and the method of extracting it. Although not mentioning opium directly, he speaks of the development of tolerance to certain drugs. About 40 A.D.

---

[14] *The Works of Lucian of Samosata,* trans. H. W. Fowler and F. G. Fowler, II (Oxford, 1905), 166-168.

Scribonius Largus mentions the method of obtaining opium from the capsules and differentiates it from the juice of the whole plant, meconium. From the references of Dioscorides (77 A.D.) it appears that opium was widely used in his day; the method used in obtaining the juice from the poppy capsule has varied little since his description. Pliny and Celsus both describe opium's medicinal uses, and Galen speaks enthusiastically of its virtues. Although there are frequent references to opium by writers of ancient Greece and Rome, and although popularity of the drug became so great that it fell into the hands of shopkeepers and quacks, it is difficult to say whether there was any concept of addiction in ancient times, or whether consistent opium use was simply regarded as a bad habit.[15]

T. W. Africa points out that Marcus Aurelius Antoninus took a daily dose of theriac, a well known opium preparation of his day. Africa suggests that the emperor's bizarre dreams and his tendency to see beauty in such strange things as the foam of a wild boar and poison, was a result of his using opium. "Temporal and spatial dimensions were accelerated until Europe was but a speck and the present a point and men insects crawling on a clod."[16]

Although unable to determine the size of the dose which Marcus Aurelius took, Africa believes that the Emperor was addicted, in that he did not sleep well when he had not taken his nightly potion. Africa suggests that this uneasiness may have been a symptom of withdrawal pains.

In the Middle Ages references to opium in European works are infrequent. It is known that Avicenna used opium and recommended its use to combat diarrhea and diseases of the eye, and it is believed that Avicenna himself died from an overdose of opium. Two other Arabic physicians of repute, Maimonides and Averroës, wrote treatises on the drug.

---

[15] The references of the preceding paragraph were taken from C. E. Terry and M. Pellens, *The Opium Problem* (New York, 1928), *passim*.

[16] T. W. Africa, "The Opium Addiction of Marcus Aurelius," *Journal of the History of Ideas*, 22 (1961), 101. All the material concerning Marcus Aurelius was drawn from the above cited article.

The Arabs have been held responsible for the introduction of opium into the East. Arabic trade with Canton was established as early as 300 A.D., and it is in the eighth century, when the Arabs conquered Sind, that the first opium references occur in Sanskrit literature.[17] The history of opium in the Orient is not well defined, but the Arabs and Indians had already established an opium trade with Burma, China, the East Indies, and the Malay Peninsula by the time the Portuguese began to explore the Orient.[18] One can see from a letter of Don Alfonso de Albuquerque to the king of Portugal in 1513 that the poppy was considered a most profitable item of the eastern trade. Van Linschoten, a Dutchman who was in the East in the late sixteenth century, describes the drug and its effect in the following manner:

> Amfion is made of sleepe balls or poppie and is the gumme which cometh forth from the same, to ye which end it is cut up and opened. He that useth to eate it must eate it daylie, otherwise he dieth and consumeth himself.... Such as use it go as if they were alwaies halfe a sleep, thay eate much of it because they would not feele any great labour or unquietness when thay are at work but they use it most for lecherie.[19]

One can see from this quotation that opium's addicting properties and a notion of its ability to cause physical dependence, as well as its mythical qualities as an aphrodisiac, were well known to Van Linschoten.

Opium seems to have been used in China principally for its medicinal value, but a quotation from an unidentified Chinese poet indicates that its ecstatic properties were not unknown:

> I see here the Hermit of the Shade
> And the long-robed Buddhist priest.
> When they sit opposite I forget to speak.
> Then I have but to drink a cup of this poppy-seed
>   drink.

---

[17] David E. Owen, *British Opium Policy in China and India* (New Haven, 1934), p. 2.
[18] Owen, p. 2.
[19] Ibid., pp. 2-3.

I laugh,
I am happy,
I have come to Ying-Chuan,
And am wandering on the banks of its river.
I seem to be climbing the slope of the Lu
    Mountain
In the far west. [20]

The opium trade increased under the auspices of the Portuguese and in the last part of the eighteenth century and in the early nineteenth century grew to enormous proportions under the famous East India Company. This finally led to the series of hostilities known as the Opium Wars, of which the two principal conflicts, from 1839 to 1842 and from 1857 to 1860, were undertaken to force the Chinese to accept Indian opium as return cargo for Chinese tea and other goods.

As a result of the increased number of markets and the awareness of opium's potential as a commercial product, opium sale and production increased greatly all over the world in the second half of the nineteenth century.

In Western Europe from the time of Galen the use of opium has continued under various forms. However, it was frequently mixed in such varied concoctions that distinction between the important and the useless ingredients could not be determined. In the twelfth or early thirteenth century the leading surgeon of the day, Hugo de Lucca, used opium as an element in his soporific sponge, a basic prescription of the mediaeval physician which was used as an inhalation anesthetic. [21] Opium was generally regarded as a panacea where all other medication failed. [22] Its miraculous powers, not at all understood, evoked awe among many physicians who used it. [23] The various authori-

---

[20] Ibid., p. 12.

[21] Collom, p. 620.

[22] Some of the many ailments for which opium was used: diarrhea, cough, smallpox, tuberculosis, cholera, various dysenteries, syphilis, dropsy, gout, headaches, palpitations, abortions, urinary calculi, and psychological states such as melancholia and mania.

[23] The awe which opium inspired can be sensed in John Jones' work, *The Mysteries of Opium Revealed*, published in 1700. He writes that most men consider it impossible to explain the mysterious effects of opium be-

ties note with some wonder that one is put to sleep and that when he awakens he is completely well. In a learned Latin treatise published in 1620, Doctor Döring speaks with great respect concerning opium's ability to raise people almost from death:

> Inducit somnos dolori minimè obnoxios, neque soporem ac stuporem infert, veluti reliqua ad levandos dolores apparata; verùm somnum tam diu detinet, quo usque; Pharmacum penetrârit, et caussas dolorum dissolverit. Et sanè multi ex aegris à somno surrexerunt, adeò concoquendi facultate praestantes, ut obliti sint, an unquam aliquid à principio doluerint. [24]

Opium has long been associated with one of the most controversial physicians of the sixteenth century, Philippus Aureolus Theophrastus Bombast von Hohenheim, better known as Paracelsus. It is often stated that much of his success as a physician was due to his extensive use of opium. Even though not a part of his famous laudanum mixture, opium formed a part of many of the physician's preparations. "He is said to have carried opium in the pummel of his saddle and called it the 'stone of immortality.'" [25] Opium was praised highly by the followers of Paracelsus. Sylvius de la Boe, the famous Dutch physician, claimed that his practice of medicine would have been impossible without opium. Another physician and chemist, Van Helmont (ca. 1640), employed the drug so frequently that he was called Doctor Opiatus. [26] Thomas Sydenham, whose famous laudanum preparation became a standard prescription from the

---

cause they are persuaded "... that it operates by an occult Quality, wholly unexplicable, and particularly reserved from the *Knowledge of Mankind*" (p. 41).

[24] M. Döring, *'Akróama medico-philosophicum de opii usu, qualitate calefaciente, virtute narcotica, et ipsum corrigendi modo* (Jenae, 1620), p. 15. It induces sleep by no means harmful to one grieving and not deep sleep and unconsciousness as the other preparations for lightening pain. But it holds sleep until the drug penetrates and dissolves the causes of pain; and many have awakened from sleep healed from sickness and so recovered in the faculty of digestion that they have forgotten whether they suffered any pain in the beginning.

[25] Terry, p. 57.
[26] Ibid.

seventeenth century forward, expresses as follows the high opinion which many held concerning the virtues of opium:

> Here I cannot but break out in praise of the Great God, the giver of all good things, who hath granted to the human race as a comfort in their afflictions no medicine of the value of opium, either in regard to the number of diseases it can control or its efficiency in extirpating them. Medicine would be a cripple without it and whoever understands it well will do more with it alone than he could well hope to do from any such medicine. [27]

Throughout the period of the Middle Ages and Renaissance, just as in ancient times, it is difficult to determine whether there was any conception of addiction to opium. Records do not disclose any definite knowledge that persons could become addicted. John Jones' work, *The Mysteries of Opium Revealed* (London, 1700), shows that he was aware that a tolerance to opium develops, and that severe pain results from cessation of its use. Yet Jones does not seem to be aware of addiction. By 1793, however, Samuel Crumpe, in his *Inquiry into the Nature and Properties of Opium*, recognizes that opium users lose voluntary control of the habit. With Sertürner's discovery in 1806 of morphine (an essential soporific element in opium) and with increased study of opium itself, there resulted a more definite knowledge of the drug's actions. Although many were still dissenting as late as 1900, a large number of physicians were well aware of opium's addicting properties by 1860.

Opium is occasionally mentioned in European literature of the late Middle Ages and Renaissance. Chaucer's "Knight's Tale" has the following passage concerning the poppy as a narcotic:

> That soone after the mydnyght, Palamon,
> By helpyng of a friend, brak his prison.
> And fleeth the citee faste as he may go.
> For he hade yeve his gayler drynke so
> Of a claree maad of certeyn wyn,
> Of nercotikes, and opie of Thebes fyn,

---

[27] A. D. Wright, "The History of Opium," *Transactions of the College of Physicians of Philadelphia*, 29 (1961), 22.

> That al that nyght thogh that men wolde hym shake,
> The gayler sleep, he myght nat awake. [28]

Opium's power to induce a death-like slumber is found also in the tenth story of the fourth day of Boccaccio's *Decamerone*. Here the story has the famed Salerno physician, Master Mazzeo, make up an opium potion as an anesthetic for an amputation. By mistake, the lover of the physician's wife drinks the potion. Thinking that his deep sleep is death, she puts him into a chest. Discovered there, the lover is taken for a thief and sentenced to be hanged. He is saved by the clever play of the lady's maid, and all live a merry life thereafter. In this instance the drug serves no other purpose than to cast the lover into a deep sleep.

In Shakespeare's *Othello*, Act III, scene 3, line 330, reference is made to sleep brought on by opium and mandragora:

> Not poppy, nor mandragora,
> Nor all the drowsy syrups of the world,
> Shall ever medicine thee to that sweet sleep
> Which thou ow'dst yesterday. [29]

In this speech, Iago indicates that Othello's nights of peaceful sleep are gone forever. Nevermore will he taste "sweet sleep" even by using narcotics, for the sweet narcotic-induced slumber resolves none of the woes which one must face when awakened. Even more interesting is the thought that the dreams which a narcotic might bring are tempered by one's state of mind. For Othello, life can be only a nightmare once he doubts Desdemona.

* * *

Since hashish has been used far less than opium for medicinal purposes, it is far more difficult to trace its development from early times to the present day. Whereas opium is mentioned in many medical texts because of its ability to relieve pain, references to hashish are confined to a more fanciful, vague world of

---

[28] Collom, p. 622.
[29] Ibid. Cited from Shakespeare's *Othello*, Act III, scene iii, lines 330-333.

religious and mystical experience. The drug's wondrous ability to set man's imagination free, to change the shape and color of his world, has caused it to be used quite differently from opium and for purposes more related to man's spiritual existence.

What may be the earliest extant reference to the hemp plant is found in a Chinese compilation between 1200 and 500 B.C. called the *Rh-Yh*;[30] and there is recognition of the narcotic properties of hashish among the Assyrians as early as the seventh or eighth century before Christ.[31] It appears that the Assyrians used the drug in religious rites as an incense; and it has even been suggested that their apparent experience of the drug's narcotic effects through inhalation may clarify Herodotus' (486-406 B.C.) interesting remarks concerning the Scythians:

> When the Scythians obtain the seed of this kannabis, they throw it on to red-hot stones in the fire. It burns like incense, sending up more smoke than any Greek vapour bath. This they then inhale and begin to rave.[32]

Hashish has also been used in religious rites in the Congo. The Kassai and Baluba tribes have employed the plant as a religious fetish, and considered it as a means of protection from physical sickness as well as a symbol of peace.[33]

Hashish is frequently associated with religious ceremony and mysticism, especially in reference to the religious priests in India. J. Campbell Oman states in his book *The Mystics, Ascetics, and Saints of India*:

> It would be an interesting philosophical study to endeavor to trace the influence of these powerful narcotics (charas and bhang) on the minds and bodies of the itinerant monks who habitually use them. We may be sure that these hemp drugs, known since very early times in the

---

[30] R. P. Walton, *Marihuana: America's New Drug Problem* (Philadelphia, 1938), p. 1.

[31] Ibid., p. 5.

[32] P. B. Wilkinson, "Cannabis Indica; an Historical and Pharmacological Study of the Drug," *British Journal of Inebriety*, 27 (1929), 72.

[33] Lewin, pp. 113-114.

East, are not irresponsible for some of its wild dreamings. [34]

It has been suggested that the stupefaction which the Hindu monk calls "fixing his mind on God" is an intoxication of the drug.

Robinson relates that old Arabic and Persian writers ascribe the discovery of the narcotic properties of hashish to a certain austere monk named Haider:

> Haider was a rigid monk who built a monastery on the mountains between Nishabor and Ramah. For ten years he never left his hermitage, never indulged in even a fleeting moment's pleasure. One burning summer's day when the fiery sun glared angrily upon Mother Earth as if he wished to wither up her breasts, Haider stepped out from his cloister and walked alone to the fields. All around him lay the vegetation weary and without life, but one plant danced in the heat with joy. Haider plucked it, partook of it, and returned to the convent a happier man. The monks who saw him immediatley noticed the change in their chief. He encouraged conversation, and acted boisterously. He then led his companions to the fields, and the holy men partook of the hasheesh, and were transformed from austere ascetics into jolly good fellows. At the death of Haider, in conformity with his desire, his disciples planted the hemp in an arbor around his tomb. [35]

The earliest Chinese reference to the narcotic powers of hashish is by the physician Hoa-tho (ca. 220 A.D.) who supposedly used a preparation from the hemp plant as an anesthetic in operations. It is noted that the medicine was taken in wine.

Another supposed early reference, also claimed for opium, concerns the famous narcotic, Nepenthès, which Helen gives to Telemachus in the fourth book of the *Odyssey*. [36]

---

[34] Louis J. Bragman, "The Weed of Insanity," *Medical Journal and Record*, CXXII (1925), 418.

[35] Victor Robinson, *An Essay on Hasheesh* (New York, 1912), p. 23.

[36] The Greek word, Nepenthès, means "banishing pain and sorrow" and is reputed to have come from Egypt. Homer states in the famous potion-giving passage in Book IV: "Such cunning drugs had the daughter of Zeus, drugs of healing, which Polydamna, the wife of Thon, had given her, a woman of Egypt, for there the earth, the giver of grain, bears

Pliny does not mention hashish directly, but he quotes the following passage from Democritus concerning plants thought possibly to have been hemp. The first is theangelis:

> Taken in drink it produces delirium, which presents to the fancy visions of a most extraordinary nature. The theangelis, he says, grows upon Mount Libanus in Syria, upon the chain of mountains called Dicte in Crete, and at Babylon and Susa in Persia. An infusion of it imparts powers of divination to the Magi. The gelotophyllis, too, is a plant found in Bactriana, and on the banks of the Borysthenes. Taken internally with myrrh and wine all sorts of visionary forms present themselves, excite the most immoderate laughter. [37]

That the pleasurable and narcotic effects of the hemp plant were known to the ancients is attested by the following quotation from Galen's "De cannabis semine":

> Its fluid extract is poisonous. Yet mixed with other drugs, it is eaten after meals by some people to induce pleasurable sensations. Shortly after taking it they experience a feeling of warmth and finally lose consciousness. [38]

It has been claimed by C. Creighton that there are a half dozen mistranslated passages in the Old Testament which in fact refer to hashish. Creighton's suppositions are fascinating, but have been denied by scholars for lack of proof. [39]

---

greatest store of drugs, many that are healing when mixed, and many that are baneful..." (Homer, *The Odyssey*, trans. A. T. Murray [London, 1919], p. 123.)

E. W. Lane believed that the Greek word derives from the Coptic plural of "Bendj": "Bendj the plural of which in Coptic is 'nibendj,' is without doubt the same plant as the 'nepenthe,' which has so perplexed the commentators of Homer. Helen evidently brought the nepenthe from Egypt, and bendj is there still reputed to possess all the wonderful qualities which Homer attributes to it" (Walton, p. 7).

[37] Walton, p. 8.
[38] Wilkinson, p. 72.
[39] Creighton's arguments, if true, would accord hashish its traditional role as an aphrodisiac, and as giver of courage before battle, and of the power to make one particularly sensitive to the charms of music. An example of his method of argument is the following: In Canticle 5.I the passage has been translated: "I am come into my garden, my sister, my

48 THE ARTIFICIAL PARADISES IN FRENCH LITERATURE

It is not certain how well hashish was known to Europe in the Middle Ages, when its fame seems to have spread chiefly through the famous story of the Old Man of the Mountain and the Assassins. But by the time of the Renaissance, hashish begins to appear in literature and in works of travel and medicine.

In a treatise by Prosper Alpinus, *De Medicina Aegyptorum* (1592), there is a rather lengthy description of the effects of hashish; and in 1620 Dr. Döring wrote of the drug "assis":

> Est autem Assis nihil aliud, quâm pulvis è Cannabinis foliis confectus, et cum aqua dulci in massam coactus. De hac massa quinque vel plures Bolos, totidem Castaneis magnitudine respondentes, ubi deglutierint, post horam quasi inebriati suas produnt amentias, atque Ecstaticorum instar visionibus suis expetitis delectantur. Hoc Medicamentum cum vili veneat, apud plebem in frequenti usu exsistit. [40]

But aside from such occasional references, the drug was still known principally as the agent used by the Old Man of the Mountain.

---

spouse; I have gathered my myrrh with my spice; *I have eaten my honeycomb with my honey;* I have drunk my wine with my milk." In this passage, the Hebrew word *yagar* was translated *favum* (honeycomb) by St. Jerome. Where the word *honeycomb* is specifically called for elsewhere the words *tzooph* and *nohpheth* are used. In the fifty or sixty other places where *yagar* is used, it clearly means wood, forest, planted field, herbage, etc. Creighton contends, since the context suggests an aphrodisiac, and since cannabis is often taken with honey as a confection for this very purpose, that the person has taken *hemp* not *honeycomb* with *honey*. Creighton also feels that Jonathon (I Sam. 14, 27) dipped his staff in a hemp confection and not *honey-wood* (*yagar*), for upon tasting the honey — "his eyes were enlightened." Jonathon's bravery in the ensuing fight is also ascribed to the hashish. Among other interpretations, Creighton considers that Saul was a hashish eater and thus easily moved by the playing of David's harp, and he attributes the wild fantasmagoria in the first chapter of Ezekiel to hashish hallucinations. These suggestions are exciting from a literary standpoint, but are considered by scholars too suppositional for acceptance. (C. Creighton, "On Indications of the Hachish-Vice in the Old Testament," *Janus*, 8 [1903], 291, 297.)

[40] Döring, p. 78. Hashish is, however, nothing but powder made from the leaves of Cannabis and with fresh water mixed into a mass. After an hour, when they have swallowed five or more morsels of this mass, corresponding in bulk to as many chestnuts, like drunken men they betray their madness

HISTORICAL CONSIDERATION OF OPIUM AND HASHISH

The legend of the Old Man of the Mountain and his followers became well known in literature and to the people of Mediaeval and Renaissance Europe; and the fame of the Assassins spread as a result of the many murders of important personages committed by members of the cult. In all this, it was not primarily the spectacular murders themselves which aroused popular interest, but the mysterious belief that the Old Man of the Mountain held his subjects under a spell through magic powers or through the virtues of a magic potion. To understand this widespread fascination, it is necessary to review briefly the historical evidence concerning the colorful legend of the Assassins and its spread to Europe.[41]

In 1090 a certain Hasan-i Sabbâh conquered the rock fortress at Alamût[42] in the Persian province of Mazandaran at the center of the Elbruz chain of mountains south of the Caspian Sea.[43] Hasan and his zealous religious followers formed part of the Ismâ'îlîs, a sect of the part of Islâm known as the Shî'a.[44] The Shî'a originated as a faction of one of the Muslim leaders of the first generation after the death of Mohammed. They supported the claims of 'Alî (d. 661), cousin and son-in-law of the Prophet.[45]

---

and like those in ecstasy they take delight in their wished for visions. When this medicament may be purchased cheaply it is frequently used by the people.

[41] The historical information concerning the Assassins has been drawn in large part from the work of M. G. S. Hodgson, *The Order of the Assassins* (The Hague, 1955).

[42] The name of the Fortress, Alamût, had been called in former times Aluh Amût which means "Eagle's Nest" or perhaps "Eagle's teaching." In view of the legendary assassination policy of the sect, it is of interest that the unpointed Arabic for Alamût would be the same as the word for "death." (M. G. S. Hodgson, *The Order of the Assassins*, pp. 49, 138.)

[43] This district was known during the period as the *Muleete* (heretic) district.

[44] The other division of Islâm, the Sunnî, supported the traditional portion of Muslim Law and disputed the claims of the Shî'a.

[45] At his death (632 A. D), Mohammed was succeeded by Abu-Bakr, Omar, and the weak Othman. The Sunnî supported this succession. After Othman's death, 'Alî gained the Caliphate in 656 and ruled until his death in 661. The Shî'a, supporting the claims of 'Alî, attempted to keep the succession within Mohammed's family.

These had in common the notion that 'Alî and his successors in Mohammed's family were the only legitimate rulers from the start, after Mohammed's death; and moreover the only authoritative religious teachers, *imâms*. [46]

The particular sect of the Shî'a known as the Ismâ'îlîs insisted that each imâm since 'Alî had designated his successor and that the designated imâm alone had the right to determine points of law and ritual. There was strong loyalty among the Ismâ'îlîs to the imâm, considered to be almost divine.

> ... the Ismâ'îlîs tied him to philosophical tradition as the microcosm par excellence, in whom the metaphysical soul of the universe was personified. He had access to metaphysical reason itself, personified in the inspired Prophet.... [47]

In the eleventh century, when the Fâtimid dynasty, favorable to the Shî'a, fell, and the Seljuk Turks gained power, the scattered Ismâ'îlîs attempted, through sheer devotion to their cause, to storm the Seljuk cities and to destroy their power bit by bit. In 1090, as we have seen above, Hasan-i Sabbâh and his followers captured the fortress at Alamût. This group, known as the Assassins [48] was a religious and military organization bent on realizing for all Islâm the mythical Imâm's power and on accomplishing by force the destruction of the power of the Sunnî and the Seljuk Turk.

Hasan believed that God could not be attained by the individual intellect or by didactic means, but only by following

---

[46] Hodgson, p. 8.
[47] Ibid., p. 10.
[48] The word "assassin" derives from the Arabic word, hashîshiyya, the name given to the sect led by Hasan-i Sabbâh. Christians apparently did not know why the sect had been given this name. In this matter even William of Tyre, one of the best historians of the period, admitted his ignorance: "Notre peuple, aussi bien que les Sarrasins les appelle *Assissins*, sans qu'il me soit possible de savoir d'où leur est venu ce nom ..." (Guillaume de Tyr, *Histoires des croisades*, in *Collection des mémoires relatifs à l'histoire de France*, ed. M. Guizot, XVIII [1832-1835], 297). It is difficult to say when the term first came to be used generically in Europe. Dante's reference in the *Divina Commedia*, cited below, is the first known general use of the term.

the teachings of the mystical and mythical imâm. Hasan claimed to be the imâm and hence the only person who could possess this knowledge and make it known to others. He was the personification of the divine substance and supreme authority and thus omnipotent and infallible.

Not a great deal is known concerning the true activities of the Assassins and life at Alamût. The policy of assassination is difficult to determine, since one has only news of the spectacular killings. It does not seem to have been the intent to kill all Sunnî, but rather to assassinate military leaders, viziers and occasionally sultans who had attacked their strongholds. [49]

In the early years the life at Alamût is considered to have been highly religious, following the strict order imposed by Hasan. The legend of the garden may be the result of irrigation which made the area around Alamût seem like a garden in comparison with the barrenness of the surrounding area. It has been suggested that, if any garden really existed, it was a retreat for contemplation and edification fitting into the sect's code of austerity and discipline. When Alamût was ransacked in 1256, a large library, an alchemic laboratory, and a collection of perfect astronomical instruments were found.

The fame of the strictness of Hasan and the loyalty of his followers spread throughout the Near East and Europe. It is related that Hasan killed one of his sons for misconduct, and another for disobeying the regulation against drinking wine. It was also said that Hasan's followers willingly put themselves to death at his request.

Adding to the Assassins' reputation as heretics was the proclamation of the Grandmaster Hasan II in 1164. This leader undertook three revolutionary innovations: 1) He ended the sway of the *shari'a* the ritual law. 2) He proclaimed the resurrection of the dead, the end of the world having finally come. 3) He proclaimed himself Caliph and divinely appointed ruler. These innovations produced a great change at Alamût, since they modified the strict purist rule which had predominated before.

---

[49] It is surmised that the Assassins were employed later as general hirelings for murder. (Hodgson, p. 113.)

Much of the legend concerning Hasan and his followers was created by orthodox Muslims in their attempts to explain stories which they had heard concerning the sect. Since the Assassins were an heretical group, it was inconceivable to the orthodox that a truly religious zeal could inspire their evident loyalty. It has been suggested that the name *hashīshiyyan*, given to the sect, was a term of orthodox contempt, inferring that only a man who was drugged or not in his right senses could so willingly give up his life. There is no evidence that the drug was used in any form of initiation by Hasan or by later leaders of the sect.

The fame of the Assassins spread throughout Europe as a result of frequent contact with the Crusaders and through reports of the spectacular murders which the Assassins performed. The death of Conrad, the Marquis of Montferrat, during the Third Crusade especially gained notoriety, since Richard Cœur de Lion became implicated. The fame of these murders became so great that the term Assassin came to be used as a general term rather than as a specific designation for a member of the sect. Dante uses the term in a general sense in *Inferno* XIX of the *Divina Commedia*:

> Io stava come'l frate che confessa
> Lo perdido assessin, che poi ch'è fitto,
> Richiama lui, per che la morte cessa. [50]

The story of the garden-paradise and the indoctrination of youth to do the leader's will struck the fancy of the European mind. Both Frederick the Second and Richard Cœur de Lion were accused of having their own group of assassins which they had raised and indoctrinated in the manner of the Old Man of the Mountain. The tale of the dream of paradise induced by a magic potion became a favorite which chroniclers told whenever they discussed a murder by the sect of the Old Man of the Mountain. There are two characteristic types of this legend before

---

[50] *La Divina Commedia*, ed. C. H. Grandgent (Boston, 1933), *Inferno*, Canto XIX, pp. 171-172. "I stood like the friar confessing a treacherous assassin who, after being put in the hole (to be buried alive), calls the confessor back to delay his death" (Dante Alighieri, *The Divine Comedy*, trans. by H. R. Huse [New York, 1954], p. 92).

the famous story found in Marco Polo's *Il Milione*. Both are found in early German chronicles. In the first type the joys of Paradise exist only in the dream vision of the drugged assassins. Thus Arnold von Lübeck relates the legend of the Old Man of the Mountain in his *Chronica Slavorum* around 1210:

> About this Old Man I am told a ridiculous story, but one that is attested to me by reliable witnesses. This Old Man, by his magic art, knows how to deceive the people of his land, so that they believe in no other God but him. He also fills them by supernatural means with the hope of eternal joy and happiness, so that they prefer Death to Life. For often many of them, upon a sign or order from him, have hurled themselves from a high wall, on which they were standing; so that they died with a broken neck below. Those he declares the most blessed who spill human blood and in such an act of revenge find their own death. If some of them have chosen to die in this manner, that they agree to kill someone by treachery, hoping to die more blessed because of it, he himself hands them daggers especially sanctified for this purpose, and by a certain potion puts them into a state of ecstasy, rapture, and transport, and lets them see through his magic powers fantastic visions full of joy and pleasure, or rather of folly, promising them these joys in eternity if they carry out such a deed.[51]

In the second type a different device is employed by the Old Man to make his followers believe that they are in Paradise. Children are early locked in a dark, ugly place and never allowed to gaze upon the beauty outside. Once released from this dungeon, they are amazed by the beauty of the world and believe themselves to be in Paradise. Since it is the Old Man who lets them into "Paradise," they consider him to be God and are ready to obey him.[52]

By the time Marco Polo made his famous journey to China, the fortress at Alamût and the sect of the Assassins had been

---

[51] W. Fleischhauer, "The Old Man of the Mountain: The Growth of a Legend," *Symposium*, IX (1955), 80.

[52] Fleischhauer, p. 81.

destroyed.[53] However, the legend was still popular among the people of the area. It is Marco Polo's story and that of Odoric de Pordenone which became so well known to later European literature.

Polo says that the Old Man had enclosed a valley between two mountains and had made the area into a beautiful garden. Every variety of fruit, beautiful pavilions, rivers of wine, milk, honey, and water, as well as ladies and damsels, could be found in the garden. No one was allowed there except those whom the Old Man would make his "Ashishen." He kept many youths between twelve and twenty years of age at his court and told them tales of Paradise. Then he would give some of them a certain potion which put them into a deep sleep. While asleep, they were carried into the garden, which the waking youths took to be the Paradise of which they had heard. After a period of enjoyment, the Old Man again had them drugged and returned to the palace. He then told them that he would have his angels return them to the Paradise if they would accomplish his will.[54]

The fascination which the legend of the Assassins had for the European can be seen in its appearance in five Provençal poems that were probably composed around 1200.[55] The theme in each poem concerns an aspect of courtly love which is comparable to the faithfulness of the Assassin. In the poem "Pos descobrir ni retraire" of Aimeric de Peguilhan, probably written between 1195 and 1230, the poet writes:

> Car mieills m'avetz ses doptanssa,
> Qe'l Vieills l'Asasina gen,

---

[53] The sect's fortress was destroyed in 1256 A. D. by the forces of Hulagu Kahn. Only after a long siege did Kahn's forces succeed in starving the besieged into submission.

[54] *The Book of Ser Marco Polo*, trans. and ed., with notes by Sir Henry Yule (3rd ed.; London, 1929), pp. 139-146.

[55] Chambers suggests that Philip Augustus' accusation in 1192 that Richard Coeur de Lion had hired Assassins to have him killed may have stimulated a special interest in the sect. This increased curiosity may have influenced the poets to use some aspect of Assassin fidelity or obedience as an analogy in their poems. (Frank M. Chambers, "The Troubadours and the Assassins," *Modern Language Notes*, LXIV [1949], *passim*.)

> Qu'il vant, neis s'eron part Franssa,
> Tant li son obedien,
> Aucir sos gerriers mortals. [56]

Whereas Aimeric speaks of being in his Lady's power just as the Assassin is in the power of the Old Man, Bernart de Bondeilhs writes that he will serve love as unfailingly as the Assassins serve their master. [57] In a very interesting passage found in a love letter written to his Lady, an anonymous poet writes:

> Lo vostre verais ancessis,
> Que cre conquestar paradis
> Per far toz vostres mandamens. [58]

Thus not only the idea of fidelity, but the reward of paradise which the Old Man promised enters into the poet's comparison.

Two final references, one by Aimeric de Peguilhan and the other by Giraut de Bornelh, compare respectively the heart and love to the Assassin. In the poem by Aimeric, the heart is killing the poet:

> Mas faich avetz ansessi
> Mon cor que per vos m'auci. [59]

And in the poem by Giraut, it is his love for his lady which, like the Assassin, is destroying him:

> Ren als no·lh sai comtar
> Mas que s'amors m'auci.
> Ai, plus mal assesi
> Noca·m saup envirar. [60]

The Assassins made an impression on mediaeval society which can scarcely be exaggerated. It is even said that the Knights

---

[56] "You have me more fully in your power than the Old Man his Assassins, who go to kill his mortal enemies, even if they were beyond France." (Ibid., p. 245.)

[57] Ibid., p. 246.

[58] "I am your Assassin who hopes to win Paradise through doing your commands" (Ibid., p. 247).

[59] Ibid. Chambers loosely summarizes, "He likens his heart to an Assassin since it kills him for his lady's sake."

[60] Ibid., p. 248. Chambers summarizes the essential idea: "My Lady's love (i. e., my love for her) is an Assassin, which kills me."

Templar, formed in 1108 by Bernard de Clairvaux to protect Christians in their travels to the Holy Land, were organized upon the model of this strange sect.[61]

In literature the story told by Marco Polo found its way into numerous chronicles and became the basis for Boccaccio's eighth story of the third day in the *Decamerone*. Here a Tuscan abbot uses the magic potion employed by the Old Man of the Mountain to put aside temporarily the bumpkin husband, Ferondo, of a lady he wishes to seduce. Still asleep from the drug, Ferondo is transported into a black vault where, once awake, he is made to reside thinking that he has died and is now in Purgatory. When the lady becomes pregnant, Ferondo is again put under the potion's powers and allowed to return to life to assume responsibility for the child which will be born.

In the seventeenth century La Fontaine retells this story from the *Decamerone* in one of his *Contes* ("Féronde ou le Purgatoire"), but places the tale of the Old Man and his followers in a kind of preface to the narrative.

Interest in the legend of the Assassins remained active long after the sect had been disbanded in the latter half of the thirteenth century. In 1603, a certain Denis Labey de Batilly, Conseiller du Roy, Maistre des Requestes de son hostel à la couronne de Navarre, et commis par sa Maiesté à l'exercise de l'Estat de President en la Ville de Mets ... attempted to set forth the true historic origin of the term *Assassin*, which had recently become a lively topic.[62]

In 1659, Henricus Bangertus edited with commentary Lübeck's *Chronica Slavorum*, which contains an account of the Assassins, and Herbelot included the story of the sect in his *Bibliothèque*

---

[61] Nowell makes the following comparison between the organization of the Knights Templar and the organization of the Assassins: "The Christian order, in its lower branches, consisted of lay-brothers, esquires, and knights, which were duplicated in the Lasiqs (laymen), Fidâ'is (agents), and Rafîqs (companions) of the Assassins. Templar knights were required to wear white mantles, on which was the familiar mark of the red cross. Assassin Rafîqs, the group corresponding to the knights, also wore white and completed the parallel with red finishings; not crosses but caps." (C. E. Nowell, "The Old Man of the Mountain," *Speculum*, XXII [1947], 504-505.)

[62] Bernard Lewis, "The Sources and History of the Syrian Assassins," *Speculum*, XXVII (1952), 475.

Orientale of 1697.[63] Interest continued during the eighteenth century with Falconet's essay[64] and flourished in the nineteenth century as a result of an increased interest in Oriental studies. The monumental work of Silvestre de Sacy in the early nineteenth century[65] and the widely circulated study of J. von Hammer,[66] the most comprehensive to that date, stimulated interest in the legend of the Old Man of the Mountain and made the legend well known to the *literati* of the period.

---

[63] M. d'Herbelot, *Bibliothèque orientale* (Paris, 1697).

[64] M. Falconet, "Dissertation sur les Assassins, peuple d'Asie," *Mémoires de Littérature Tirés des Régistres de l'Académie Royale des Inscriptions et Belles-Lettres*, XVII (1751), 127-170.

[65] Silvestre de Sacy, "Mémoire sur la dynastie des Assassins," *Mémoires de l'Académie des Inscriptions et Belles Lettres*, IV, part 2, Paris, 1818.

[66] J. von Hammer, *Histoire de l'ordre des Assassins*, trans. by J. J. Hellert and P. A. de la Nourais (Paris, 1833).

Chapter III

OPIUM AND HASHISH IN THE LITERARY SOCIETY
OF THE NINETEENTH CENTURY

From the evidence presented one can see that opium was well known to European physicians by the nineteenth century. A survey of studies on opium from 1500 to 1850 indicates the great interest of the medical profession in the drug. From 1500 to 1700 more than fifteen works were written concerning opium and its marvelous effects. Interest in the drug increased noticeably from 1700 to 1800, as more than forty full length studies appeared concerning its effects and possible therapeutic uses. This remarkable trend continued in the nineteenth century. After 1800 there is, on the average, more than one full length study a year. For the most part these works concern only the medical aspects of the drug, although its famed powers as an aphrodisiac are occasionally discussed. Hashish, on the other hand, was rarely mentioned and there are few studies on it before 1800.

Even though the persistent and increasing interest in opium as a therapeutic medical agent can be shown, one must wonder how the use of opium and hashish became such a fad in the early nineteenth century among literary and artistic people.[1] How did these drugs gain reputations as stimulants to artistic inspiration, and in what way were they used in connection with the literary

---

[1] Even a partial list of French writers and painters believed to have indulged in opium or hashish indicates the widespread interest in these drugs. Lamartine, Nodier, Musset, Hégésippe Moreau, Murger, Grandville, Nerval, Balzac, Barbey d'Aurevilly, Sue, Boissard, Karr, Gautier, Dumas, Baudelaire, et al., tried opium or hashish at some time during their lives.

pursuits of the period? To answer these questions, one must consider the great interest in the Orient [2] which developed in France during the seventeenth and eighteenth centuries, for it is in the fascination with the Orient and everything exotic that one can see the closest link between opium and hashish and the romantic literature of the early nineteenth century.

The beginning of French interest in the Orient is traditionally placed around 1664 with the successful formation of the Compagnie des Indes Orientales. [3] Under Louis XIV France entered into direct relations with the Far East. Various trade ventures and missionary endeavors established permanent ties between France and the Far East, and caused a commercial and political exchange which attracted those who were curious about strange peoples and countries. It became fashionable to own oriental objects and furnishings, and the curious were even piqued into adopting unusual habits and mannerisms which were reported common in the distant lands. Maugras mentions, in his *La Cour de Lunéville*, that Stanislas de Lorraine amused himself by smoking "dans une grande pipe à la turque de six pieds de long." [4] From the correspondence of Mme du Deffand one learns that the "Marquis des Alleurs informait soigneusement Mme du Deffand du mode de vivre des Turcs; il lui donnait des conseils forts autorisés sur la manière de fumer l'opium." [5]

This fad for the Orient included furnishings for apartments, clothing, curiosities, and various spices and perfumes. The great interest seemed to lie in the exotic aspect of these items, which people wished to acquire simply because of their strangeness. It was not so much a question of artistic taste or admiration which caused individuals to want to own the statuettes of the mysterious

---

[2] I use the word Orient here to signify both the Far East and the Near East.

[3] There was, of course, interest in the Orient prior to 1660, but only a few attempts had been made to establish contact. Companies were formed in 1604, 1615, and 1635 in an effort to initiate trade with the Orient, but they ended in failure. (Pierre Martino, *L'Orient dans la littérature française* [Paris, 1906].)

[4] Martino, p. 347.

[5] Ibid., p. 91.

Indian divinities or the Chinese pagodas, but rather because they were symbols of exoticism, symbols of a strange way of life.

The taste for exoticism was greatly aroused by the numerous fabulous travel accounts which entertained the readers in the eighteenth and nineteenth centuries; and it is in this form of literature that one begins to see the Orient become associated with stimulants and narcotics. Before 1660 there were about ten travel accounts on India, three or four on China and Persia, and several on the Near East. After 1660 and the formation of commercial ties, the number of travel accounts increased rapidly. At least forty to fifty can be cited in the last third of the seventeenth century, and numerous accounts appeared until 1746, when the twenty-volume publication known as the *Histoire générale des voyages* was begun. Such accounts often contained exaggerated description of the manners and customs of the people and quite naturally delighted in relating anything which would amaze the French reader. For this reason the travelers took pleasure in describing the bizarre custom of using opium or hashish or drinking tea or coffee, and in describing their effects upon the individual.

In his description of Persia, Chardin devotes a section of his work to various drugs commonly used by the Persians, including opium and "bueng," a preparation from hemp. He notes that in taking opium, "les Persans trouvent qu'elle produit dans le cerveau des visions agréables et une manière d'enchantement." [6] Other characteristics which he indicates, such as the immoderate laughter provoked by the drug, suggest that the opium was mixed with hashish. Chardin relates that a certain P. Ange de Saint-Joseph, a missionary to Ispahan who had taken the drug, "... voyait des fantômes et mille chimères lui passer devant les yeux, qui lui paroissoient grotesques, et le divertissoient merveilleusement ...." [7] In the descriptions of both opium and "bueng," Chardin indicates that each is a dangerous, habit-forming drug which tends to shorten one's life. Once a person was habituated to the drug, death would occur if his supply were removed.

---

[6] *Voyages du Chevalier Chardin en Perse, et autres lieux de l'Orient,* ed. par L. Langlès (Paris, 1811), p. 74.
[7] Chardin, p. 76.

Chardin feels that the primary motivation for taking these drugs is to find relief from "ennui": "... vous les voyez [les cabarets] pleins de gens qui cherchent, dans cet enivrement, une trêve à leurs ennuis, et une trêve à leur misère." [8]

Also fascinating to the romantic artist must have been accounts such as the one by Dubois, which told of the use of opium in occult and religious ceremonies. Dubois states that many forbidden items —meats, liquor, and drugs (opium was especially noted)— were brought before the idol of Vishnu and indulged in to excess. After such overindulgence, all kinds of sexual excesses were permitted. [9]

As mentioned above, some accounts treated coffee and tea in much the same manner as the drugs. An indication of the respect for coffee as a stimulant can be seen in the long essay written by La Roque in connection with his *Voyage de l'Arabie heureuse*. Le Mousti d'Aden, Gemaleddin Abou Abdallah, "... s'apperçut bientôt des autres propriétés du café, et sur tout de celles qu'il a de dissiper la pesanteur de la tête, d'égaier l'esprit, et d'empêcher le sommeil, sans en être incommodé. Il fit particulièrement son profit de cette dernière qualité, prenant du café avec les Derviches, ou Religieux Mahométans, à l'entrée de la nuit pour la passer en prières, et dans les autres exercices de sa Religion, avec plus de liberté d'esprit." [10]

The oriental tale is another important medium through which the Romantics were introduced to drugs as stimulants. Especially popular among such works was the *Mille et une nuits*. Frequently in this group of stories a potion is used by a faithless wife to put her husband to sleep so that she may pursue her love affairs, and in several instances a mixture of hashish or bhang is specifically mentioned. One particular story, "The Tale of the Hashish-Eater," though not found in Galland's translation of the *Mille et une nuits*, may yet have been known to the Romantics, and is of interest for its representation of many aspects of hashish about which they

---

[8] Ibid., p. 82.
[9] J. A. Dubois, *Description of the Character, Manners, and Customs of the People of India; and of Their Institutions, Religious and Civil* (Philadelphia, 1818), pp. 240-242.
[10] La Roque, *Voyage de l'Arabie heureuse* (Amsterdam, 1716), p. 276.

were concerned. The tale is told by the slave woman Bakun in an effort to put to sleep Kanmakin, a man she has been sent to kill. In the story, a hashish-eater, who had become poor through squandering his money on fair women, goes into a bath to tend a bleeding finger. Finding no one in the bath, he decides to take some hashish and begins to have a hallucination. He imagines that he is being waited upon by a lord and two slaves occupied in giving him a shampoo. The scene changes, and he is brought into a room filled with the sweet fragrance of fruits and flowers, and the scent of burning incense and perfumes. In a way characteristic of many hashish hallucinations, he retains an awareness of reality, realizing that what he is experiencing cannot be real: "Haply they are now blundering; but after an hour they will know me and say, this fellow is a beggar; and take their fill of cuffing me on the neck." [11] He is carried into a hall of beautiful, magnificent furnishings, such as befit only a king, and placed on a divan where he is kneaded to sleep. While asleep, he has a very erotic dream in which he is about to have intercourse with a beautiful slave girl. At this point he is awakened by a crowd of people who are laughing at his erotic posture. Just as he had predicted earlier in his moment of lucidity, he was soundly cuffed on the neck.

Many of the effects of hashish which fascinated the Romantic are present in this short tale. The hashish-eater realizes what he is experiencing and yet he is unable to determine where reality is. He is placed in beautiful surroundings and all the while is victim of a hallucination which makes use of or conforms to the actual setting. And in the dream within the hallucination, one sees the erotic effect which hashish was supposed to have.

Most of the Romantics took great delight in the *Mille et une nuits*, and Martino describes well its attraction for them:

> ... ce qui charma aussi ... ce fut le caractère Fantastique du récit. L'homme, dans les *Mille et une Nuits*, semblait échapper aux lois naturelles. Traversée par des génies, bouleversée par des catastrophes faciles et innoffensives,

---

[11] Sir Richard Burton, *Arabian Nights* (Benares edition, 1885-1887), III, 92.

encombrée de gnomes, de magiciens et de sorciers, pleine de talismans et d'animaux extraordinaires, la terre n'était plus la contrée de plate misère, où s'allongent côte à côte des existences monotones; c'était un champ ouvert aux plus audacieuses énergies et créé pour les plus déconcertantes aventures; le ciel et l'enfer, la surface du globe, tout voisinait indistinctement. [12]

Napoleon's campaign to Egypt at the beginning of the nineteenth century increased the Romantics' acquaintance with hashish and caused them to associate it with the Near East. Brotteaux states that Sonnerat was the first to bring hashish to France after his return from a voyage to the Indies in 1782. Although it is believed that hashish was actually known in France prior to Sonnerat's voyage, very little attention was paid to the drug before 1800. During his campaign, Napoleon was forced to give an order forbidding all French soldiers to indulge in hashish. Some of the soldiers brought the habit to France, however, as did many other Frenchmen who worked for the government or traveled in the Near East. Later in the century it was frequently stated that France's problem of addiction was largely a result of the return of addicted government functionaries from the colonial possessions. [13]

The increased interest in Oriental studies at the end of the eighteenth and the beginning of the nineteenth centuries inspired several works which had much to do in spreading the fascination with hashish. Chief among these were the writings of Silvestre de Sacy. In 1809 de Sacy published a study in the *Bulletin des Sciences Médicales* entitled "Des préparations enivrantes faites avec le chanvre"; and two other publications by the same author in 1818 became very popular among the romantic writers. De Sacy's *Mémoire sur la dynastie des Assassins et sur l'étymologie de leur nom* and his *Chrestomathie arabe* furnished Gérard de Nerval much of his information concerning the Druses and the Caliph Hakem and brought to the attention of most Romantics the fascinating story of the Old Man of the Mountain and his

---

[12] Martino, p. 256.
[13] R. Dupouy, *Les opiomanes, mangeurs, buveurs et fumeurs d'opium* (Paris, 1912), pp. i-ii.

exotic use of the drug hashish. This story, referred to or retold by Dumas, Gérard de Nerval, Baudelaire, Gautier, and Moreau de Tours, among others, was perhaps as responsible as any other single factor for the widespread interest in hashish. Exotic in the true sense of the word, it provided an escape and an exhibition (supposedly from history) of the intense faith which the Romantics so earnestly sought.

Through their curiosity about the Orient, then, and their desire for the exotic, the Romantics were introduced to the various stimulating drinks and drugs from which they hoped to find a means of escape to an exciting, exotic, poetic world which would have all the charm of Paradise. It is curious that the early European concept of the Orient from which the wondrous spices were brought was that it was a Paradise. Belevitch-Stankevitch writes that...

> Beaucoup de personnes étaient convaincues que les épices fines, exquises au point d'être nommées "paradisiaques," venaient tout droit du paradis. Or, comme on savait qu'elles arrivaient à Alexandrie par le Nil, ce fleuve fut identifié avec le Gehon, fleuve du paradis. Pour les crédules, les épices et les bois précieux étaient les fruits et les branches des arbres, croissant sur les bords, qui étaient tombés dans ses eaux et emportés par le courant jusqu'à l'Égypte, où l'on ne faisait que les repêcher.[14]

Joinville says of the Nile that it is "un fleuve qui vient d'Égypte et du Paradis terrestre; et que l'on pêche dans ses eaux la rhubarbe, le gingembre, l'aloès et la cannelle, bois sec tombé des arbres du Paradis quand il fait du vent."[15]

Scarron's poem in the seventeenth century indicates the concept of an Orient-Paradise suggested by the exotic beauty of the articles found there:

> Menez-moi chez les Portugais
> Nous y verrons à peu de frais
> Les marchandises de la Chine,

---

[14] H. Belevitch-Stankevitch, *Le goût chinois en France au temps de Louis XIV* (Paris, 1910), p. xv.
[15] Emile Deschanel, *Physiologie des écrivains et des artistes* (Paris, 1864), p. 39.

> Nous y verrons de l'ambre gris,
> De beaux ouvrages de vernis,
> Et de la porcelaine fine
> De cette contrée divine
> Ou plutôt de ce paradis. [16]

The Romantics, having learned through the Orient of the stimulating effects of drugs and beverages, hoped that exotic stimulants (perfumes, tobaccos, beverages and drugs) would carry their vivid imaginations far from the banal world around them that seemed engulfed in "ennui." Flaubert speaks of the wondrous effect of tea and how it carries his mind to the exotic lands from which it comes. Balzac's *Voyage de Paris à Java*, an amusing parody on the many exotic travel accounts which were being written, has an interesting section worth quoting concerning the relative values of wine, coffee, tea, and opium, "les quatre grands stimulants ... qui compromettent singulièrement l'immatérialité de notre âme." [17] Wine, he says, is gross and brings a drunkenness of the body, whereas coffee

> ... procure une fièvre admirable! Il entre dans le cerveau comme une ménade. A son attaque, l'imagination court échevelée, elle se met à nu, elle se tord, elle est comme une pythonisse, et, dans ce paroxysme inspirateur un poëte jouit de facultés centuplées; mais c'est l'ivresse de la pensée comme le vin amène l'ivresse du corps. [18]

Of the four stimulants, opium is the most all-consuming:

> ... l'opium absorbe toutes les forces humaines, il les rassemble sur un point, il les prend, les carre ou les cube, les porte à je ne sais quelle puissance, donne à l'être entier toute une création dans le vide. Il fait rendre à chaque sens sa plus grande somme de volupté, l'irrite, le fatigue, l'use; aussi l'opium est-il une mort calculée. [19]

---

[16] Belevitch-Stankevitch, pp. 145-146.
[17] Honoré de Balzac, *Oeuvres complètes d'Honoré de Balzac* (Paris: Conard, 1938), XXXIX, 574.
[18] Ibid., p. 576.
[19] Ibid.

On the whole, however, tea holds first place; for in tea all the beautiful visions and joys of opium can be had without its dangers:

> Le thé, pris à grandes doses et bu dans les contrées, où, comme à Java, la feuille, fraîche encore, n'a rien perdu de ses précieux parfums, le thé vous verse tous les trésors de la mélancolie, les rêves, les projets du soir, même les conceptions inspirées par le café, même les jouissances de l'opium. Mais ces caprices arrachés au cerveau se jouent dans une atmosphère grise et vaporeuse. Les idées sont douces. Vous n'êtes privé d'aucun des bénéfices de la vivacité corporelle. Votre état n'est pas le sommeil, mais une somnolence indécise semblable à la rêvasserie du matin. [20]

In Balzac's *Voyage de Paris à Java* we see something of what the Romantics hoped to attain through the use of stimulants. Without making an actual voyage, which he well knew would not take him to an exotic paradise, Balzac sought escape, through his heightened senses, to another plane of reality where all was beauty and harmony. Because of the hypersensitivity caused by the stimulants, little impetus was needed to stir the imagination. The fragance of an exotic perfume, such as ambergris or musk, or a scent recalling a Javanese girl's hair was enough to carry one into an entire exotic setting:

> Puis plongé dans une infertile méditation, fruit défendu aux gens de peine at aux gens de lettres, ... je vais flairant les parfums indiens. Je me perds au milieu de ces pays grandioses auxquels l'Angleterre restitue aujourd'hui leurs antiques magies. [21]

In the preface to *Une âme en peine* by Amédée Kermel, the author offers to escape with his love "dans l'Orient, abîmés que nous serions dans les ivresses extatiques de l'opium, bercés par le chant des Almées et des Bayadères." [22]

Thus interest in the Orient helped introduce the Romantic to the "stimulants." What he hoped to achieve in employing them

---

[20] Ibid.
[21] Ibid.
[22] Louis Maigron, *Le romantisme et les moeurs* (Paris, 1910), p. 18.

was in part the exotic reality which he imagined the Orient itself to be. Hence the words *opium, hashish,* and *tea* are frequently introduced into writings merely to add an exotic atmosphere.

At a time when the literary figures in France and England were fascinated by the aspects of horror and phantasmagory of the "conte fantastique" and the Gothic novel, it is no wonder that such a work as De Quincey's *Confessions of an English Opium-Eater* found immediate acclaim. De Quincey's opium dreams suggested new possibilities of horror and charm through the hallucination of the senses. As its influence on Balzac shows, the idea of hallucination provided a stimulus to imagination and seemed to add life to imaginative works of this kind.

Together with the oriental fashion of the day, De Quincey's writing encouraged the fad of taking drugs and had great influence on the literature of the nineteenth century. The number of references to the *Confessions* in doctors' theses indicates that the work was well known to the medical profession in France by the 1830's. Doctor Botta's thesis on the use of opium (1829) cites "O just, subtile, and mighty opium" from De Quincey as an epigraph. [23]

Published first in the *London Magazine* in 1821, the *Confessions of an English Opium-Eater* was not translated in France until Alfred de Musset published a version of the 1823 edition in 1828. Musset's work, entitled *L'Anglais mangeur d'opium,* has suffered diverse criticism because of its author's failure to translate the complete text of De Quincey, and because of certain errors in translation and deviations from the English text. It should be noted, however, that Musset obviously intended to adapt the text and frequently deleted details which did not agree with his adaptation and the episodes he had added. While errors were made in translation, it is hardly justifiable to say that Musset knew little English. Long passages are accurately rendered and occasionally Musset is able to condense a complicated digression with admirable clarity into a few sentences. The weakest part is the added episode on De Quincey's later encounter with Ann

---

[23] P. E. Botta, *De l'usage de fumer l'opium* (Paris, 1829). The epigraph is on the title page.

and the subsequent duel scene, romanesque and puerile in conception. It is of interest that he attempted to change the relationship between Ann and De Quincey, always maintained as a sisterly, human affection, to one that conforms more to a romantic notion of love. In one passage where De Quincey says that he would like to see Ann again, whether in brothel or grave "there to awaken thee with an authentic message of peace and forgiveness, and of final reconciliation," [24] Musset writes that he would bring to her there "le cri de mon amour, de mon respect, de mon admiration . . . . "[25] It has been stated that the French have always been fascinated by De Quincey's episode with Ann, even more than by the opium descriptions. Musset's adaption is, no doubt, in part responsible for this. His added romantic episode gives the impression that De Quincey's relationship with Ann was the most important single incident in the book.

Because of Jacques Crépet's statement that Musset's translation passed "complètement inaperçue" at the time of its publication, it was long believed that his work had little influence on the literature of the nineteenth century. As the story is related, neither Musset, nor his brother, nor any of Musset's biographers considered the translation from De Quincey of any consequence. Thus Musset's *L'Anglais mangeur d'opium* supposedly passed unnoticed until a certain Charles Soto uncovered it in 1868 and subsequently passed it on to Arthur Heulhard, who published it in the *Moniteur du Bibliophile* in 1878.

It is true that Baudelaire does not mention Musset's adaptation when speaking of his own, although he seems to indicate a knowledge of its existence when he says that the *Confessions* of De Quincey have never been completely translated. Moreover, few references to Musset's adaptation can be found among the writings of the 1830's and 1840's.

However, it has been shown that *L'Anglais mangeur d'opium* influenced a number of writings during the period, and that Balzac knew the work early and thought highly of it. In the

---

[24] Thomas De Quincey, *The Collected Writings of Thomas De Quincey*, edited by David Masson, VIII (London, 1897), 362.

[29] Alfred de Musset, *Œuvres complètes* (Paris: Éditions de Seuil, 1963), p. 576.

amusing little story, "Les litanies romantiques" (1830), where Balzac speaks of the great literary critic M. S..., who cannot find complete delight in the poetry of any work, no matter how good, he mentions the *Mangeur d'opium* as one of the excellent works so fated. In Balzac's short work "L'opium" (1830) there are many similarities to Musset's adaptation from De Quincey. The most convincing proof of influence is that Balzac borrows whole phrases from the short scene in Spain which is not in the English text, but was added by Musset. In Balzac's "L'opium" two men watch an Andalusian woman "... abritée par un store de soie rouge." In Musset's work the Andalusian woman is seen behind a "jalousie" (also mentioned in "L'opium") and the sun shines beautifully "... à travers la soie rouge des stores ...." [26] Much later, Balzac incorporated almost the whole of "L'opium" in *Massimilla Doni*. Randolph Hughes also notes considerable influence on Balzac's *La peau de chagrin*, whose beginning is very similar to a passage in De Quincey's "Tortures de l'opium." [27]

Maurice Saillet points out a number of instances where authors were influenced by De Quincey's well-known hallucination occasioned by the phrase *consul romanus*, a phrase of great significance to the avid reader of Livy.

In Balzac's *La peau de chagrin* the hero, Raphael de Valentin, in his visit to a shop of antiquities, sees various things from Egypt and India and recalls the dream of De Quincey:

> Armée du pouvoir des talismans arabes, la tête de Cicéron évoquait les souvenirs de la Rome libre et lui déroulait les pages de Tite-Live. Le jeune homme contempla *Senatus Populusque Romanus:* le consul, ses licteurs, les toges brodées de pourpre, les luttes du Forum, le peuple courroucé défilaient lentement devant lui comme les vaporeuses figures d'un rêve. [28]

---

[26] Randolph Hughes, "Vers la contrée du rêve," *Mercure de France*, No. 239 (1939), 563.

[27] Ibid., p. 545.

[28] Saillet also points out quotations from Gérard de Nerval, Gautier, and Baudelaire which show definite drug influence, but which are too general in nature to be identified with certainty as borrowings from De Quincey. Later in the century, both Huysmans and Jarry borrowed from the famous *consul romanus* passage. Des Esseintes, the hero of *A rebours*, has a vision whose similarity is acknowledged by the author: "De même qu'après une

Another influence which acquainted the Romantics with drugs and fostered their use is related to the great interest in Swedenborgianism or in a general Neo-Platonic philosophy, and to romantic interest in mysticism, sorcery, magnetism and the occult. Baudelaire, Balzac, Gautier, and Gérard de Nerval, to name a few, were all interested in and influenced by the general philosophic system which proposes that this life is only the reflection of a Greater Reality which exists in the mind of God. All is created by God and therefore is only a manifestation of the Divine Thought. Hence, everything in this life bears an analogy to the Greater Reality. Man is the microcosm, a perfect duplication in miniature of the macrocosm. Since all created things are made from the same substance, the Divine Thought, everything bears analogy to every other thing, and all matter physically has contact with all other matter within the universe. Birth and death are only entrances into two different states of being. And thus time and space are simply two conditions of observation, two modes of being, two ways that the soul perceives.

Behind the variations of the Neo-Platonic notion of a Greater Reality, which became so popular in the eighteenth century and grew in popularity in the nineteenth century, was a common bond which united mystics, occultists, and magnetists, etc. against the growing force of materialism. In the practices of all these groups drugs played an important part. Experimentation with drugs seemed to allow the users to move into the other area of reality proclaimed in their beliefs. Since it was the poet's accepted task to apprehend and reveal the relationships between the exterior world and the interior world, he looked upon the drugs as an excellent means of producing that traditional state of ecstasy or frenzy which gives the poet greater vision.

---

touche d'opium, de Quincey, au seul mot de Consul Romanus, évoquait des pages entières de Tite-Live, regardait s'avancer la marche solennelle des consuls, s'ébranler la pompeuse ordonnance des armées romaines; lui, sur une expression théologique demeurait haletant, considérait des reflux de peuple, des apparitions épiscopales, se détachant sur les fonds embrasés des basiliques; ces spectacles le tenaient sous le charme, courant d'âges en âges, arrivant aux cérémonies religieuses modernes, le roulant dans un infini de musique, lamentable et tendre." (Maurice Saillet, *Sur la route de Narcisse* [Paris, 1958], pp. 90-91.)

Bosc points out that sorcerers of the Middle Ages used drugs to enter into contact with divine spirits and in the preparation of aphrodisiacs;[29] and Michelet tells us that all who were considered sorcerers used mandragora, datura, henbane and belladonna in their practices.[30]

From Allendy's definition it is easy to see how closely opium was allied to the three principal endeavors of alchemy.

> L'Alchimie présente un triple caractère; elle poursuit un but chimique, avec la Pierre philosophale; physiologique avec la Palingénésie et l'Homunculus, et thérapeutique, avec la Panacée Universelle. Elle est basée tout entière sur un système philosophique: L'Hermétisme, dont elle est l'application pratique aux choses de la nature. Elle cherche à transformer la forme extérieure des corps, à transporter, à reproduire la vie. Elle est donc la Science des transmutations, et elle veut être une sorte de Physiologie intégrale des trois règnes.[31]

Opium enjoyed the reputation of being the universal panacea, the medicine which seemed to work through an ". . . *occult Quality*, wholly unexplicable, and particularly reserved from the *Knowledge of Mankind*."[32] Opium was called the "Stone of Immortality" by Paracelsus and the "universal Panacea" by De Quincey himself.

Occultists used opium experimentally throughout the nineteenth century. In *L'opium à Paris,* Fabrice takes his reader into many of the places where opium is smoked. He introduces him to a group of occultists whose leader is a certain Stan... de G... (apparently Stanislas de Guaita). The author asks, "... vos amis et vous vous livrez à des expériences d'occultisme expérimental. Quelle valeur peuvent avoir vos observations si vos cerveaux sont troublés?"[33] One of the friends of Stan... de G... replies:

> Vos observations, judicieuses et justes pour les phénomènes de la vie terrestre, ne sauraient s'appliquer à l'Au-Delà. Nous croyons fermement que tous les excitants

---

[29] Eugène Bosc, *Traité théorique et pratique du haschich et autres substances psychiques* (Paris, 1895), p. 27.
[30] Jules Michelet, *La sorcière* (Paris, 1952), p. 179.
[31] R. F. Allendy, *L'alchimie et la médecine* (Paris, 1912), p. 15.
[32] J. Jones, *The Mysteries of Opium Revealed* (London, 1700), p. 41.
[33] D. Fabrice, *L'opium à Paris* (Paris, 1914), pp. 166-168.

> cérébraux, et l'opium au premier rang, sont de merveilleux extériorisateurs de la pensée. Le fumeur d'opium, après quelques pipes, entre dans un état de tranquillité parfaite. La vie d'ici-bas n'existe plus pour lui. Son corps est une loque dont il n'a cure. Toute sa force s'est concentrée dans son cerveau ... ses premiers effets sont toujours de stimuler et d'exalter l'homme, de le purifier; et cette partie épurée de son être et ses perfections morales jouissent de leur maximum de souplesse, et, avant tout, son intelligence acquiert une lucidité consolante et sans nuages ... C'est seulement sous cette influence ... que les initiés distinguent mieux et plus subtilement les phénomènes de l'Occulte. Des indices, des insignifiances éparses, les frappent. Ils les réunissent, en forment un faisceau et finissent par en tirer des conclusions.
>
> Et puis quelle force possède un cerveau dégagé de toute matérialité pour agir, commander même à l'Au-Delà! [34]

Desoille states that occultists make use also of hashish to give themselves a vision of the Great Beyond. He relates the following method suggested by Lancelin:

> Près de chaque oreille, on suspend une montre dont le tic-tac monotone produit comme une sorte de bercement du sens, tandis que dans l'obscurité complète de la pièce, à une certaine distance de l'opérateur, une petite lampe à l'alcool est allumée où brûle de l'alcool ordinaire, mais dans lequel on a fait macérer préalablement, pendant 24 heures, une forte pincée de *fleurs de chanvre* par litre. La lumière obtenue par ce moyen, à la fois vacillante et fascinante, répand des émanations narcotiques très douces ... [35]

Interest in magnetism, somnambulism and spiritualism was great throughout most of the nineteenth century. Balzac's interest in magnetism and the anecdote concerning his mother's cure by a magnetist are well known. Gautier attended the "séances" of Mme de Girardin and was ardently interested in all things con-

---

[34] Ibid.
[35] Henri Desoille, "Croyances et états mentaux des occultistes actuels," *Hygiène Mentale*, 25 (1930), 130.

cerning the world of the spirits. Alphonse Karr has two articles on magnetism which challenge men of science to disprove the existence of any such force rather than make empty accusations against it. [36] Such articles, written seriously for public consumption, indicate the interest of individuals in magnetism and their belief in it.

Dr. Alphonse Cahagnet's book, *Sanctuaire du Spiritualisme*, published in 1848, shows best perhaps the relationship which hashish and other drugs had to the literary world and the world of thought in the middle of the nineteenth century. [37]

Cahagnet begins by expounding his philosophic beliefs concerning life, the universe, and creation. Of central importance to his Neo-Platonic conception of life is the belief that man is the microcosm in which the universe is found in miniature. Hence, man can know all that can be known by looking within himself. Cahagnet relates how he began to try various drugs which might allow him to escape from his material form and to look within his spiritual self. First he tried opium, but had no success. After an unsuccessful attempt with hemp, which he had grown in his own garden, he burned incense, hemp seed, coriander, belladonna, aniseed, and gum arabic, all without success. None produced the ecstasy he was seeking. Finally, one day, while walking down the Rue de l'Ancienne Comédie, he noticed an apothecary's sign which read "Haschish d'Orient." He purchased some and tried three grams in a cup of coffee. After a few hours the drug took effect and he experienced the desired feeling of ecstasy. Interestingly enough, Cahagnet did not consider his experience a mere hallucination, an aberration of the senses. Rather he states that such terminology should be removed from scientific vocabulary:

> Let us hope that in a short time the words *madness, hallucination,* and *imagination* will be erased from our scientific language to be replaced by those of *internal life,* and *external life.* [38]

---

[36] Alphonse Karr, *En fumant,* "Du magnétisme" (Paris, 1882), p. 178.

[37] The following information was taken from a translation of Cahagnet's work by M. Flinders Pearson. The translated title is *The Sanctuary of Spiritualism.* Pearson's translation was published at London in 1851. The French original was not available to me.

[38] Ibid., p. 184.

Cahagnet looked upon hashish as a means of gaining the inner reality which the rational, waking life obscured:

> These phenomena demonstrated to me that these hallucinations, so called by all those who have taken this beverage, and on whom similar effects have been produced, were intended to establish sacred truths... [39]

While under the influence of hashish, Cahagnet experienced and proved to himself all the principles of existence which he had surmised to be true:

> This state is so different from the material state, that it is wholly impossible, while subjected to its influence, to appreciate the time that slips away, and the space that exists between the succession and continuance of these images. I felt a conviction that I hovered over the centre and above this microscopic universe, which nevertheless presented to me the semblances of form and space, producing the same effect and impression as material forms and spaces. Being swayed by the idea of observation and comparison between this state and the material state, I could not but pronounce in favor of the former. The material state appeared in all respects inferior — that is to say, the towns, monuments, public places, gardens, sky and earth, were of incomparable beauty. I found myself in the spots I desired to visit, without ceasing to observe that I perceived them in myself — that they were my domain. I had got the solution I had been in search of; I understood what man was — I was a universe in miniature; and I appreciated how it was a clairvoyant could be in Egypt or China without journeying thither... [40]

Cahagnet draws twelve conclusions from his experience and urges the individual to whom he is speaking to take advantage of this lesson:

> I teach you thereby the means of instructing yourself, and of verifying the truths I have revealed to you to the present time; learn how to profit by them. [41]

---

[39] Ibid., p. 66.
[40] Ibid., p. 67.
[41] Ibid., p. 68.

Cahagnet next records a group of experiments which he conducted with hashish on people from various levels of society. In most instances the person's visions tended to confirm the doctrine which he had set forth based on the works of Swedenborg. Finally, Cahagnet sums up the beliefs which he holds and suggests that others can prove these truths to themselves by employing hashish.

Cahagnet's view that hallucination is simply another reality, and his use of hashish to produce an ecstasy which would permit him to see and understand this reality were not unique ideas in 1848. His view is one to which many subscribed who were interested in madness and working diligently to understand the workings of the mind.

The early nineteenth century saw a considerable growth of interest in the psychological phenomena of insanity; and one may cite as evidence Esquirol's work, *Maladies mentales,* just after the turn of the century. Again opium plays an important role and one which surely introduced it into the medicine cabinet of many an artist. Esquirol, though not advising it, points out that a preparation of opium and musk was a favorite medicine for those thought to be suffering from melancholy, a serious psychological state traditionally said to be contracted in the heat of late summer or early autumn, and which supposedly developed into insanity in the cold months of winter. [42] This keen psychological interest in the human mind, manifested in literature by the psychologically-oriented development of the "conte fantastique" and the question of reality and insanity, attracted not only doctors but all those who held philosophically to the idea of a Greater Reality. Alphonse Esquiros, who believed ardently in magnetism and attended the hashish sessions at the Hôtel Pimodan, exhibits this interest in an article written for the *Revue des Deux Mondes* in 1847. He sums up the good work being done in the study of idiocy, and praises highly the current work on the physiology of thought aimed at finding the seat of the soul. He also mentions the wonderful

---

[42] E. Esquirol, *Des maladies mentales* (Paris, 1838), p. 25.

experiments in the study of hallucination, "... cette forme extraordinaire des maladies de l'esprit...."[43]

The question of reality, and of what reality there was in the hallucinations of a psychologically disturbed individual, was interesting to both literary men and doctors. Hashish becomes important to this area of study largely as a result of the ideas of Moreau de Tours, an eminent doctor from the asylum at Bicêtre.

Moreau de Tours believed that there is an essential identity between dreams and madness. In both the mind is characterized by a noted disorganization in the thought process, "une dissociation des idées."[44] Moreau de Tours considered this phenomenon to be the fundamental disturbance, the "fait primordial" of all delirium. It was in this regard that hashish attracted his attention as a possible therapeutic agent in treating insanity.

Initially drawn to the drug by curiosity, he quickly came to realize that hashish might be used to gain an insight into the workings of a psychologically disturbed mind. He found that one of the principal problems he encountered in treating the insane was his inability to understand the motivations and drives which the insane person gave as reasons for his actions. Since one could not get inside the mind of the disturbed individual, it seemed impossible to determine his trouble. Moreau de Tours thought that by using hashish the doctor could at last attain a state of mind analogous to that of a person psychologically disturbed and thus perhaps gain an insight into the world of involuntary hallucination. Hashish was considered an especially good medium since it seemed often to provide a duality of character allowing one to retain a critical outlook, even though he was powerless to prevent the hallucinatory effects of the drug. The phenomenon of duality aroused great interest in the hallucinations produced by hashish, for it seemed to prove that there were two orders of reality, or, as Moreau de Tours proposed, that man has two existences: one with the exterior world while he is awake, and the second with

---

[43] Alphonse Esquiros, "Maladies de l'esprit," *Revue des Deux Mondes*, Nouvelle Série, 18 (1847), 288.

[44] The following information was drawn from the work by Jean Moreau, *Du haschisch et de l'aliénation mentale; études psychologiques* (Paris, 1845).

an ideal world while he is dreaming or under the influence of an hallucinogenic drug:

> ... tant que les choses sont dans cet état [d'équilibre (i. e., sans confusion de ces deux aspects de conscience)], il y a *santé morale* parfaite, c'est-à-dire régularité des fonctions intellectuelles dans l'étendue des limites qui ont été tracées pour chacun de nous. Mais il arrive que sous l'influence de causes variées, physiques et morales, ces deux vies tendent à se confondre, les phénomènes propres à l'une et à l'autre, à se rapprocher, à s'unir dans l'acte simple et indivisible de la conscience intime ou du *moi*. Une fusion parfaite s'opère, et l'individu, sans avoir totalement quitté la vie réelle, appartient, sous plusieurs rapports, par divers points intellectuels, par de fausses sensations, des croyances erronées, etc., au monde idéal. [45]

Moreau de Tours became interested in the use of hashish as a result of his association with another doctor, Aubert-Roche, whose book, *De la peste, ou typhus d'Orient,* published in 1840, stimulated considerable interest in hashish intoxication. He began experiments with Aubert-Roche in 1841 and was approached sometime thereafter (perhaps in 1843), by Théophile Gautier, who expressed interest in trying the drug himself. Little is known concerning these meetings with Moreau de Tours, or concerning the famous "Club des hachichins" which Gautier describes in his short work of the same name.

Because of Gautier's "Le club des hachichins" and "Le hachich," there has always been considerable interest in this unique club, which seems to have held regular monthly meetings in François Boissard's room in the Hôtel Pimodan. Our only information concerning this interesting group comes from Gautier's work, several letters of invitation from François Boissard, and isolated statements which seem to pertain to the club.

From Boissard's letters, it is apparent that the group was meeting in the presence of Moreau de Tours in 1845; and from Gautier's statement concerning Baudelaire's first introduction into the club, it seems that meetings were being held at least as late as 1849. Gautier's statement that he first met Baudelaire at the

---

[45] Ibid., p. 42.

club in 1849 has caused much conjecture, since both Gautier and Baudelaire lived in the Hôtel Pimodan from 1843 to 1845, and since Baudelaire stated that he first met Gautier in 1843. It is indeed difficult to believe that Baudelaire could have lived in the same building and not have participated in some of the hashish sessions. It is likewise hard to believe that Gautier tried hashish only a few times in his life in view of his keen interest in drugs and his association with individuals who indulged in drug taking. This would be all the more unlikely since there was at the time no moral stigma attached to drug use as there is today. At all events, the hashish evenings were held and many writers and artists of the period attended at one time or another.

In his book, *Du haschisch et de l'aliénation mentale* published in 1845, Moreau de Tours presents the results of his experiments with hashish. Basically, he divides the effects of the drug into eight phenomena, some of which are of unusual literary interest. From his brief review of the important effects of hashish, one can see why its attraction was so great for writers, and one can begin to suspect something of the influence which the use of hashish may have had on the literature of the early nineteenth century.

Basically, the effects of hashish hallucination are of twofold significance for artistic creation: (1) they change the relationship between the rational faculty and the imaginative faculty, and (2) they change the impressions which one receives through the senses.

The individual who is under the influence of hashish is drawn into a world of new relationships. The rational faculty, though retained to a certain degree, is powerless to direct the individual's experience; and it no longer controls the choice of sensations or memories that come forth from his mind. Once this controlling factor is inoperative, thoughts and memories from the mind's great storehouse come forth at random. Associations are made which the rational faculty would never have allowed. Thus the sources of imagination are set free and dominate the rational, critical faculty.

In the belief of the time, hashish allowed one to enter into the inner world of the Greater Reality and yet retain a certain degree of awareness. Traditionally it is the poet's task to seize the relationship between this world and the spiritual world of which it is a symbol. Thus poets were interested in the drug as a means of giving free reign to the imaginative faculty (or, as we would say, of releasing the subconscious), while at the same time retaining enough critical awareness to be able to employ the relationships which were revealed to them in their ecstasy.

Among the changes in sense perception which seemed to broaden experience and to change the dimension in which man lives were the changes in time and space. Under the influence of hashish past and present time are confused. The rush of thoughts and images through the mind makes one feel that much time has passed when in truth it has been only moments. Spatial distances between objects lose their importance, and there is greater interest in the position itself of one object in relation to another. A stairway may seem interminable and may take an "eternity" of time to negotiate.

Certain sensations of physical identification often take place which cause the individual to feel that his physical self has changed its shape:

> J'aurais pu me croire métamorphosé en oiseau, en ballon, en proie à la crainte d'être emporté par un coup de vent, ou crevé par le moindre choc, incendié par une étincelle; m'attribuer le pouvoir de m'élever dans les airs, de franchir l'espace à tire d'ailes ... [46]

One artist felt his body to be of such elasticity as to have been able to enter a bottle and to remain there with ease.

Another phenomenon of hashish which attracted the attention of artists and writers of the period was the increased sensitivity it often gave to the five senses. Under the influence of hashish, a person can experience intense joy or pain from hearing certain sounds. Harmonies are felt strongly as well as rhythms.

Synaesthetic sensations are sometimes experienced. Individuals reported that they sensed the existence of new relationships between perceptions of the various senses. Sounds, colors, and smells were frequently experienced in simultaneous association. So great was one's sensitivity that he might be transported in

---

[46] Ibid., p. 164.

hallucination to an exotic setting through the mere fragance of an exotic perfume.

It is not difficult to imagine the fascination which hashish and opium held for the romantic mind, eagerly seeking an escape from the "ennui" of reality and ardently searching for a mystical experience which would bring a measure of peace. Hashish and opium seemed to offer the artist the deeply emotional experience which he felt was needed to create a work of art. It offered release to all the imaginative genius locked in the poetic mind. Here was the opportunity to reach down into the rich fount of the subconscious, to look into one's own soul in search of something new.

Chapter IV

OPIUM AND HASHISH IN THE LITERATURE OF FRENCH ROMANTICISM

The means by which the Romantics became acquainted with opium and hashish leaves little doubt why such keen interest was shown in these drugs by the artists and authors of the early nineteenth century. The powers of the drugs seemed to respond to the needs and interests of the romantic temperament. Interested in the exotic and in local color, the Romantics were easily attracted by the oriental association which opium, hashish, and tea evoked. These stimulants also suggested a means of escape from the humdrum existence of everyday life, an escape into a pleasurable, vicarious existence where the brighter hues of the sunny oriental paradise offered a world of unending charm.

Secondly, the Romantic's love for the mystery of all things occult attracted him to opium and hashish, which seemed to offer a means of transcending the prosaic and abhorrent world of scientific reality. Here was the opportunity for the soul to free itself from the rational overlord, and to impose its world of spiritual reality.

The fad of indulging in the stimulants, if only from the standpoint of curiosity, became widespread in the early nineteenth century. Writers and painters experimented freely in the use of opium and hashish and were greatly impressed by the changes which these drugs produced in the human psyche and sensibility.

As might be expected, the influence which one finds from opium and hashish on the literature of the first half of the nineteenth century in France is related to the sources which introduced the Romantics to these drugs. Both opium and hashish are frequently used to contribute to the local color of an oriental setting or to help create an exotic, oriental atmosphere. Opium or hashish is often introduced in reference to a certain character or situation when the author wishes to create an aura of mystery around him. Naturally, there is a certain amount of journalistic literature written with the intent of capitalizing on the great interest which the drugs provoked. Perhaps its most important use, however, was as a means of presenting the world as a place in which one cannot really find reality. It has been used effectively by authors in connection with a character who participates in two distinct existences, both of which appear to be authentic. Finally, there appears to have been some influence from the drug experience itself, from the visions and aesthetic experience which it evoked.

In this chapter examples illustrating these various types of influence will be shown in works by Balzac, Flaubert, Puycoussin, Dumas, Théophile Gautier, Gérard de Nerval, and Eugène Sue.[1]

I

Perhaps of all the literary figures who were concerned with the stimulants, with the exception of Baudelaire, Balzac is the most interesting. One of the earliest writers to show an interest in opium and obviously fascinated by all the "excitants," Balzac was nevertheless fearful of them and frequently condemned their use. Balzac was an avid coffee drinker and praised its powers of stimulation. Contrarily, he condemns its excessive use in the "Traité des excitants modernes" as a serious danger to man's physical health. His attitude toward hashish shows this same contradiction.[2] Gautier relates that he brought Balzac to a meeting of the "Club des Hachichins," but that he was unable to persuade him to try any hashish. Balzac was afraid that his

---

[1] The influence of opium and hashish on the life and works of Charles Baudelaire will be treated in Chapter V.

[2] Balzac seemed to take every opportunity to condemn the use of any of the stimulants. In his "Traité des excitants modernes" Balzac warns against the pernicious effect of alcohol, sugar, tea, coffee, and tobacco.

rational faculty would lose control of his actions, a thought which was frightening to him. In a letter of December 23, 1845, Balzac states that he finally succumbed to his curiosity and tried some of the famed hashish preparation. Because of his own mental resistance, the drug was slow to take effect, and he left the gathering seemingly undisturbed. As he was leaving, however, he began to feel the effects from the hashish which he described to Mme Hanska:

> Néanmoins, j'ai entendu des voix célestes et j'ai vu des peintures divines; puis j'ai descendu pendant vingt ans l'escalier de Lauzun; j'ai vu les dorures et les peintures du salon dans une splendeur féerique.[3]

Thus, in these brief remarks concerning Balzac's personal contact with the stimulants, one can see his evident fascination with their powers and his fear of them.

Balzac's literary use of the stimulants displays this same contradictory attitude. Intrigued by the strange visions which the author of *L'Anglais mangeur d'opium* described, Balzac composed a short work entitled "L'opium," which he published in 1830 in *La Caricature* under the pseudonym, Le Comte Alex de B.... Balzac early recognized the important part which opium visions might play in a genre such as the "conte fantastique," and he treats the drug's effects in "L'opium" with an aura of fascination; yet he felt that he must condemn the use of this pernicious drug.

In the first paragraph Balzac sketches a man who is debauched, a non-believer, and tired of life. He begins to take opium in the company of an Englishman, who "... cherchait la mort, une mort voluptueuse; non celle qui arrive à pas lents sous la forme de squelette, mais la mort des modernes ... une mort tout à fait fashionable!"[4]

By the use of opium, the two men hoped to escape to exotic places:

---

[3] Honoré de Balzac, *Œuvres complètes*, XXIV (Paris, 1856), 482.

[4] Honoré de Balzac, *Œuvres complètes*, ed. M. Bouteron and H. Longnon, II (Paris, 1938), 193.

> Ils demandaient à l'opium de leur faire voir les coupoles dorées de Constantinople, et de les rouler sur les divans du sérail au milieu des femmes de Mahmoud ... L'opium leur livrait l'univers entier! [5]

Or, at times, they enjoyed a scene of domestic bliss:

> ... un foyer, une soirée d'hiver, une jeune femme, des enfants pleins de grâce, qui, agenouillés, priaient Dieu, sous la dictée d'une vieille bonne ... [6]

Even the boundaries of time could be broken. One could relive the magic splendor of ancient times:

> ... ils rebatissaient même les conceptions gigantesques de l'antiquité grecque, asiatique et romaine... Ils reconstruisaient les écuries de Saloman, le temple de Jérusalem, les merveilles de Babylone et tout le moyen-âge avec ses tournois, ses châteaux, ses chevaliers et ses monastères! [7]

However, the ultimate effects of opium soon became apparent. Splendid visions were soon replaced by nightmares as horrible as the dreams had been beautiful, and the two opium takers entered a period of severe grief followed by death. "C'est là ton dénouement, ô prestigieux opium...." [8]

Balzac often condemned the dangerous effects of the stimulants, but he makes frequent use of hallucinations in many of his works, especially the type of hallucination in which inanimate objects seem to move. In a short work entitled "Le Dôme des Invalides," with the sub-title "Hallucination," published in the *Annales Romantiques* (1832), Balzac describes an interesting experience of the central figure in the tale. Invited to lunch at the Baron de Werther's, the narrator is affected strangely by his host's music and by the wine which he drank. At least he assumes that this must have been the reason for the unusual experience he had upon leaving the luncheon:

---

[5] Ibid., p. 194.
[6] Ibid.
[7] Ibid.
[8] Ibid.

... Werther s'assit à une petite table, et, levant une partie de couvercle, il tira, d'un instrument allemand, des sons qui tiennent un juste milieu entre les accents lugubres d'un chat implorant une chatte ou rêvant des joies de la gouttière, et les notes d'un orgue vibrant dans une église. Je ne sais ce qu'il fit de ce terrible appareil de mélancolie, mais jamais mon intelligence ne fut plus cruellement bouleversée. Le souffle de l'air, dirigé sur des métaux produisait des vibrations harmoniques si fortes, si graves, si perçantes, que chaque note attaquait immédiatement une fibre, et cette musique de vert-de-gris, ces mélodies pleines d'arsenic, introduisirent violemment dans mon âme toutes les rêveries de Jean-Paul, toutes les ballades allemandes, toute une poësie fantastique et douloureuse qui me mit en fuite, moi gai, moi jovial, mais souffrant, mais agité. Je me trouvais comme dédoublé. Mon être intérieur avait quitté cette forme extérieure ... L'air n'était plus de l'air; mes jambes n'étaient plus des jambes; c'était une nature molle et sans consistance qui pliait, et les pavés s'enfonçaient, les passants dansaient, et je trouvais Paris singulièrement gai.[9]

Having left the luncheon between four and five in the afternoon, the narrator walked down the rue de Babylone. Suddenly the "Dôme des Invalides," which he had taken for his guiding point, began to walk toward him. It laughed as it followed him, and the narrator imagined that the "Dôme" now belonged to him just as if he had found a stray pet. What a fortune he would make displaying his walking "Dôme" around Europe. How upset Parisians would be over his ownership of the "Dôme." Suddenly he saw a gig run into his "Dôme" and smash it to pieces. When the vehicle had passed, the "Dôme" picked itself up and gradually re-formed. The narrator felt his own form take shape again:

... je me trouvai près des Invalides, devant une grande nappe d'eau où se mirait le Dôme des Invalides.[10]

Many of the features of this hallucination remind one of descriptions given by those under the influence of hashish and occasionally those under the influence of opium. The narrator

---

[9] Ibid., p. 458.
[10] Ibid., p. 460.

mentions that he became sensitive to music, and that he experienced a strange doubling of the self. His inner being seemed to escape from its exterior form, and the world seemed to become gay. Each of these phenomena can be found again and again in the descriptions of those who have experimented with hashish or opium. Perhaps Balzac was again recalling the impressive descriptions of De Quincey.

Although Balzac probably never tried opium and reportedly tried hashish only once, he was one of the first Romantic authors in France to refer to opium and to spread interest in the drug.

II

One can draw a parallel between Balzac's attitude toward opium and Flaubert's attitude toward hashish. Like Balzac, Flaubert was tempted to try the drug, but he was apprehensive of its effects. In a letter to Baudelaire he writes that "Ces drogues-là m'ont toujours causé une grande envie. Je possède même d'excellent haschisch composé par le pharmacien Gastinel. Mais *ça me fait peur*, ce dont je me blâme." [11] Unlike Balzac, however, he did not condemn the drug, but rather felt that it might be employed in a way beneficial to mankind.

Oddly enough, Flaubert felt that Baudelaire was perhaps unjust in finding so much evil in the use of opium and hashish. In a letter to Baudelaire in 1860 concerning his friend's work on opium and hashish, Flaubert criticizes Baudelaire for his harsh attitude toward the drugs.

> Il me semble que, dans un sujet traité d'aussi haut, dans un travail qui est le commencement d'une science, dans une oeuvre d'observation naturelle et d'induction, vous avez (et à plusieurs reprises) insisté trop (?) sur *l'Esprit du mal*... J'aurais mieux aimé que vous ne blâmiez pas le haschisch, l'opium, l'excès. Savez-vous ce qui en sortira plus tard? [12]

---

[11] Paul Dimoff, "Autour d'un projet de roman de Flaubert: *La Spirale*," *RHL*, XLVIII (1948), 314. The following material concerning Flaubert's projected novel has been drawn from Mr. Dimoff's excellent article.
[12] Ibid.

Flaubert was fascinated by the possibilities which the drugs afforded and was keenly interested in Baudelaire's *Un mangeur d'opium* and his *Poème du haschisch*. Flaubert himself planned to write a work which would show the possible benefit from the use of hashish. The notes for his projected novel, *La Spirale*, have been studied carefully by Mr. Dimoff and give an excellent idea of Flaubert's intention.

Flaubert wrote to Louise Colet in 1852 that he was planning a "roman métaphysique et à apparitions." [13] It was long thought that Flaubert was here referring to *La Spirale;* but Dimoff feels that Flaubert's actual idea for the novel came only after he had become acquainted with Baudelaire's *Les paradis artificiels*, sometime in 1860 or 1861.

> Nul doute donc qu'en 1860 Flaubert n'ait aussitôt reconnu, dans le mangeur de haschisch de Baudelaire, un personnage quasi fraternel, aussi bien par sa sensibilité et son imagination exceptionelles, que par ses tentatives d'évasions hors de la réalité. [14]

Dimoff proposes that Flaubert's letter to Louise Colet indicates only that the idea to write such a novel was constant with Flaubert and consistent with his basic need to escape from everyday reality. Flaubert had a great longing and need for the exotic. In a letter to Emmanuel Vasse he wrote:

> Pour vivre, je ne dis pas heureux (ce but est une illusion funeste), mais tranquille, il faut se créer, en dehors de l'existence visible, commune, et générale à tous, une autre existence interne et inaccessible à tout ce qui rentre dans le domaine du contingent, comme disent les philosophes. [15]

In *La Spirale*, the development of the hero's character follows the development of personality which Baudelaire describes for one who is under the influence of hashish. Gradually one feels that he has become God. Flaubert's hero, although suffering many

---

[13] Dimoff, p. 328.
[14] Ibid.
[15] Ibid., p. 325.

adversities and consigned to a home for the insane, reaches the point where he feels peacefully superior to all humanity.

Dimoff asserts that Flaubert saw much of his own nature in this character. Only the fact that the hero's personality would be attributed in large part to his constant use of hashish would have allowed Flaubert to publish the novel without feeling embarrassment. Flaubert's own great need to escape from ordinary existence into another order of reality was accomplished by his hero through the use of hashish.

In the novel the hero is a painter who had acquired the habit of taking hashish in the course of his voyage to the Orient.

> Un usage prolongé de celui-ci, une faculté exceptionnelle d'imagination, sans doute aussi une disposition spéciale à la rêverie, l'ont amené peu à peu à cet état extraordinaire qui est le sien. Par l'accoutumance, son système nerveux, saturé de la drogue, est devenue capable de visions et d'extases, sans autre adjuvant que l'odeur de la boîte qui la contient; puis le besoin de cet adjuvant ne s'est même plus fait sentir: à chaque instant, extases et visions naissent maintenant d'elles-mêmes, moyennant certaines conditions favorables; le personnage en arrive à vivre dans un rêve presque continu; il est dans une espèce de "somnambulisme permanent" qui le rend insensible à la douleur.[16]

But Flaubert felt that a character who lived only within his own dream world would hold little interest for a reader. Thus he felt the necessity of establishing a close connection between the dream and reality by making the one depend upon the other. He gave his hero a character that was good by nature and sensitive. Hence any moral remorse acted upon him strongly and caused such great grief that he was unable to enjoy the ecstasies of his dreams. Contrarily, each time he did something good he enjoyed his dream world even more. In this way Flaubert established a close link between the hero's world of dream and the

---

[16] Dimoff, p. 311. Flaubert's lack of knowledge concerning the effects from the habitual use of hashish is apparent from this idea that one becomes more sensitive to the drug the longer and more regularly that one takes it. One develops neither a greater sensitivity nor a tolerance to hashish.

world of reality. In order for him to enjoy his hashish experience, it would be necessary for him to participate actively in life in a good way. Flaubert compared this in his notes to a " 'purgation,' qui purifie l'âme, et grâce à laquelle le Paradis tout doucement arrive." [17] M. Dimoff says of it:

> Le roman aurait alors montré comment l'étrange rêveur, aiguillonné par le désir d'extases nouvelles, est capable, malgré les épreuves croissantes que la réalité lui impose, de continuer à faire sans cesse le bien, poussant jusqu'à ses dernières limites l'esprit de sacrifice, et comment il est récompensé de cet effort par des visions splendides, transfigurant pour lui les laideurs et les brutalités de la vie réelle. Le contraste entre la réalité et le rêve serait allé s'accentuant de plus en plus jusqu'au dénouement: l'on y aurait vu le héros trouver le bonheur parfait dans ses visions, au moment même où, ruiné, raillé, incompris de tous, il aurait été enfermé dans une maison de fous. [18]

Some of the experiences he would have had in real life include being abandoned and deceived by his friends, robbed of his wealth, and deserted by the woman he loved. He was to watch the girl he loved marry an unworthy fellow and then find it necessary to protect her from him. They were to have a child which he would eventually have to raise. In spite of these obstacles, the hero was to surmount his difficulties with the aid of his dream-world produced by hashish, and win victories over himself and others.

According to Dimoff:

> La conclusion de ce livre, que Flaubert voulait faire 'exaltant et moral,' eût été que le bonheur consiste à être fou —au sens où l'entend le commun des hommes—, c'est-à-dire à tenir les visions, que notre imagination tire de la vie réelle, pour plus vraies que cette vie elle-même. Il n'est que de se croire roi pour goûter en esprit les plaisirs d'un roi, grand musicien, pour se donner en rêve les plus vives jouissances musicales. Aussi le héros du roman voit-il, en ses compagnons d'asile, dont chacun se

---

[17] Ibid.
[18] Ibid., pp. 311-312.

figure être ce qu'il n'est pas, les véritables sages et les seuls heureux sur terre.[19]

It is curious that Flaubert, who had such fear of hashish and probably never tried it, should conceive of such a unique benefit to be derived from the paradise which the drug was capable of producing. Not having experienced the harsh reality of drug habituation with which Baudelaire was acquainted, he was unable to comprehend the bitter implication of Baudelaire's title "paradis artificiels." Baudelaire, too, longed for escape from the "ennui" and frustration which plagued him in everyday life. But in the drugs he found only the "Esprit du mal," the illusion of paradise which Satan Trismegistus, perverse alchemist that he is, created to ensnare mankind, to subject man to his will like a puppet dangling on a string. Only Flaubert's desperate need for escape and his lack of experience with the drugs could have blinded him so to the bitter reality which Baudelaire knew so well.

III

An interesting little "conte fantastique," "La nuit du 31 décembre," originally attributed to Gérard de Nerval, but now generally credited to Edouard Puycoussin, uses opium as the means of explaining the strange events in the story, and the experience of the principal character. A very short story of no more than ten pages, it is divided oddly by the author into twelve parts. Each part seems to have only the slightest relationship to the next, and one senses that he is witnessing a reality lacking in the logical continuity which our own lives seem to possess.

In part one a man who is hurrying down the street stops to enter various shops. It is December 31. Part two introduces a young English girl named Betty, who has come to visit a rich old aunt from whom she is to inherit. While she is lying in her room musing about England, a man comes to visit. One sees from his description that it is the man who was walking down the street in part one. It is in part five that one begins to observe

---

[19] Ibid., p. 313.

that something is strange in the situation. Betty's aunt states that Betty could not possibly have received the calendar from the postman, for all the postmen had died suddenly the previous night. When Betty remarks that this is impossible, her aunt answers in a threatening tone that nothing is impossible. Betty withdraws to her room slightly frightened. After staring at the calendar for a quarter of an hour, she feels a dizziness come over her. All becomes dim before her eyes as if she were looking through dense fog. Then a luminous point on the wall begins to grow and the calendar's appearance changes radically. She shuts her eyes and turns away, but finds that she is able to see through her eyelids. Gradually the room becomes distorted, and the walls catch on fire. Without transition, she suddenly finds herself in a cathedral made of neither stone nor marble but wholly of "rayons de jour entrelacés et tressés entre eux comme un arc-en-ciel," and penetrated on all sides by a diaphanous light. [20] The cathedral has a wondrous altar made entirely of crystal, and the inside of the church is filled by the fragance of perfumes and the lovely sound of harmonious voices. While Betty is under the sway of these wonderful sensations, a silver door at the back of the cathedral is opened. A young man with a sapphire lyre, blue wings, and many wedding rings on his finger enters. Betty thinks that it is Lord Edward, the person whom she wants to marry; but it is a strange, pale young man who calls himself the First of January. (He lives during these twenty-four hours each year.) He confesses love for Betty, and says that he must die forever if she will not have him. Again Betty remarks that this is impossible, and the young man answers in a hoarse voice that she should not say that it is not possible. In part eleven Betty begins to return to herself, and meditates on the impossibility of not having a first of January. While she is meditating, her aunt is carried before her. In part twelve she receives a letter with an engagement ring inside from Edward who is coming to marry her. She learns that her aunt, who was an inveterate opium addict, has just died. Betty now realizes that she had unwittingly drunk her aunt's usual early morning opium mixture.

---

[20] Gérard de Nerval, *Le Marquis de Fayolle* (Paris, 1928), p. 406.

Puycoussin uses opium as a means of explaining the mysterious sequence of events. But in looking at the events one should note that he included most of the phenomena which occultists and medical people attributed to the drug. Betty's hallucinations represent a carefully worked out description of many of the aspects of the drug experience. First of all, the basic events around which the hallucinations centered had a sound basis in Betty's reality. The beautiful cathedral and the young First of January were suggested by her preoccupation with her forthcoming marriage. Interestingly enough, she has a moment of clairvoyance when the First of January offers her the ring, for she receives a ring from Edward shortly afterwards. Magnetists and somnambulists frequently used drugs in order to attain the somnambulistic state in which clairvoyance was supposedly possible through a communication of spirits. Betty's sense of personal well-being and heightened sensitivity, and her colorful vision of the cathedral, with its sweet perfumes and harmonies of sound, complete the experience which so many have described in similar terms.

IV

In his long novel *Le Comte de Monte-Cristo,* published in 1844-1845, Alexandre Dumas, who had dabbled in hashish himself, made use of the keen interest in the drug and the story about the Old Man of the Mountain to add an aura of mystery and grandeur to his principal character, the Count. The chapter called "Simbad le Marin," from the fictitious name used by the mysterious gentleman who owned the luxurious underground palace, is relatable to the wide interest in the Orient and exotic stories of the *Thousand and One Nights,* and to the sophisticated use of hashish as an after dinner dessert.

Late one afternoon near sundown after a particularly bad day of hunting, Franz is persuaded by Gaetano and the men who are ferrying him in their boat, to go to the deserted island, Monte Cristo, where hunting is excellent. Although the sun is going down and the party will have to return at night or remain on the barren island until morning, Franz is charmed by the notion of an uninhabited island in the Mediterranean and decides in favor of the trip. Dumas adds an aura of suspense and mystery when Gaetano informs Franz that the island is used as a base for smugglers.

One senses that Gaetano and his men are also smugglers. They arrive at the island after dark and see by a fire in the distance that there is apparently a group of contrabandists on the island at this very moment. Dumas maintains the suspense excellently as Franz must wait silently in the boat out in the water as Gaetano makes arrangements with the mysterious island bandits. After some time the party goes ashore and eats of the smugglers' dinner.

Franz has been invited to dine with a mysterious gentleman who owns a luxurious palace somewhere beneath the rock of the barren island. Since no one is to know the entrance or location of the palace, Franz is blindfolded until he is inside.[21] Upon removal of the blindfold, he is amazed by the beautiful furnishings, the Turkish rug, the lamp of expensive Venetian glass and bejewelled Arabic weapons. The host, who calls himself Simbad, serves hashish for dessert and tells Franz that "... cette sorte de confiture verte n'est ni plus ni moins que l'ambroisie qu'Hébé servait à la table de Jupiter!"[22] Simbad advises him to take some, and he will see whatever delights his mind:

> Êtes-vous un homme positif et l'or est-il votre dieu, goûtez à ceci, et les mines du Pérou, de Guzerate et de Golconde vous seront ouvertes. Êtes-vous un homme d'imagination, êtes-vous poète, goûtez encore ceci, et les barrières du possible disparaîtront; les champs de l'infini vont s'ouvrir, vous vous promènerez libre de cœur, libre d'esprit dans le domaine sans bornes de la rêverie.[23]

Take some, says Simbad, and you will be king on this earth.

Franz asks what the "confiture verte" is, and his host relates the story of the Old Man of the Mountain as recounted by Marco

---

[21] It is of interest that Dumas not only retells the story of the Old Man of the Mountain in reference to the hashish but even uses the mechanics of the legend to introduce Franz into the wonderful palace. When he awakens after the experience with hashish, he finds himself in a dark cave. This corresponds to one of the two principal legends about the Old Man mentioned in Chapter II.

[22] Alexandre Dumas, *Le Comte de Monte-Cristo* (Paris, 1956), p. 401.

[23] Ibid.

Polo. Franz decides that he will try the drug, and Simbad says that he must allow his mind to be carried into another reality.

> ... it faut que la réalité cède au rêve; et alors le rêve règne en maître, alors c'est le rêve qui devient la vie et la vie qui devient le rêve ... [24]

Simbad warns Franz that when one leaves this blissful state it is like leaving paradise. He will never wish to live in the world of reality again.

After taking the hashish, Franz begins to feel light, as though he could fly around the world in a day. The horizon seems to expand, "... un horizon bleu, transparent, vaste, avec tout ce que la mer a d'azur, avec tout ce que le soleil a de paillettes, avec tout ce que la brise a de parfums...." [25] Again he sees the panorama of his trip to the island. He begins to relive the reality in dream.

Franz sees the isle appear again, but this time it appears to be an oasis instead of a barren rock. A harmony of sound comes forth from the island, creating an aura of enchantment. Once again he enters the underground palace, but this time amid greater splendor with a background of enchanting melody. He passes into a room of statues where Cleopatra, Phryne and Messalina vie for his love.

After an erotic scene where the passion becomes so intense as to be painful, Franz awakens in a bleak cave of the island. Twice he searches at length for the underground palace, but he is unable to find its entrance. Franz begins to doubt the reality of the stranger and the magnificent palace, but Gaetano points him out on a distant boat sailing for Corsica. Through glasses, Franz sees Simbad standing alone on the deck.

In this chapter Dumas used the cave motif from the Old Man of the Mountain story, the mysterious qualities of hashish, the enchanted, undiscoverable palace, and the mysterious stranger with the exotic name to cast an aura of enchantment around the episode. Franz re-enacts the reality within the dream so that the dream, as Simbad remarked, "règne en maître" — and becomes the

---

[24] Ibid., p. 405.
[25] Ibid., p. 409.

reality. Only when Gaetano points out the mysterous stranger in the distance is Franz sure that it was not all a dream. And even then the stranger is at such a distance, and his ship disappears so quickly over the horizon that he retains an aura of mystery which suggests enchantment.

V

To what extent Théophile Gautier used opium and hashish during his lifetime remains largely a mystery. He himself states that he tried hashish only a few times, and according to his own statement, he attended the monthly meetings of the "Club des Hachichins," but rarely indulged in the drug. So far as can be ascertained, Gautier tried opium at least once in 1838. From this experience, he wrote "La pipe d'opium." In 1843 he tried hashish for the first time and wrote a description of his experience called "Le hachich." In 1846 he published another work on his experience with hashish, "Le club des hachichins."

Although it seems unlikely that Gautier could have associated for such a long period of time with individuals who used hashish and not have participated frequently in these experiments himself, it must be said that there is nothing which would indicate that he ever became habituated to any drug. Indeed his reaction to the experiences he had suggests that his use of drugs never reached beyond the stage of curiosity.

There is evidence that Gautier used some of his drug experiences in his prose writing, but little indication that he used them extensively in his poetry. Gautier seems to have been interested in opium and hashish in two respects: 1) As a writer for the feuilleton, he seems to have found in the drug experiment an opportunity to participate in a curious, new experience; and, realizing that the effects of the drug would be interesting to the general public, he took advantage of the opportunity and published descriptions of his hallucinations under its influence. 2) As a novelist and short story writer, Gautier recognized the value of the drug experience in describing the transition from the world of physical reality to the greater world of spiritual reality. He never seemed to consider the use of hashish as having any real significance for life. To him it seemed to represent an adornment or a novel amusement rather than a serious threat to the integrity of one's being.

One can trace much of the succeeding popularity of opium and hashish to Gautier's short accounts of his experiences. The descriptions of his three hallucinations recorded in "Le hachich" have become classic accounts of the effects of hashish. Even today one occasionally senses that certain purported hashish experiences have been colored greatly by Gautier's famous passages.

In his first work concerning drugs, "La pipe d'opium," published in feuilleton form in *La Presse* on September 27, 1838, Gautier describes a dream which he had one night after having smoked opium at the residence of Alphonse Karr. The dream is not greatly different from other dreams recorded in literature, but certain aspects of this experience are interesting in that they reappear rather frequently in Gautier's prose works.

Gautier uses basically the same procedure in relating his experience with opium that Dumas uses in describing the hallucination of Franz in the *Comte de Monte-Cristo*. In both instances the individual who has taken the drug (in Franz's case it was hashish) relives the reality which has just taken place. But in the dream the events are colored by the drug's influence.

One day Gautier finds his friend, Alphonse Karr, smoking opium and takes a few puffs on the pipe before going to dinner and the theater. Thereafter he returns home and goes to bed. During his sleep, which is troubled by the opium he has inhaled, Gautier relives the sequence of events which had occurred earlier in the day. Once again he is visiting Alphonse Karr, who is sitting on his divan smoking opium. Gautier participates in the smoking and lies back on the pillows to gaze at the ebony ceiling, which soon begins to change colors. The ebony becomes a beautiful blue, and the beams become transparent. He thinks that his friend, Esquiros, could probably explain all this if he were only present. No sooner does he think of Esquiros than his friend appears, having come directly through the closed door. After a moment Gautier becomes aware of a woman sitting in the corner. Her delicate transparency reveals that she is a spirit. The spirit informs him that she may yet have six more months of life if Gautier has the courage to seek out her dead body and give her a kiss. The author departs on a wild mysterious ride in a driverless carriage to an unknown town. He finds the body of the girl, kisses her, and suddenly finds himself with Karr in a room which he has never seen before. The spirit of the girl is there and comes to embrace him. In the midst of his embrace, Gautier is awakened by his cat.

From the brief description of the events in the dream, one can see that the story is scarcely different from the ordinary "conte fantastique." It is of interest, however, that certain descriptive aspects of the dream are repeated by Gautier and that even certain of the situations in the dream were employed again in later works where Gautier was obviously trying to impart an aura of mystery to either the characters or the situation.

Gautier's description of Esquiros when he appears unexpectedly in the room, seemingly as a result of Gautier's wish, is similar to the description of many characters whom he wishes to present in a mysterious light.

> ... il me regardait d'un air étrange, et ses yeux s'agrandissaient d'une façon démesurée; ils étaient ardents et ronds comme des boucliers chauffés dans une fournaise, et son corps se dissipait et se noyait dans l'ombre, de sorte que je ne voyais plus de lui que ses deux prunelles flamboyantes et rayonnantes. [26]

In *Avatar* the mysterious doctor Cherbonneau, whose magnetic powers permit him to transfer souls from one body to another, has the same burning eyes, frequently described by Gautier as glowing in the shadows:

> Quoique la figure du docteur fût baignée d'ombre et que le haut de son crâne, luisant et arrondi comme un gigantesque œuf d'autruche, accrochât seul au passage un rayon du jour, Octave distinguait la scintillation des étranges prunelles bleues qui semblaient douées d'une lueur propre comme les corps phosphorescents.... [27]

---

[26] Charles Baudelaire, *Les paradis artificiels*, précédé de "La pipe d'opium," "Le hachich," et "Le club des hachichins" par Théophile Gautier, édition établie et présentée par Claude Pichois (Paris, 1961), p. 6. Hereafter cited as Pichois.

[27] Théophile Gautier, "Avatar" in *Romans et Contes* (Paris, 1923), p. 9.

In both instances the eyes of these men emit rays of magnetic power which the person senses. In the opium dream Gautier feels the magnetic impulses enter his body:

> Des réseaux de feu et des torrents d'effluves magnétiques papillotaient et tourbillonnaient autour de moi, s'enlaçant toujours plus inextricablement et se resserrant toujours; des fils étincelants aboutissaient à chacun de mes pores, et s'implantaient dans ma peau à peu près comme les cheveux dans la tête. J'étais dans un état de somnambulisme complet. [28]

In *Avatar* Octave also feels the magnetic penetration of the rays from the doctor's eyes:

> ... il en jaillissait un rayon aigu et clair que le jeune malade recevait en pleine poitrine avec cette sensation de picotement et de chaleur produite par l'émétique. [29]

Immediately after Gautier's description of Esquiros, he sees "... des petits flocons blancs qui traversaient l'espace bleu du plafond comme des touffes de laine emportées par le vent ...." [30] He asks what these are and is told that they are spirits. It is then that he sees in the corner one of the spirits in the form of a young girl, whose life he can save for six months by kissing her corpse. The ensuing ride in the driverless carriage and the kiss which the corpse returns, coupled with the vision of the "flocons" remind one of two works of Gautier which bear a certain analogy to elements of the opium dream. His seeing "des petits flocons

---

[28] Pichois, p. 6.
[29] "Avatar," p. 9. Many of Gautier's more mysterious characters have unusually penetrating, scintillating eyes which seem to have a kind of magnetic power. The eyes of Paul d'Aspremont, the principal character of "Jettatura," are described as follows: "... s'ils se fixaient sur quelque personne ou quelque objet, les sourcils se rapprochaient, se crispaient, et modelaient une ride perpendiculaire dans la peau du front: les prunelles, de grises devenaient vertes, se tigraient de points noirs, se striaient de fibrilles jaunes; le regard en jaillissait aigu, presque blessant ..." (Théophile Gautier, "Jettatura," *Romans et contes* [Paris, 1923], p. 142.) Other similar descriptions in Gautier's works can be found in "Le pied de momie" (the shop owner), "Militona" (Juancho the bullfighter), and "La morte amoureuse" (Clarimonde the vampire).
[30] Pichois, pp. 6-7.

blancs" as spirits in the air, and the young girl who died before being able to experience any of the joys of this life seem directly related to Gautier's novel, *Spirite*.

In *Spirite*, a young girl of seventeen dies without ever having had any of the joys of terrestrial life. She too is allowed to spend some time immediately after death near earth and appears to the man she loves as a spirit in the form of a "diaphane flocon blanc." [31] Other elements of the dream, such as the girl's being given new life by means of a kiss, and the wild ride to the village where the corpse lay remind one of Gautier's *conte*, "La morte amoureuse," published two years before "La pipe d'opium." Even the scene in "La morte amoureuse" where the priest kisses the lips of the dead Clarimonde is reminiscent of the scene described in Gautier's opium dream. In both instances the body is dead, but the lips respond ardently to the life-giving kiss. [32]

Gautier's second text concerning a drug experience was "Le hachich," published in *La Presse* on July 10, 1843. In this short article, he describes an evening of hashish and three successive hallucinations which the drug produced. Although fewer direct analogies can be cited between these hallucinations and his other writings, this is probably the most frequently cited of Gautier's three works on drugs and is probably the one which most excited interest in hashish among literary figures of the period and of later generations. Each of the hallucinations seems to have been planned carefully to include certain of the hallucinatory phenomena which would be appealing to the *literati*. Much of the

---

[31] Note that Lavinia's name is unknown to Malivert just as Carlotta's is unknown to Gautier in "La pipe d'opium." In the visions of the spiritual world that Lavinia describes, the spirits are also represented as sparks of light.

[32] In "La pipe d'opium" Carlotta's body responds in this way: "Ses lèvres humides et tièdes, comme si le souffle venait à peine de les abandonner, palpitèrent sous les miennes, et me rendirent mon baiser avec une ardeur et une vivacité incroyables." (Pichois, p. 10.) Clarimonde responds similarly to the kiss of Romuald in "La morte amoureuse": "O prodige! un léger souffle se mêla à mon souffle, et la bouche de Clarimonde répondit à la pression de la mienne: ses yeux s'ouvrirent et reprirent un peu d'éclat, elle fit un soupir, et, décroisant ses bras, elle les passa derrière mon cou avec un air de ravissement ineffable." (Théophile Gautier, "La morte amoureuse," *Romans et contes* [Paris, 1923], pp. 279-280.)

interest in hashish as a possible aid to the imagination in artistic composition can be traced undoubtedly to the enchanting hallucinations which Gautier presents in this short work.

Gautier's first hallucination presents a myriad of colors and designs, the metamorphosis of objects and individuals, the transposition of one language into another, and the interesting phenomenon of being able to see through the outer surface of one's own body:

> Au bout de quelques minutes, un engourdissement général m'envahit. Il me sembla que mon corps se dissolvait et devenait transparent. Je voyais très-nettement dans ma poitrine le hachich que j'avais mangé sous la forme d'une émeraude d'où s'échappaient des millions de petites étincelles; les cils de mes yeux s'allongeaient indéfiniment, s'enroulant comme des fils d'or sur de petits rouets d'ivoire qui tournaient tout seuls avec une éblouissante rapidité. Autour de moi, c'étaient des ruissellements et des écroulements de pierreries de toutes couleurs, des arabesques, des ramages sans cesse renouvelés, que je ne saurais mieux comparer qu'aux jeux de kaléidoscope; je voyais encore mes camarades à certains instants, mais défigurés, moitié hommes, moitié plantes, avec des airs pensifs d'ibis debout sur une patte, d'autruche battant des ailes si étranges, que je me tordais de rire dans mon coin ... L'un de ces messieurs m'adressa en italien un discours que le hachich, par sa toute-puissance, me transposa en espagnol. [33]

After a period of relative calm and lucidity, Gautier has a second hallucination of beautiful figures and unusual combinations of objects in design. It is this vision which became so famous because of its reference to the phenomenon of synaesthesia. Fascinated by the idea of the unity of the arts and the *correspondances*, Romantics were keenly interested in this passage. Gautier suggests the possibility of detaching one's soul from the physical body and experiencing the corresponding unity of the physical senses:

---

[33] Pichois, pp. 16-17. Note that the lengthening of one's eyelashes is a phenomenon which Gautier describes in "La pipe d'opium."

Mon ouïe s'était prodigieusement développée; j'entendais le bruit des couleurs. Des sons verts, rouges, bleus, jaunes, m'arrivaient par ondes parfaitement distinctes. Un verre renversé, un craquement de fauteuil, un mot prononcé bas, vibraient et retentissaient en moi comme des roulements de tonnerre ... plus de cinq cents pendules me chantaient l'heure de leurs voix flûtées, cuivrées, argentines. Chaque objet effleuré rendait une note d'harmonica ou de harpe éolienne ... j'étais si fondu dans le vague, si absent de moi-même, si débarrassé du moi, cet odieux témoin qui vous accompagne partout que j'ai compris pour la première fois quelle pouvait être l'existence des esprits élémentaires, des anges et des âmes séparées du corps. J'étais comme une éponge au milieu de la mer ... tout mon être s'injectait de la couleur du milieu fantastique où j'étais plongé. Les sons, les parfums, la lumière, m'arrivaient par des multitudes de tuyaux minces comme des cheveux dans lesquels j'entendais siffler les courants magnétiques. [34]

Gautier states that time seemed suspended. He felt that he had lived an eternity in what was really just a quarter of an hour.

The third hallucination, less interesting than the first two, seemed to lose continuity. A parade of grotesque figures was seen in rapid succession, each strange, imaginative, and unique. The fantastic creatures found in this last hallucination appear in isolated places in Gautier's work, but it would be difficult to say that they are a direct product of his experience with drugs.

Gautier's "Le club des hachichins," published in the *Revue des Deux Mondes* on February 1, 1846, is perhaps the most famous of his three works dealing with opium and hashish. Its importance, however, lies not in its literary value, but as an historical document. Its fame can be seen in the numerous references which are made to the famous club of hashish eaters by both French and English critics and writers in the second half of the nineteenth century. The widespread fame of the club rests almost solely on Gautier's article, and little is known about the club's supposed meetings, except what Gautier relates in his text. The popularity

---

[34] Ibid., pp. 17-18. In describing a hashish experience which he once had, Alphonse Karr asserts that his hearing became so keen that he was able to distinguish the conversation of two gentlemen talking in low tones at the opposite end of the room.

which this article has enjoyed is less a result of the hashish experience than of the fascinating idea of such a mysterious club. The article itself is a description of a typical evening of the club at the Hôtel Pimodan and the hallucination which Gautier had after having taken some of the prepared hashish.

As interested as Gautier was in the effects of hashish and opium upon the imagination and the senses, he seems to have been influenced little by this experience in composing his poetry. It is true that there is a "macabre" element in some of Gautier's work which might suggest influence of the drug, but, for the most part, Gautier's imagery suggests little that could be attributed directly to his experience with drugs.

Randolph Hughes indicates a few places where he feels that Gautier was influenced by the work of De Quincey. He suggests that much of the "macabre" element in the *Albertus* (1831) was a result of De Quincey's influence.

>   C'était des bruits sans nom, inconnus à l'oreille
>   Comme la voix d'un mort qu'en sa tombe réveille
>   Une évocation, de sourds vagissements
>   Sortant de dessous terre, et des rumeurs lontaines,
>   Des chants, des cris, des pleurs, des cliquetis de chaînes,
>   D'épouvantables hurlements. [35]

Besides the many strange, grotesque figures in Gautier's work, there are a few passages which suggest opium to add an exotic atmosphere. In a poem called "Gazhel" of the *Poésies nouvelles*, Gautier writes of the many things he likes. Among the pleasures of an oriental nature, he loves the sweet, perfidious opium which brings pleasure to the desolate soul:

>   J'aime aussi l'odeur fine
>   De la fleur des Houris;
>   Sur un plat de la Chine
>   Des sorbets d'ambre gris,
>   L'opium, ciel liquide,
>   Poison doux et perfide,
>   Qui remplit l'âme vide
>   D'un bonheur étoilé;

---

[35] Hughes, p. 565.

> Et, sur l'eau qui réplique,
> Un doux bruit de musique
> S'échappant d'un caïque
> De falots constellé. [36]

Some of Gautier's most charming lines are those concerning the exotic, fragrant Orient. In referring to the mysterious elixir, opium, Gautier is particularly adept at using the textures of sense impressions to correspond with the emotional pleasure of the exotic. The strong fragrance of ambergris unites with the pleasurable visions and sensations produced by the sweet but perfidious liquid. Especially happy is the phrase "ciel liquide," which causes one to think both of the pleasurable liquid opium preparation and the extraterrestrial vision it presents, as well as of the frequent impression the sky gives of being a clear blue liquid.

However, aside from scattered references to opium or hashish used to heighten the exotic atmosphere of a given poem, Gautier's experience with these drugs seems not to have had great effect on his poetic composition. [37]

* * *

It has been shown in a previous chapter how magnetists of the nineteenth century were experimenting with hashish in order to

---

[36] Théophile Gautier, *Poésies complètes*, II (Paris, 1932), 235.

[37] In several instances Gautier includes the smoking of opium to lend the proper local color to an oriental setting. Abou Kasar, Sultan of Baghdad in the short play, "La négresse et le pacha," smokes opium regularly. However, the effects of the opium do not play an integral part in the text. (Spoelberch de Lovenjoul, *Histoire des œuvres de Théophile Gautier*, I [Paris, 1887], 465-492.) Opium smoking is also mentioned in reference to the completely oriental residence created by Fortunio in the middle of Paris. Here the opium smoking of Fortunio's mistress is included only as a touch of local color. (Théophile Gautier, "Fortunio," in *Nouvelles* [Paris, 1923].) In a poem entitled "Étude de mains" from the collection *Émaux et camées*, Gautier describes a piece of sculpture which is so beautiful that it suggests more to the mind than

> Romans extravagants, poèmes
> De haschisch et de vin du Rhin,
> Courses folles dans les bohèmes
> Sur le dos des coursiers sans frein ...

(Gautier, *Poésies complètes*, III, 11.)

experience the greater spiritual reality in which they believed. It should be recalled that Cahagnet did not consider the hashish experience to be a mere hallucination, but rather a spiritual experience which carried one into an inner reality where, under ordinary circumstances, the rational mind could not enter. This interesting notion of the ambiguity of reality and the reality of the drug experience was used by Théophile Gautier, Gérard de Nerval, and Eugène Sue to create an atmosphere of doubt around a group of events or around a particular character.

All three writers present personages whose "real" existence becomes confused with their imagined existence under the influence of a drug.

The influence from opium and hashish on Gautier's writings seems most evident in his prose work concerning the relationship between the physical reality of life and the world of the spirit. In the *conte* called "La mille et deuxième nuit" and in the short, pantomime-ballet, "La Péri," Gautier treats man's desire to unite himself with the spiritual. In both instances opium plays a part in freeing man's spirit from his terrestrial bonds so that he can participate in a more perfect spiritual existence.

In the pantomime-ballet, "La Péri," [38] Gautier presents the Arabic architect, Achmet, who is fatigued by the boredom of the pleasures in his world. Although surrounded by all the pleasures and advantages which life can offer, he is unhappy and seeks consolation in the spiritual reality of opium:

> Achmet est un peu poëte; les voluptés terrestres ne lui suffisent plus; il rêve des amours célestes, des unions avec les esprits élémentaires; la réalité n'a plus d'attraits pour lui, et il demande à l'opium des extases et des hallucinations. [39]

Bored with the company of his harem, Achmet dismisses it and asks for his opium pipe. He soon falls asleep and begins to have an opium dream which carries him to a realm of splendid beauty:

---

[38] First presented at the theater of the "Académie royale de musique" on July 17, 1843.

[39] Théophile Gautier, "La Péri, "in *Théâtre* (Paris, 1905), pp. 281-282.

> Les contours des objets se confondent dans la chambre; des vapeurs bleuâtres et rosées s'élèvent dans le fond, et en se dissipant, laissent apercevoir un espace immense, plein d'azur et de soleil, une oasis féerique avec des lacs de cristal, des palmiers d'émeraude, des arbres aux fleurs de pierreries, des montagnes de lapis-lazuli et de nacre de perle, éclairé par une lumière transparente et surnaturelle. [40]

During the dream, a group of peris approaches the divan on which he is lying. Immediately he recognizes the queen of the peris as the perfect soul he had imagined in his dreams. Before she leaves, she gives him a talisman [41] by which he can recall her any time it pleases him. When he awakens from his dream and has related the vision he had, he is told by his eunuch that his dream was simply the work of the opium pipe which he had smoked.

Up to this point in Gautier's scenario, nothing extraordinary has occurred. Under the influence of opium Achmet has had a beautiful dream which corresponds to his desires. Roucem, the eunuch, tells him that his dream had no reality except in his imagination. However, in the next scene, when it seems that Achmet is about to be charmed by the favorite of the harem, Nourmahal, the angry queen of the peris appears and replaces the talisman in his hands. It is true that the peri is only visible to Achmet, but another dimension has still been added to reality, for Achmet is no longer under the influence of opium.

According to a rather widespread belief, opium and hashish freed the soul from its physical prison so that it could participate in another order of reality. Gautier explains his idea to Gérard in a notice concerning "La Péri" published in July 1843.

> Achmet et la Péri, c'est-à-dire la matière et l'esprit, le désir et l'amour, se rencontrent dans l'extase d'un rêve, comme dans un champ neutre; ce n'est que lorsque les yeux du corps sont endormis que les yeux de l'âme s'éveillent. Les liens charnels sont dénoués, et le monde invisible se révèle, les esprits du ciel descendent, ceux

---

[40] Ibid., p. 282.
[41] The talisman is a bouquet of flowers with a star from the crown of the peri placed in the center. Achmet can make her appear by kissing the star.

de la terre montent, et des unions mystérieuses s'accomplissent dans un vague crépuscule où l'on pressent déjà l'aurore du jour éternel. [42]

Thus what was for Achmet only a reality under the influence of opium has now become a reality to him even when he is not under the influence of the drug. As the play develops the spiritual reality of the peri becomes concrete and participates in the physical world of Achmet. [43]

In the physical form of Leila, the peri is no longer only a spiritual reality which Achmet can see, but a physical reality as well. As a result of the freedom of soul obtained by means of the opium, Achmet enjoys a reality which is in every way as authentic as the reality to which he was bound before his opium experience. In the conclusion of the ballet, the reality which was revealed by the opium replaces the physical reality of which he was a part, for as he is thrown out of the window into the "gouffre":

> Les murs de la prison s'évanouissent, des nuages se lèvent portant des groupes de Péris: le ciel s'ouvre, et l'on aperçoit un paradis musulman, merveilleuse et fantastique architecture dont Achmet divinisé monte les degrés étincelants en tenant la main de celle dont il est désormais inséparable. [44]

In the short story, "La mille et deuxième nuit," Gautier uses essentially the same story which he used in his pantomime-ballet,

---

[42] Ibid., pp. 296-297.
[43] At this time a slave girl escapes from the harem of the pacha. As she is fleeing, she is killed by her pursuers. The queen of the peris decides to give new life to the dead slave by replacing the departed soul with her own. Feigning to be only slightly wounded, the peri (who now takes the name Leila) begs Achmet to give her shelter. Achmet is soon pleased with his new slave and begins to love her with as much fervor as he had loved the peri. The pacha hears that his slave is still alive and demands her return. When Achmet refuses, he is thrown into prison. In prison he is put to the final test by the peri, who comes to offer him freedom if he will only turn Leila over to her master. Achmet chooses to sacrifice his own life rather than betray the girl he loves. The pacha orders Achmet's execution, but he is saved by the peri. As he is thrown out of the window to be torn by iron hooks sticking out from the wall, the entire scene vanishes to be replaced by a scene of the Mohammedan Paradise.
[44] Ibid., p. 292.

except that the principal character's love for Leila ends in marriage on earth, and opium is not introduced directly in the story to create another order of reality.[45] It is true that Mahmoud-Ben-Ahmed (he corresponds to Achmet in the ballet) is smoking his narguileh at the precise moment that he meets the runaway slave, Leila; but his smoking does not seem to play an important role in the development of the narrative. However, the framework in which the story is told strongly suggests that Gautier is describing an afternoon of opium or hashish in which the unique idea for the arrangement of the tale was suggested.

Gautier begins his story by saying that he had taken all precautions not to be disturbed for the afternoon so that he might enjoy his favorite pastime, doing nothing:

> ... j'avais pris toutes mes mesures pour savourer à mon aise ma volupté favorite ... je ne voulais pas être dérangé dans cette importante occupation.[46]

---

[45] Gautier tells the story of Mahmoud-Ben-Ahmed who hoped to fall in love with a peri: "A force de fumer son narguilhé et de rêver à la fraîcheur du soir sur les dalles de marbre de sa terrasse, la tête de Mahmoud-Ben-Ahmed s'était un peu exalté: il avait formé le projet d'être l'amant d'une péri ou tout au moins d'une princesse du sang royal." (Théophile Gautier, Romans et contes, p. 326.) The peri, Boudroulboudour, hears his wish and decides to grant it. But she wants to see whether or not she could make him love her in human form. The next day Mahmoud-Ben-Ahmed catches a glimpse of the Princess Ayesha (the peri has taken her form), and immediately falls in love with her. That evening, while smoking his narguileh, Mahmoud-Ben-Ahmed hides a young slave girl named Leila, who has run away from the harem of the Sultan, Abu-Becker. Still intrigued by his love for Ayesha, Mahmoud-Ben-Ahmed does not notice the beauty of his newly acquired slave. A short time later he is granted a private rendez-vous with Ayesha, and reads her some of his poetry. He becomes so engrossed in his own verse that he fails to notice that Ayesha has turned into a peri. By the time he has finished reading, the peri has again become Ayesha and departs mysteriously. Mahmoud-Ben-Ahmed is not granted another rendez-vous. After a period of time, he becomes aware of the beauty of Leila and finally sees that she resembles Ayesha. Having won his love as a human, the peri shows her true form and explains that she was both Ayesha and Leila. She had left him on the previous occasion because she feared that he was only in love with his own poetry and not with Ayesha. She determines to remain Leila to society, but will be the peri to him.

[46] Gautier, Romans et contes, p. 347. Baudelaire advises in his "Le Poëme du haschisch" that one should be completely free from all cares and obligations if he wishes to enjoy the hashish experience.

Lying down comfortably by the fire, he would not have changed his position for all the gold in the world.[47] In this solitude, his mind begins to wander from reality. In the "délicieuse somnolence qui suit la suspension volontaire de la pensée ... le sentiment de la vie réelle m'abandonnait peu à peu, et j'étais enfoncé bien avant sous les ondes insondables de cette *mer d'anéantissement* où tant de rêveurs orientaux ont laissé leur raison, déjà ébranlée par le hatschich et l'opium."[48]

Gautier, who has turned off the clock, becomes aware of the complete silence in the room:

> Le silence le plus profond régnait dans la chambre; j'avais arrêté la pendule pour ne pas entendre le tic-tac du balancier, ce battement de pouls de l'éternité; car je ne puis souffrir, lorsque je suis oisif, l'activité bête et fiévreuse de ce disque de cuivre jaune qui va d'un coin à l'autre de sa cage et marche toujours sans faire un pas.[49]

Suddenly Gautier hears the ringing of the outside bell. The noise is disturbingly loud to him, but does not even disturb his cat:

> Tout à coup, et kling et klang, un coup de sonnette vif, nerveux, insupportablement argentin, éclate et tombe dans ma tranquillité comme une goutte de plomb fondu qui s'enfoncerait en grésillant dans un lac endormi; sans penser à mon chat, pelotonné en boule sur ma manche, je me redressai en tressaillant et sautai sur mes pieds comme lancé par un ressort ...[50]

Gautier's servant enters and introduces two women into the room. They are not ordinary women, but Scheherazade and Dinarsarde, the two famous sisters from the pages of the *Thousand and One*

---

[47] The lethargy brought on by opium and hashish is well known. All movement is avoided because of the great effort which seems to be required. In "Le Poëme du haschisch" Baudelaire states that one must "développer un long courage pour remuer une bouteille ou une fourchette." (Charles Baudelaire, *Œuvres complètes* [Paris, 1961], p. 370.)

[48] Gautier, *Romans et contes*, p. 318.

[49] Ibid.

[50] Ibid. Hypersensitivity to the sound of the clock and to the ringing bell is often described by individuals who have experimented with hashish or opium.

Nights. Scheherazade, desperate for another story to tell the next night, has come to Gautier hoping that he can provide her with a new one. It is in this strange atmosphere of hypersensitivity to sound, silence, and wandering of the mind that Gautier tells the story of Mahmoud-Ben-Ahmed and Leila.

In the novel *Spirite* Gautier again treats the marriage of a soul on earth to a soul of the spiritual reality. For Lavinia to be united in eternity with the soul that was destined to match hers, Guy Malivert must not become united in his earthly life. Gautier does not employ either opium or hashish to bring Guy Malivert into communication with Lavinia, but the visions which Malivert has of the spiritual world remind one of the descriptions of hashish hallucinations concerning it.

Malivert's first vision recalls Gautier's own hashish experience:

> ... les plis des rideaux prenaient l'aspect de vêtements féminins et semblaient palpiter comme agités par le mouvement d'un corps, mais ce n'était qu'une pure illusion. Des bluettes, des points lumineux, des taches de dessin changeant, des papillons, des filets onduleux et vermicules dansaient, fourmillaient, s'agrandissaient, se rapetissaient devant son regard fatigué, sans qu'il pût discerner rien d'appréciable. [51]

Lavinia's description of her flight into the spiritual realm includes most of the sensations commonly reported from taking opium or hashish. She feels herself passing from a world of time to a world of eternity, from the finite to the infinite:

> Des mots humains ne peuvent rendre la sensation d'une âme qui, délivrée de sa prison corporelle, passe de cette vie dans l'autre, du temps dans l'éternité et du fini dans l'infini. [52]

Her soul moves from darkness into a dazzling light, into an environment of expanding, limitless horizons. She feels an indescribable joy from these wonders:

---

[51] Théophile Gautier, *Spirite* (Paris, 1904), p. 32.
[52] Ibid., p. 164.

> A une intermittance d'ombre profonde avait succédé un éblouissement de splendeurs, un élargissement d'horizons, une disparition de toute limite et de tout obstacle, qui m'enivraient d'une joie indicible. [53]

Just as in so many hashish experiences, the problems of life are all answered. She understands the reasons behind the great mysteries. Distances no longer exist for her soul, and she can transport herself wherever she desires to be:

> Des explosions de sens nouveaux me faisaient comprendre les mystères impénétrables à la pensée et aux organes terrestres. Débarrassée de cette argile soumise aux lois de la pesanteur ... je m'élançais avec une alacrité folle dans l'insondable éther. Les distances n'existaient plus pour moi, et mon simple désir me rendait présente où je voulais être. [54]

As was so often observed by the persons who experimented with the drug under the direction of Dr. Cahagnet, the souls and created objects of the universe were represented by dazzling sparks of light emanating from the overwhelming source of light of the Creator:

> Une lumière fourmillante, brillant comme une poussière diamantée, formait l'atmosphère; chaque grain de cette poussière étincelante, comme je m'en aperçus bientôt, était une âme. Il s'y dessinait des moires comme dans cette poudre impalpable qu'on étend sur les tables d'harmonie pour étudier les vibrations sonores, et tous ces mouvements causaient dans la splendeur des recrudescences d'éclat. [55]

---

[53] Ibid.
[54] Ibid., pp. 164-165.
[55] Ibid., p. 165. M. Lecocq's vision under the influence of hashish bears a certain resemblance to the vision seen by Malivert: "I next perceived... a luminous circle, similar in color and brilliancy to that which I had previously observed; and from the centre of this creative focus sparkling jets, composed of luminous points of all colours, were continually escaping, which accumulated to an inappreciable quantity, and assumed the form of an ever moving sphere, all intermingling with each other, without the least confusion." (Cahagnet, p. 123.)

As in the vision of M. Lecocq, the souls have a single source of light and are of many colors:

> Elles avaient pour monade constitutive l'étincelle céleste. Ces âmes étaient blanches comme le diamant, les autres colorées comme le rubis, l'émeraude, le saphir, la topaze et l'améthyste. [56]

The descriptions of musical harmonies, light patterns, numerical significances, etc., provide a continuous vision of ecstasy. It is not to be thought that Gautier wrote these beautifully descriptive passages while under the influence of a drug; nothing is less likely. But it does seem probable that he drew inspiration from his own experiences or from those of which he had read. The nature of the descriptions and of the perceptions in these visions presents a striking similarity with those of numerous drug experiences recorded over the years.

Frequently in Gautier's prose works one encounters a strange description, an unusual vision, or a certain atmosphere which reminds one of Gautier's account of his hashish experience; and one is never entirely certain because of this similarity that the passage is not a direct result of this experience. "Le pied de momie" is a *conte* which renders just such an impression. Throughout the story there is a strange atmosphere of ambiguity. One cannot be certain where reality is and where it is not. The presence of the figurine at the end of the story further casts doubt upon the reality of the dream which has just been related. Yet, perhaps if one looks closely at this figurine, it may suggest what Gautier intended in his work.

There are numerous features in the story which indicate that the events are taking place in an atmosphere which little resembles the reality of everyday life. Certain aspects of the tale remind one of the characteristics of hashish intoxication. As the story begins, the narrator enters a curiosity shop to purchase a paperweight. He is met by the strange store owner, who immediately reminds one of the frequent mystery characters in Gautier's works. His eyes and expression resemble those of

---

[56] *Spirite*, p. 166.

Esquiros described by Gautier in "La pipe d'opium." The shopkeeper has a "... crâne immense" and the "... scintillement de deux petits yeux jaunes qui tremblotaient dans leurs orbites comme deux louis d'or sur du vif-argent." [57] For a paperweight, the narrator buys a real foot from the mummified body of the Princess Hermonthis, the daughter of an Egyptian Pharoah.

A second aspect of the story which reminds one of the hashish hallucination is the narrator's ridiculous feeling of superiority because he owned a mummyfoot paperweight:

> ... j'allai me promener avec la gravité convenable et la fierté d'un homme qui a sur tous les passants qu'il coudoie l'avantage ineffable de posséder un morceau de la princesse Hermonthis, fille de Pharaon.
>
> Je trouvai souverainement ridicules tous ceux qui ne possédaient pas, comme moi, un serre-papier aussi notoirement égyptien, et la vraie occupation d'un homme sensé me paraissait d'avoir un pied de momie sur son bureau. [58]

The narrator returns home from a dinner at a friend's and falls asleep conscious of the strong odor of oriental perfume. During his sleep, he has a dream or what he thinks is a dream. Many features of the dream recall the altered phenomena of perception which one experiences under the influence of hashish. First of all, the narrator is not sure whether or not he is dreaming. Just as the hashish eater seems to be able to observe himself under the influence of hashish, so does the narrator feel that he is awake, although he knows that he is sleeping:

> Les yeux de mon âme s'ouvrirent, et je vis ma chambre telle qu'elle était effectivement: j'aurais pu me croire éveillé, mais une vague perception me disait que je dormais et qu'il allait se passer quelque chose de bizarre. [59]

Just as in a hashish hallucination, inanimate objects begin to move and to take on peculiar significance:

---

[57] *Romans et contes*, p. 399.
[58] Ibid., p. 403.
[59] Ibid., p. 405.

> Cependant, au bout de quelques instants, cet intérieur si calme parut se troubler, les boiseries craquaient furtivement; la bûche enfouie sous la cendre lançait tout à coup un jet de gaz bleu, et les disques des patères semblaint des yeux de métal attentifs comme moi aux choses qui allaient se passer. [60]

After a moment, he becomes aware that the paperweight has begun to move:

> Au lieu d'être immobile comme il convient à un pied embaumé depuis quatre mille ans, il s'agitait, se contractait et sautillait sur les papiers comme une grenouille effarée ... [61]

The narrator's dream trip with the Princess Hermonthis also reminds one of a hallucination. [62] In their flight back to the tomb where he is to meet Hermonthis' father, the narrator has a number of sensations and observations common to one who is under the influence of hashish. They pass through corridors of interminable length and other corridors filled with designs of strange figures, "... bizarres d'éperviers, de serpents roulés en cercle ...." [63] Finally they arrive at a room which is so vast in size that it seems limitless:

> Enfin nous débouchâmes dans une salle si vaste, si énorme, si démesurée, que l'on ne pouvait en apercevoir les bornes; à perte de vue s'étendaient des files de colonnes monstrueuses entre lesquelles tremblotaient de livides étoiles de lumière jaune; ces points brillants révélaient des profondeurs incalculables. [64]

---

[60] Ibid.
[61] Ibid.
[62] The Princess Hermonthis enters the room by the window in hopes that she can retrieve her lost foot. (The shopkeeper who sold the foot to the narrator was formerly the suitor of the Princess, but her father was not favorable to his suit. To gain revenge, the shopkeeper had paid to have her foot removed.) The foot refuses to abandon its new owner, but the narrator gallantly returns the foot to the Princess. The Princess then takes him on a fantastic flight to introduce him to her father.
[63] Ibid., p. 411.
[64] Ibid.

The narrator also experienced among the countless kings a sense of timelessness which is so characteristic of the hashish experience:

> Plus loin, dans une vapeur poussiéreuse, à travers le brouillard des éternités, je distinguais vaguement les soixante-douze rois préadamites avec leurs soixante-douze peuples à jamais disparus.[65]

He is awakened from his sleep by a friend just as he is shaking hands with Hermonthis' father. Thus it would seem that this was only a dream. But, in looking at the place where the mummy's foot should have been, he saw much to his surprise the "... petite figurine de pâte verte mise à sa place par la princesse Hermonthis!"[66]

It should be recalled that the figurine was in the form of Isis, "conductrice des âmes," and that it was made of a "pâte verte," the description given to the hashish preparation used by Moreau de Tours and the frequenters of the Hôtel Pimodan. It is difficult to determine the significance of any such reference to hashish, but it was undoubtedly intended to add to the mysterious ambiguity of reality which the figurine itself suggests.

VI

In the "Histoire du Calife Hakem," first published in the *Revue des Deux Mondes* on August 15, 1847, Gérard de Nerval relates the strange history of the Caliph and his double, Yousouf.[67]

---

[65] Ibid., p. 412.
[66] Ibid., p. 414.
[67] During the course of a conversation with the sheikh of the Druses, Gérard asks concerning the famous Caliph Hakem, who claimed to be the incarnation of God on Earth, and he takes down the account of the Caliph's adventures. The story begins in an *okel* (an establishment where refreshments are served) along the banks of the Nile. Yousouf, a young fisherman, enters the *okel* with the intent of enjoying some hashish. A stranger in old clothes enters by an opposite door at nearly the same moment and takes a seat in the corner. Seeing the stranger's uncertainty, Yousouf invites him to take some refreshment with him in the form of hashish. He feels an immediate intimacy with the stranger and confides to him a dream which he has

Each of the main characters in the story lives a multiple reality caused in part by his use of hashish.

When Yousouf first appears in the story coming toward the *okel*, he is presented as a man who is familiar with the surroundings, an individual who has visited the *okel* on many previous occasions:

---

been having regularly while under the influence of the drug. Hakem in turn relates a secret that he has never told to anyone before. He is in love with his sister Sétalmulc, whom he considers to be the soul which was destined for him in eternity. The next evening, after having taken the hashish, Hakem returns to the palace to announce to his sister that he wishes to marry her. Unwilling to marry her own brother, she schemes with the grand vizier, Argévan, who raids the hashish *okel* the next evening and seizes the unwitting Hakem. Outraged, he announces that he is really the Caliph. Although Argévan knows who he is, he pretends that the man is raving and takes him to the insane asylum. While he is in the asylum, another Caliph sits on the throne, a man who resembles the true Caliph enough to be his double. One learns later that this double is Yousouf. Apparently Yousouf's dream has become a reality, although he is not exactly sure how much of the dream is actually reality and how much is hallucination. Each evening with his eyes covered, Yousouf is led into a magnificent palace where he is treated just as if he were really the Caliph. One evening, upon his arrival, he sees that the palace is arrayed for a wedding, his wedding to the beautiful girl whose identity remains a mystery to him. Meanwhile, an attacking army has caused enough turmoil to allow Hakem to escape from the insane asylum and once again establish himself as Caliph. On the evening of the wedding between the Caliph's sister and Yousouf, Hakem returns early from his usual all-night sojourn, having decided not to take any hashish for the evening. Seeing the magnificent preparation for some important event, Hakem wonders what the occasion may be, and he wonders for a moment about the reality of what he is witnessing. He looks into the room where the usurping Caliph is and is taken aback by the fact that the false Caliph is his double. Since such an encounter was considered an unfavorable omen, Hakem withdraws from the palace and soon sees two figures leave. One of the figures is Yousouf, who relates to him what has befallen him since their last meeting (Hakem never discloses to Yousouf that he is the Caliph). The next evening, Hakem goes as usual on his nocturnal visit. He is attacked by three men and stabbed to death. However, one of the men, none other than Yousouf, recognizes immediately whom they are stabbing and turns on the other two assailants. Both Hakem and Yousouf are left for dead. But when an attempt is made to find the two bodies, only the clothes are discovered. It is explained by the Sheikh that Yousouf, not knowing the true identity of his friend, had agreed to kill the Caliph on the sister's behalf. The two servants had been instructed to kill Yousouf if he hesitated in carrying out the task. Realizing too late whom he was sent to kill, Yousouf turns on the servants and is killed in the ensuing struggle.

> Un soir, une barque dirigée avec la certitude que donne la connaissance des lieux, vint aborder dans l'ombre de la terrasse, au pied d'un escalier dont l'eau baisait les premières marches, et il s'en élança un jeune homme de bonne mine, qui semblait un pêcheur, et qui, montant les degrés d'un pas ferme et rapide, s'assit dans l'angle de la salle à une place qui paraissait la sienne. Personne ne fit attention à sa venue; c'était évidemment un habitué.[68]

Because of the phrases "dirigée avec la certitude" and "un pas ferme et rapide," one feels a certain stability and firmness in Gérard's presentation of Yousouf. However, Yousouf only "semblait un pêcheur" and took a seat which "paraissait la sienne." In reality he is of the same lineage as the king[69] and is only dressed as a fisherman because he is unaware of his true identity. Gérard complicates Yousouf's existence by having him experience a third reality while under the influence of hashish. After a brief praise of hashish as the liberator of the spirit from its material prison, Yousouf relates a dream which he experiences every night in his boat as he returns up the Nile from the *okel*:

> ... lorsque je me retire dans ma cange, chancelant sous la splendeur de mes visions, fermant la paupière à ce ruissellement perpétuel d'hyacinthes, d'escarboucles, d'émeraudes, de rubis, qui forment le fond sur lequel le hachich dessine des fantaisies merveilleuses ..., comme au sein de l'infini j'aperçois une figure céleste, plus belle que toutes les créations des poètes, qui me sourit avec une pénétrante douceur, et qui descend des cieux pour venir jusqu'à moi. Est-ce un ange, une péri? Je ne sais. Elle s'assied à mes côtés dans la barque, dont le bois grossier se change aussitôt en nacre de perle et flotte sur une rivière d'argent, poussée par une brise chargée de parfums.[70]

---

[68] Gérard de Nerval, "Histoire du Calife Hakem," *Œuvres*, II (Paris, 1961), 359.

[69] In one version of the story Hakem and Yousouf are actually brothers who have been brought up under different circumstances in order that the father might determine which has the touch of divinity. In this version the assassination attempt fails and Hakem retires to the desert. Yousouf becomes his prophet under the name Hamza. (Ibid., p. 1351.)

[70] Ibid., p. 361.

But Gérard deliberately puts into doubt what seems to be a clear distinction between Yousouf's reality as the fisherman and his dream by adding an element of doubt to the dream.

One night, when Yousouf had taken a smaller dose of hashish than usual and felt that he was no longer being affected by the drug, he experienced a dream which was almost identical with the dream he customarily had while under the influence of the hashish.

> Une nuit, j'avais pris une dose moins forte; je me réveillai de mon ivresse, lorsque ma cange passait à la pointe de l'île de Roddah. Une femme semblable à celle de mon rêve penchait sur moi des yeux qui, pour être humains, n'en avaient pas moins un éclat céleste; son voile entr'ouvert laissait flamboyer aux rayons de la lune une veste raide de pierreries. Ma main rencontra la sienne; sa peau douce, onctueuse et fraîche comme un pétale de fleur, ses bagues, dont les ciselures m'effleurèrent, me convainquirent de la réalité. [71]

Yousouf is certain that he was not dreaming, and yet the ocurrence is the same, except for his claim that he was not under the influence of hashish. Yousouf's description of the woman's sudden appearance in the boat and the description of his emotions cause doubt concerning the reality of the scene.

> ... il me paraissait tout naturel que cette femme, qui réalisait si complètement mon idéal, se trouvât là dans ma cange, au milieu du Nil, comme si elle se fût élancée du calice d'une de ces larges fleurs qui montent à la surface des eaux. Sans lui demander aucune explication, je me jetai à ses pieds, et comme à la péri de mon rêve, je lui adressai tout ce que l'amour dans son exaltation peut imaginer de plus brûlant et de plus sublime; il me venait des paroles d'une signification immense, des expressions qui renfermaient des univers de pensées, des phrases mystérieuses où vibrait l'écho des mondes disparus. Mon âme se grandissait dans le passé et dans l'avenir; l'amour que j'exprimais, j'avais la conviction de l'avoir ressenti de toute éternité. [72]

---

[71] Ibid., pp. 361-362.
[72] Ibid., p. 362.

Moreover, Yousouf's description of the sensation he felt when he looked into her eyes reminds one of Gautier's description of Esquiros in "La pipe d'opium":

> A mesure que je parlais, je voyais ses grands yeux s'allumer et lancer des effluves; ses mains transparentes s'étendaient vers moi s'effilant en rayons de lumière. Je me sentais enveloppé d'un réseau de flammes et je retombais malgré moi de la veille dans le rêve. [73]

Because the situations are so similar, one is left in doubt concerning the reality in which Yousouf participates while under the influence of hashish. It is this doubtful world of dream which will later so impose itself that Yousouf will consider it to be reality.

Like Yousouf, Hakem is a person who is living a multiple existence. During the day he is the Caliph; but at night, he dresses in his slave's clothes and goes into town to mix with his people. This particular evening, having entered the *okel*, he takes some hashish with Yousouf. It soon takes effect and Hakem is carried into a world of novel sensations and new thoughts:

> La drogue agissant avec plus de force sur eux, ils commencèrent à rire, à s'agiter et à parler avec une volubilité extrême, l'étranger surtout, qui, strict observateur des défenses, n'avait jamais goûté de cette préparation et en ressentait vivement les effets. Il paraissait en proie à une exaltation extraordinaire; des essaims de pensées nouvelles, inouïes, inconcevables, traversaient son âme en tourbillons de feu; ses yeux étincelaient comme éclairés intérieurement par le reflet d'un monde inconnu, une dignité surhumaine relevait son maintien, puis la vision s'éteignait, et il se laissait aller mollement sur les carreaux à toutes les béatitudes du kief. [74]

Asked what he thinks of the drug, Hakem responds, "Le hachich rend pareil à Dieu." [75]

From this point forward Hakem's troubles are a direct result of his hashish intoxication and his insistence that he is God. In

---

[73] Ibid.
[74] Ibid., pp. 360-361.
[75] Ibid. p. 361.

this first encounter with hashish, Hakem, who blasphemes openly concerning the prophets, Mohammed and Christ, and commits the sacrilege of claiming to be God, is saved from the angry crowd which had gathered at the *okel* only by the intervention of Yousouf.[76] Yet the reality of the situation is not so clear that one can attribute Hakem's feeling that he is God to the effects of the hashish. Once again the element of truth in the hashish experience is underscored by an element of verification from reality. Hakem is approached at several important moments during the story by a blind Syrian priest who recognizes in Hakem the presence of God. Just as there is doubt about the reality of Yousouf's dream, so does the Syrian priest's recognition of the caliph's divinity cause the reader to wonder whether there is some truth in Hakem's own claim of divinity.

Several days later, after having hashish for the second time, Hakem is again seized by an "idée fixe." Under the influence of the hashish, he returns to the palace to announce to his sister Sétalmulc that he intends to marry her:

> Sétalmulc, dit Hakem, J'ai pensé longtemps à te donner un mari; mais aucun homme n'est digne de toi. Ton sang divin ne doit pas souffrir de mélange. Il faut transmettre intact à l'avenir le trésor que nous avons reçu du passé. C'est moi, Hakem, le calife, le seigneur du ciel et de la terre, qui serai ton époux; les noces se feront dans trois jours. Telle est ma volonté sacrée.[77]

It is because of this declaration that Sétalmulc plots agains Hakem. At her instigation, Argévan raids the *okel* during Hakem's next hashish intoxication and takes Hakem to a prison for the mad where, although in reality he is Caliph and perhaps God incarnate, he is treated as though he were insane.

The climax of the story comes after Hakem has been re-established as Caliph and has again gone out, presumably to go to town and remain until the usual hour. However, he returns

---

[76] Yousouf later explains to the proprietor that everyone has his "idée fixe" under the influence of hashish. The stranger's happens to be in thinking that he is God.

[77] Ibid., p. 372.

early, having decided not to take any hashish, and finds the palace lighted and in the process of a celebration.

It is here that the confused realities of the two friends clash. Sétalmulc, the girl in Yousouf's dream, has put Yousouf on the throne of the Caliph Hakem. Each night she causes his eyes to be covered and has him brought into the magnificent palace.[78] When his eyes are uncovered, Yousouf finds himself in such splendor that he cannot be sure that he is not seeing the wonders of a hashish vision. Yet everything is so real that he can only consider it to be reality.

Returning to the island and finding the celebration, Hakem is faced with a situation that defies his analysis. The beauty and splendor of the palace and the lack of attention paid to him by the servants cause him to think that he might be suffering from a hashish hallucination. Yet, he has taken no hashish. Although Caliph and God incarnate, Hakem has uncovered a reality which he never knew existed and which he cannot control. Since he is the Caliph, it is impossible for this to be a reality. To add to his confusion, Hakem does not see an imposter upon the throne, but a person who so resembles his own being that it can only be his double.

The solution to Hakem's problem is found only in the conclusion by his apparent death and withdrawal from this life to a more spiritual existence. The clash between Hakem's spiritual reality and the reality of the flesh is underscored by Gérard when the Caliph is taken to the prison for the insane. The reality of what is and what appears in this world is irreconcilable. Only the death in this life can reconcile the clash between one's temporal and one's spiritual reality.

VII

Whereas Gérard de Nerval saw the hashish experience as an additional aspect of an already confusing reality, Eugène Sue saw in the use of opium the possibility of creating another existence

---

[78] Again it should be noted that this episode is reminiscent of the Old Man of the Mountain story.

so complete that it might replace what one considers ordinarily to be reality. To emphasize the inability of man to determine what is real and what is not real, Sue uses two lines from Lamartine's *Harmonies* as an epigraph for his chapter entitled "Opium" in the novel *Atar-Gull*:

> Rien n'est vrai, rien n'est faux;
> Tout est songe et mensonge. [79]

Wherein lies the true reality of a man's life if half of it is spent in one existence and the other half in another which is entirely different?

In *Atar-Gull*, Sue presents just such a character in the avowed opium-eater, Brulart. Brutal captain of a pirate vessel called *L'Hyène*, Brulart leads a dual existence which divides his life equally between the beautiful, hope-filled world created by opium, and the dreary, cruel life he leads as the sadistic captain of the pirate ship. So horrible is his existence as a pirate and so disgusting his character that he has come to consider his escapades as only a hideous nightmare which he must tolerate daily. His true existence is the one he procures through the use of opium. So persuaded is he that the nightmare life he leads as a pirate is only an illusion, from which he will awaken under favorable auspices, that he deliberately commits excessive cruelties, [80] satisfied that no real harm can result from them. [81]

After having presented Brulart the pirate as an individual dedicated to sadistic cruelty and consummate in evil-doing, Sue presents the half of Brulart's life which takes place behind locked doors in his private quarters. As if he were gradually waking from a frightful dream, Brulart's expression changes completely at the sight of the little case containing his opium:

---

[79] Eugène Sue, *Atar-Gull* (Paris, 1958), p. 243.
[80] His brutal acts include throwing persons overboard, delivering Benoît, a ship's captain, to a tribe of cannibals, exploding a ship in which a number of slaves were helplessly tied, and punishing excessively members of his crew.
[81] When Brulart is about to blow up Benoît's ship on which there were many helpless slaves, he casually identifies the sadistic plan that he has divised as a *"vilain rêve."* (Sue, p. 291.)

> Sa figure, ordinairement rude, sauvage, semblait se dépouiller de cette écorce épaisse, et ses traits, fortement caractérisés, paraissaient vraiment beaux, tant une subite et inimitable expression de douceur s'y était révélée ... [82]

The contrast between the existence he is about to enter and the one he is preparing to leave is emphasized by the religious adoration he shows toward the flask of fluid capable of delivering him from his filthy existence as a pirate:

> Il le baisa [le flacon] avec onction et amour, comme on baise la main d'une vierge, et le déposa, non sur la vilaine table; oh! non, mais sur un petit coussinet de velours noir, tout brodé d'argent et de perles ... [83]

Immediately after taking several drops of the fluid, Brulart's entire bearing, appearance, and attitude begin to radiate the confidence and joy of another nature:

> Et quand il se redressa, vous eussiez baissé les yeux devant ce regard inspiré ... qui faisait presque pâlir la lumière de sa lampe; il était beau, grandiose, admirable ainsi; ses guenilles, sa longue barbe, tout cela disparaissait devant l'incroyable conscience de bonheur qui éclatait sur ce front tout à l'heure sombre et foncé ... maintenant lisse et pur comme celui d'une jeune fille ... 'Adieu terre! ... à moi le ciel'... dit-il en s'élançant sur son lit ... [84]

---

[82] Ibid., p. 236.

[83] Ibid. In his description of Brulart's complete adoration of his opium, Sue compares Brulart to a priest performing a religious ceremony: "Mais pendant toute cette cérémonie il y avait sur les traits de Brulart autant de recueillement et d'adoration que sur le visage d'un prêtre qui retire le calice du tabernacle ...

"Et ouvrant délicatement la petite fiole, il versa goutte à goutte la séduisante liqueur qui tombait en perles brillantes comme des rubis.

"Il en compta vingt ... puis il remplit la coupe d'une autre liqueur limpide et claire comme du cristal, qui prit alors une teinte rouge et dorée." (Sue, pp. 237-238).

The complete adoration of an addict for his drug can scarcely be exaggerated. Sue describes this aspect of drug taking better than any other writer of the period.

[84] Ibid., pp. 238-239.

From Brulart's opium dreams it is easy to see how he came to consider his dream-world a more authentic reality than his ordinary life. Nothing in the latter corresponds to the life he had been brought up for or to the life he hoped to lead. Shaped by bizarre circumstances and by his unfortunate relationship with a faithless girl named Marie, [85] Brulart's life no longer coincides with his inner spirit. Contrarily, the opium dreams, based upon the events of his waking life (thus retaining a valid framework of reality) and enhanced by his aspirations and longings form an existence in conformity with his desires.

Sue presents two of Brulart's opium dreams. The first shows the contrast between his world of dream and his world of reality. In the dream Brulart is a nobleman who lives a pleasant existence with a faithful Marie. Sue emphasizes Brulart's mother-mistress image of Marie, when, during the dream, the hideous memory returns and changes the dream into a veritable nightmare. Finding himself in the middle of a garden full of fruit, Brulart takes an orange and begins to peel it. Instead of juice, thick black blood oozes from the orange. Suddenly he feels the orange bite into his finger. In the midst of excruciating pain as the bite penetrates his bone, Brulart feels the kiss of a woman, his protectress:

> Alors il sentit l'impression fraîche et humide d'une bouche de femme effleurer ses lèvres brûlantes ... et une voix bien connue murmurait à son oreille: 'Ne crains rien, je veille sur toi ... attends-moi ...' [86]

---

[85] As a young man, Brulart had married this girl. After a short period of amorous bliss and great spending, they dissipate their fortune. Unable to bear the thought of living in poverty, Marie suggests that they commit suicide together. She makes a capsule supposedly filled with poison at each end and suggests that they each bite off half the capsule. In this way they could die in a last embrace. The poison in Brulart's half, however, was not potent enough, and he awakens to find that Marie is no longer beside him. Later he discovers that all was a trick on her part in an effort to rid herself of a husband who no longer has enough money to support her needs. Discovering that she has married a wealthy count and is in Marseilles, Brulart immediately goes there and kills her. It is because of this murder that he must flee the country to live the rest of his life as the pirate, Brulart.

[86] Ibid., pp. 253-254.

Once Brulart is reassured by his protectress, his dream changes to a peaceful scene where he awaits and receives his faithful Marie.

Brulart's second dream occurs much later, after he has been taken by the English ship and condemned to be hanged.[87] Brulart is allowed to keep his opium flask and determines to use the remainder of the opium to escape from his dreadful nightmare. This last dream of Brulart is interesting in that it unites his opium existence to his life as a pirate. At the beginning of the dream Brulart is a youth of only sixteen who aspires to a career in the navy. Contrary to the direction and fortune of his real life, he becomes a member of the crew aboard a ship called *Le Cygne*. In his earliest battle experience, he leads the French sailors to a victory over the English. In the second scene of the dream, his ship is caught in a storm and shipwrecked. He is washed ashore and wanders into a cave where he sees his mother in the form of a goddess. Again the mother-mistress image assures him of her protection and promises him indescribable happiness next to the woman who loves him. In the third scene he is in bed convalescing from his shipwreck and being cared for by his beautiful protectress. Sue presents this enchanting creature as Brulart's entire life — the only family and the only love he has:

> ... oui, vous êtes tout pour moi ... vous êtes la seule qui m'ayez témoigné de l'intérêt ... je vous aime de toute la tendresse que j'ai dans le coeur, je vous aime comme une mère, comme une soeur; comme une amie; ô vous ... toujours vous ... vous serez mon Dieu, ma religion, ma croyance ...[88]

Up to this point in his dream life, Marie has always been faithful to Brulart. She has been the opposite of what she was

---

[87] After having seized the ship and cargo of Captain Benoît, Brulart was pursued by an English frigate. He managed to escape the faster English vessel by setting Benoît's ship adrift, rigged with explosives. The boarding party from the frigate accidently set off the explosives which Brulart had planted, but the English ship was not sunk as he had hoped. They were delayed, however, and Brulart escaped. Later in the story Brulart, who was set adrift by the mutinous pirates of his own ship, is picked up by this same frigate and sentenced to be hanged.

[88] Ibid., pp. 421-422.

in his real life. It is here that Sue unites and completes the two existences of Brulart. While making love to Brulart in the fourth part of the opium dream, Marie allows her long tresses to fall down over Brulart's head and shoulders in a sensuous act of complete affection and love. Under the cover and protection of her beautiful hair Brulart steals a kiss from the unsuspecting Marie. Angered and surprised by this action, Marie suddenly changes character. For a moment she is the playfully malicious, pouting Marie whom Brulart had loved in real life. Using her tresses of hair like a rope, she strangles the helpless, adoring Brulart. At the moment that he is being strangled in the dream, he is being hanged aboard the English vessel.

It is ironic that both Brulart's lives should be made to end in a similar manner, and it is even more ironic that in his dream-death his faithful, adoring Marie should be his executioner as he was hers in life. Indirectly her unfaithfulness and deceit were the causes of all his misery, of his dreadful life as the brutal captain Brulart, and of his hanging. In contrast, as the faithful, loving Marie, she represented to his dream life his source of love and protection. And yet in this dream she is the direct cause of his death because of his deceit. It would seem from this description that Brulart's real life had finally destroyed his dream, that he was forced to live at last in his miserable reality. This, however, is not so. Brulart's dream-world transcends his wretched reality and his horrible death by hanging. Because of the opium, Brulart remains unaware that he is being hanged. And even though strangled in his dream by Marie, he ends in complete adoration, unconcerned about his death: "... oh ... à toi ... ma vie ... je meurs ... mon ange ...." [89] It was noted on board ship that Brulart had a peaceful, happy expression, even at the moment of strangulation:

> Et le docteur remarqua comme un phénomène physiologique que la physionomie du patient, jusque-là froide et immobile, prit, au moment de la strangulation, une inconvenable expression de bonheur. [90]

---

[89] Ibid., p. 424.
[90] Ibid., p. 425.

Note that both Gautier and Sue created realities through the use of opium which replaced the reality of ordinary life. In *Atar-Gull* reality becomes a nightmare which Brulart must endure, whereas in "La péri" the boring reality of life is completely replaced by the enchanting existence which Achmet's love for the peri has created. Only the intrusion of the pacha (like Brulart's capture by the English vessel) threatens to destroy the new reality and replace it with the old. However, in both instances, the greater spiritual reality is triumphant. Brulart dies in the complete ecstasy of his dream, totally unaware of his physical death, joyously willing to sacrifice the life in his dream to his beloved Marie. Not only is Achmet not seen to die in "La péri," but the entire scene of physical reality is transformed into the spiritual reality of which Achmet had become a part.

Chapter V

OPIUM, HASHISH AND BAUDELAIRE

Of all the writers who experimented with drugs and whose experience influenced their literary production, Baudelaire is easily the most interesting and the most important. Many of the authors previously studied seem to have regarded the use of drugs as a fascinating opportunity to experience new and mysterious sensations which ordinary reality did not provide. In many instances the drug is treated as if it were an asset to man, a means of entering a reality more meaningful than life itself. Even Flaubert, who was admittedly afraid to take hashish, felt that the drug might be of great benefit to mankind. Only Baudelaire seems to have understood completely the serious danger which opium and hashish pose for man.[1] The significance which Baudelaire placed on the danger of using opium and hashish can be seen in *Les paradis artificiels.* The title itself indicates the illusion which the drugs create, and its ironic and tragic significance to Baudelaire is strikingly clear in comparing Baudelaire's original portion, "Le poème du haschisch," with passages from his correspondence on opium and hashish, which make it obvious that Baudelaire was writing the "poème du haschisch" from his own experience with drugs. Numerous agonizing remarks concerning his own life become clear when compared with his statements concerning the harmful effects of the drugs.

---

[1] It is curious that Balzac, who apparently tried hashish only once, understood better than most the serious danger of drugs.

Baudelaire divided *Les paradis artificiels* into two parts: the first, "Le poème du haschisch," is his own composition concerning the use of hashish, while the second is a translation of De Quincey's *The Confessions of an English Opium-Eater*.[2] In the "Poème du haschisch" Baudelaire does what Gautier had done in three separate essays in the 1830's and 1840's and resumes what he himself had done in an essay called "Du vin et du hachish" written in 1851. Like Gautier he discusses the proper way to take hashish and the curious stages of intoxication which it produces. Included are descriptions of the various types of hallucinations and the final period of sleep and calm. Yet this aspect of the drug experience, the only aspect which seems to have interested Gautier, appeared trivial and insignificant to Baudelaire:

> Il est temps de laisser de côté toute cette jonglerie et ces grandes marionnettes, nées de la fumée des cerveaux enfantins. N'avons-nous pas à parler de choses plus graves: des modifications des sentiments humains, et, en un mot, de la *morale* du haschisch?[3]

He now treats what he considers the truly important consequence of drug use: the way in which the drug becomes the most important element in a man's existence, a part of the fabric of his life. Baudelaire felt that the English were right in using such terms as "enchained," "fettered," and "enslaved" in speaking of a man's relationship with opium:[4]

> Chaînes, en effet, auprès desquelles toutes les autres, chaînes du devoir, chaînes de l'amour illégitime, ne sont que des trames de gaze et des tissus d'araignée! Épouvantable mariage de l'homme avec lui-même![5]

---

[2] It is probable that Baudelaire had both opium and hashish in mind in writing this first part. He frequently refers to opium as well as hashish in drawing his conclusions, apparently believing that they caused approximately the same reactions.

[3] Charles Baudelaire, *Œuvres complètes*, éd. Y. G. Le Dantec, révisée par Claude Pichois (Paris: Bibliothèque de la Pléiade, 1961), p. 372. Hereafter cited as *Œuvres*.

[4] Baudelaire later writes that what he relates concerning opium can be applied to hashish as well.

[5] *Œuvres*, p. 372.

But what causes man to be interested in such drugs? What would lead man to begin such a dangerous relationship? Baudelaire attributes man's weakness in this respect to his unquenchable thirst for the infinite. Certain days man feels young, vigorous and poetic:

> ... le monde extérieur s'offre à lui avec un relief puissant, une netteté de concours, une richesse de couleurs admirables. Le monde moral ouvre ses vastes perspectives, pleines de clartés nouvelles. L'homme gratifié de cette béatitude, malheureusement rare et passagère, se sent à la fois plus artiste et plus juste, plus noble, pour tout dire en un mot.[6]

But what is truly unique in this state of well-being "que je puis sans exagération appeler paradisiaque, si je le compare aux lourdes ténèbres de l'existence commune et journalière..."[7] is that one has no way of knowing what caused such a wonderful feeling. Baudelaire considered it a "véritable *grâce*, comme un miroir magique où l'homme est invité à se voir en beau, c'est-à-dire tel qu'il devrait et pourrait étre; une espèce d'excitation angélique, un rappel à l'ordre sous une forme complimenteuse."[8] This state of being, however, comes only infrequently and unforewarned. It is like a paradise compared with the daily torture of life. Thus man strives, by any means possible, to find this serenity, to escape from his "habitacle de fange," even if only for a few hours:

> C'est dans cette dépravation du sens de l'infini que gît, selon moi, la raison de tous les excès coupables, depuis l'ivresse solitaire et concentrée du littérateur, qui, obligé de chercher dans l'opium un soulagement à une douleur physique, et ayant ainsi découvert une source de jouissances morbides, en a fait peu à peu son unique hygiène et comme le soleil de sa vie spirituelle...[9]

Behind this easy escape from reality, Baudelaire saw the directing hand of Satan. In such a practice, one is tempting a force which is stronger than oneself:

---

[6] Ibid., p. 347.
[7] Ibid.
[8] Ibid., p. 348.
[9] Ibid., p. 349.

> Il oublie, dans son infatuation, qu'il se joue à un plus fin et plus fort que lui, et que l'Esprit du Mal, même quand on ne lui livre qu'un cheveu, ne tarde pas à emporter la tête. [10]

Baudelaire considered opium and hashish the perfect instruments of Satan for subjecting man to his will:

> ... j'avouerai que les poisons excitants me semblent non-seulement un des plus terribles et des plus sûrs moyens dont dispose l'Esprit des Ténèbres pour enrôler et asservir la déplorable humanité, mais même une de ses incorporations les plus parfaites. [11]

During the hallucination itself man is led cleverly into blasphemy. Beginning with what is seemingly a more generous love and sympathy for one's fellow man (Baudelaire points out that close analysis of this love reveals a sense of superiority on the part of the drugged individual), the person who is under the influence of the drug gradually feels that he has become God. Because of the intense enjoyment of this artificial paradise, man's will is completely destroyed. It is in the destruction of man's will that Satan succeeds so well in subjecting and destroying the victim himself. Again and again Baudelaire warns that man's most precious possession is his will. Without control over the will, man is incapable of anything worthwhile:

> Car je ne sais pas jusqu'à quel point on peut dire qu'un homme qui ne ferait que rêver et serait incapable d'action se porterait bien, quand même tous ses membres seraient en bon état. Mais c'est la volonté qui est attaquée, et c'est l'organe le plus précieux. [12]

As an inspirational aid in writing poetry, Baudelaire especially condemned the drugs. Even if one can say that they heighten the senses, they so stifle the will that one is incapable of any daily routine. Baudelaire, in his correspondence as well as in "Le poème du haschisch," frequently praised Balzac for his miraculous

---

[10] Ibid.
[11] Ibid., p. 374.
[12] Ibid., p. 342.

will to work. He insisted that only through regular living and a daily routine of work could one bring about the inspiration sought artificially by means of the stimulants. [13]

In a short essay entitled "Du travail et de l'inspiration," Baudelaire denounces the idea that poetic inspiration has any relationship to debauchery:

> L'orgie n'est plus la soeur de l'inspiration: nous avons cassé cette parenté adultère ... Une nourriture très-substantielle, mais régulière, est la seule chose nécessaire aux écrivains féconds. L'inspiration est décidément la soeur du travail journalier. [14]

In his "Du vin et du hachish" Baudelaire confirms that he agrees completely with Barbereau in saying that

> ... l'enthousiasme et la volonté suffisent pour l'élever [le poète] à une existence supranaturelle. Les grands poètes, les philosophes, les prophètes sont des êtres qui par le pur et libre exercice de la volonté parviennent à un état où ils sont à la fois cause et effet, sujet et objet, magnétiseur et somnambule. [15]

Baudelaire's rigorous condemnation of hashish and opium undoubtedly stems from his own bitter experience in the use of these drugs. A close look at his correspondence discloses the same complaints which he attributed to the use of opium or hashish in the "Poème du haschisch."

When Baudelaire first began using opium is difficult to say. There is mention of the drug in the first poem of the *Juvenilia* (1838-1842) and definite reference to Baudelaire's use of it in a poem written to him by Auguste Dozon in 1842:

> Et quand tu sens tomber l'ennui froid et livide,
> Tu vas chercher, pensif, et d'une lèvre avide,
> La puissance et l'amour dans ce verre fêlé,

---

[13] Baudelaire felt that Balzac had made himself into a great writer through his daily effort. He became a writer of great insight as a result of hard work, not because of any great natural gift.
[14] *Œuvres*, p. 482.
[15] Ibid., p. 343.

> Dans la grosse bouteille au goulot effilé,
> Abyme qui recèle un fond souillé de fange;
> Et j'ai presque frayeur de ton regard étrange. [16]

In a letter written to Mme Aupick in June 1842, Baudelaire may well be referring to having taken opium when he writes:

> La ridicule sottise que j'ai commise hier m'a fait passer une mauvaise nuit. — Que marcher convenablement est une difficile chose! [17]

In a letter to Mme Aupick later that month he writes, "Ne m'envoie, je te prie, ni drogues, ni sirops." [18]

Baudelaire's inability to work regularly and his lack of will are emphasized in a letter to Mme Aupick written in December 1847:

> ... l'oisiveté me tue, me dévore, me mange. Je ne sais vraiment comment je possède assez de force pour dominer l'effet désastreux de cette oisiveté, et posséder encore une lucidité absolue d'esprit, et une espérance perpétuelle de fortune, de bonheur et de calme... Franchement, le laudanum et le vin sont de mauvaises ressources contre le chagrin. Ils font passer le temps, mais ne refont pas la vie. [19]

---

[16] G. T. Clapton, *Baudelaire et De Quincey* (Paris, 1931), p. 6.

[17] Charles Baudelaire, *Correspondance générale*, recueillie par Jacques Crépet, XI (Paris, 1947), 20-21. This is included in the 19 vol. Conard edition of the *Œuvres complètes*. Hereafter cited as *Correspondance générale*. Baudelaire writes in "Le poème du haschisch" that one has difficulty walking after a night of drugs: "Mais vous êtes à peine debout, qu'un vieux reste d'ivresse vous suit et vous retarde, comme le boulet de votre récente servitude. Vos jambes faibles ne vous conduisent qu'avec timidité, et vous craignez à chaque instant de vous casser comme un objet fragile." (*Œuvres*, p. 371.)

[18] *Correspondance générale*, XI, 21.

[19] *Correspondance générale*, XI, 91-92. In *Fusées* under the caption "Hygiène. Conduite. Méthode," Baudelaire frequently exhorts himself to take up a daily routine of work. One of the resolutions which he finds necessary to this resolution is the immediate suppression of all stimulants: "Je me jure à moi-même de prendre désormais les règles éternelles de ma vie... travailler toute la journée, ou du moins *tant* que mes forces me le permettront ... obéir aux principes de la plus stricte sobriété, dont le premier est la suppression de tous les excitants, quels qu'ils soient." (Charles Baudelaire, *Journaux intimes*, éd. critique établie par Jacques Crépet et Georges Blin [Paris: José Corti, 1949], p. 43.)

A letter to Ancelle in January 1850 shows perhaps how Baudelaire became acquainted with opium:

> J'ai été assez gravement malade comme vous savez. J'ai l'estomac passablement détraqué par le laudanum; mais ce n'est pas la première fois... [20]

In 1851, the year in which he published his work "Du vin et du hachish," Baudelaire wrote a letter to Mme Aupick in which he complains of the very problems which beset the drug-taker:

> Dans un mois, dans quinze jours peut-être, je serai riche, mais d'ici là... D'ici là le désordre et conséquemment *l'improduction*. Voilà mon histoire de 9 ans qui recommence aujourd'hui... je suis très inquiet et très triste. Il faut se l'avouer, l'homme est un bien faible animal, puisque l'habitude joue un si grand rôle dans la vertu. *J'ai eu toutes les peines du monde à me remettre au travail.* Encore devrais-je effacer le *Re,* car je crois que je ne m'y suis jamais mis. [21]

It is curious that the nine years which Baudelaire mentions would take his complaint back to 1842, the year in which it can be shown that Baudelaire was using drugs.

In succeeding years, Baudelaire continues to complain of his inability to work. A number of letters in 1857 and 1858 mention both his lack of will and his use of opium to control stomach pains:

> Est-ce le physique malade qui diminue l'esprit et la volonté, ou est-ce la lâcheté spirituelle qui fatigue le corps, je n'en sais rien. Mais ce que je sens, c'est un immense découragement, une sensation d'isolement insupporta-

---

[20] *Correspondance générale,* XI, 114-115.
[21] *Correspondance générale,* XI, 140-142. It should be noted that, in this same letter, Baudelaire praises Balzac's regularity of work as he did in the "Du vin et du hachish": "Et cependant il est parvenu à avoir, *à se procurer...* non-seulement des conceptions grandioses, mais encore immensément d'esprit. Mais il a *toujours* travaillé." The similar problem which Baudelaire and the drug-taker face leaves little doubt that Baudelaire's remarks in "Du vin et du hachish" and in "Le poème du haschisch" were written from personal experience.

ble,[22] une peur perpétuelle d'un malheur vague, une défiance complète de mes forces, une absence totale de désirs, une impossibilité de trouver un amusement quelconque... Si le moral peut guérir le physique, un violent travail continu me guérira, mais il faut vouloir avec une volonté affaiblie; —cercle vicieux.[23]

In January 1848, in letters to Mme Aupick and Mme Sabatier, Baudelaire again mentions that he is taking opium to calm his stomach pains. However, he adds in a letter to Mme Aupick that "l'opium a de terribles inconvénients."[24] Baudelaire's addiction to opium is very clear from the numerous references in letters throughout his lifetime. In a letter to Ancelle in February 1859 he writes:

---

[22] Note that Baudelaire criticizes hashish specifically in the "Du vin et du hachish" for being a drug which tends to isolate man from his fellow beings.

[23] *Correspondance générale*, XI, letter of 30 December 1857 to Mme Aupick, pp. 108-109. It is characteristic of all addicts that they find difficulty in being interested in anything. A letter to Mme Aupick on 25 December 1857 displays additional evidence of Baudelaire's acute addiction. In speaking of his inability to work he writes: "... car je suis tombé depuis *plusieurs mois* dans une de ces affreuses langueurs qui interrompent tout; ma table est depuis le commencement du mois chargée d'épreuves auxquelles je n'avais pas le courage de mettre la main, et il vient toujours un moment où il faut, avec une grande douleur, sortir de ces abîmes d'indolence. Ces maudites fêtes ont le privilège de nous rappeler cruellement la fuite du temps, et comme il est mal rempli, et comme il est plein de douleurs! ... Je suis dans un état assez pitoyable, d'esprit et de corps, à ce point que j'envie le sort de tout le monde." (*Correspondance générale*, XII, 104-106.) Particularly striking are Baudelaire's references to the "affreuses langueurs" (also mentioned as part of the drug effects in "Le poème du haschisch") and the cruel reminder of passing time. One can scarcely forget the dreadful lines from "L'horloge" and the similar passage in the prose poem, "La chambre double": "Horreur! je me souviens! je me souviens! Oui! ce taudis, ce séjour de l'éternel ennui, est bien le mien... le Temps règne en souverain maintenant; et avec le hideux vieillard est revenu tout son démoniaque cortège de Souvenirs, de Regrets... Je vous assure que les secondes maintenant sont fortement et solennellement accentuées, et chacune, en jaillissant de la pendule, dit: —'Je suis la Vie, l'insupportable, l'implacable Vie'" ("La chambre double," *Œuvres*, p. 234.)

[24] *Correspondance générale*, XII, 119. Baudelaire's daily struggle against using the drug is well depicted in a letter to Mme Aupick in February 1858: "... quand les nerfs d'un homme sont très affaiblies par une foule d'inquiétudes et de souffrances, le Diable, en dépit de toutes les résolutions, se glisse tous les matins dans son cerveau: Pourquoi ne pas me reposer une journée

Je suis bien noir mon cher, et je n'ai pas apporté d'opium,
et je n'ai pas d'argent pour payer mon pharmacien à
Paris.[25]

Besides frequent references to his inability to work, there are numerous allusions to physical symptoms which might well indicate a constant use of opium.[26] That Baudelaire was accustomed to taking a sizeable dose of the drug is indicated in several letters. A letter to Ancelle on December 26, 1865 relates that a doctor who did not know Baudelaire's situation prescribed a dose which would have had no effect on the poet:

Un médecin, que j'ai fait venir, ignorait que j'avais autrefois un long usage de l'opium. C'est pourquoi il m'a ménagé, et c'est pourquoi j'ai été obligé de doubler et de quadrupler les doses.[27]

Many additional letters could be cited which indicate unquestionably that Baudelaire's use of opium was more than sporadic as some scholars have suggested. It is clear from Baudelaire's correspondence that he had probably begun the use of opium by 1842, and that his use was recurrent from that time forward. It is also probable that Baudelaire, even though he may have tried opium for the first time out of curiosity or as a result of De Quincey's work, was introduced to the consistent use of opium as a result of his illness, syphilis.[28]

---

dans l'oubli de toutes choses? Je ferai cette nuit, et d'un seul coup, toutes les choses urgentes. —Et puis la nuit arrive, l'esprit est épouvanté par la multitude de choses arrièrés; une tristesse écrasante amène l'impuissance, et le lendemain la même comédie se joue de bonne foi; avec la même confiance et la même conscience. (*Correspondance générale*, XII, 127.)

[25] *Correspondance générale*, XII, 271.

[26] Baudelaire speaks of alternating constipation and diarrhea, for example, a common trouble caused by use of opium.

[27] *Correspondance générale*, XV, 192. Baudelaire is rather indignant when his mother suggests that his dizziness and vomiting may be a result of his taking opium. He reminds her that he has been in the habit of taking large doses of opium without danger for several years: "... tu sais bien que j'en ai eu l'habitude pendant plusieurs années, jusqu'à en prendre 150 gouttes sans aucun danger." (*Correspondance générale*, XV, 268-269.)

[28] Note that opium was commonly prescribed for syphilis at this time. As mentioned previously, opium was regarded as a kind of panacea and was prescribed for many illnesses, especially when there was pain. See

The association of syphilis, woman, and opium must have been striking to Baudelaire, for each was, in its way, his downfall. One need not seek far in his work to find the condemnation of woman and her association with original sin. And one is constantly reminded of Baudelaire's conclusion that opium and hashish are the perfect instruments of Satan's temptation. It would not be illogical, therefore, to suspect that Baudelaire might have associated his two nemeses, woman and drugs, very closely. Indeed, it was woman who caused this sickness which would follow him and contribute to his early death; and, indirectly, since she caused his sickness, woman was responsible for his having become addicted to drugs, the direct cause of his spiritual death and the death of his ability to write creatively.

In his preface to *Les paradis artificiels,* dedicated to the mysterious J.G.F., Baudelaire states that it will seem strange to some that he should dedicate a work of "voluptés artificielles... à une femme, source la plus ordinaire des voluptés les plus naturelles." [29] However, the physical world affects the spiritual and "la femme est l'être qui projette la plus grande ombre ou la plus grande lumière dans nos rêves. La femme est fatalement suggestive; elle vit d'une autre vie que la sienne propre; elle vit spirituellement dans les imaginations qu'elle hante et qu'elle féconde." [30] Thus does Baudelaire ascribe to woman a dual role in man's life, a role which is clearly harmful as well as beneficial. And he suggests an indirect influence which continues to haunt man beyond his direct association with her.

The proof of this close association between woman and the drug becomes clear through a careful study of Baudelaire's principal poetic composition, *Les Fleurs du Mal.* Baudelaire frequently seems to derive the same sensations from a woman's hair, eyes, or mouth as one would expect from the use of a drug. He

---

footnote 22 on page 41. Baudelaire is undoubtedly describing his own acquaintance with opium when he describes in "Le poème du haschisch" the introduction of the young *littérateur* to hashish: "... obligé de chercher dans l'opium un soulagement à une douleur physique, et ayant ainsi découvert une source de jouissances morbides, il en a fait peu à peu son unique hygiène et comme le soleil de sa vie spirituelle..." (*Œuvres,* p. 349.)

[29] *Œuvres,* p. 345.
[30] Ibid.

is carried into ecstasies and exotic, hallucinatory visions, just as if he were describing an opium or hashish experience. One also finds, curiously enough, that Baudelaire's poems of adoration, as if written to a goddess, are even more meaningful if one considers that Baudelaire may have in mind both woman and the drug. At all times there is the bitter irony that woman and opium are at once his downfall and his only sources of consolation.

It is in this way, then, that Baudelaire's drug experience influenced his poetic achievement. Certainly not primarily in stimulating the already fertile imagination of the gifted Baudelaire, but as an essential element of the tragic existence which he describes in his masterpiece.

The importance of Baudelaire's drug experience to the composition of *Les Fleurs du Mal* can scarcely be exaggerated. Some aspect of the poet's experience with opium and hashish plays an important role in every section of the volume as well as in the dedication and perhaps even in the title of the work itself.

Influence on the greatest number of poems is in the first section, "Spleen et Idéal." The drug experience as presented by Baudelaire in *Les paradis artificiels* is closely related to both elements of the title. The drug is a means of escape from spleen into an ideal reality where the cares of daily existence are set aside. Yet the drug is intimately connected with the poet's spleen, for it seems to magnify the daily cares which he had momentarily escaped. To the will weakened by use of the drug, even the slightest task seems too great.

There is less influence upon the poems in the "Tableaux parisiens," for these are not so much concerned with the poet himself as with the city of Paris seen through his eyes.

There is also little influence in the section called "Le vin," for Baudelaire generally regarded the effect of wine as beneficial, in contrast with the more pernicious "excitants." However, possible implication of opium or hashish in the last two poems suggests that this section may refer on occasion to other "excitants" than wine.

From these last poems one is led directly into the pessimism and despair of "La destruction," the first poem of the section called "Fleurs du Mal." The presence of Satan, in the first verse, here confirms the source of the destruction in this section; and one cannot help but recall Baudelaire's admonition that Satan's finest means of enslaving and ruining man is the drug.

Although no single poem can be cited in "La révolte" which would confirm an influence from opium, it is nevertheless the section which best displays the result of the use of drugs. The greatest possible blasphemy, the belief that one has become God, is the culmination of the drug experience in Baudelaire's mind. It is this great sin which makes the drug-taker the perfect partisan of Satan and hence would lead to the presumption of revolt. Looked upon as the apex of a life of sin, only death can follow.

The title of Baudelaire's collection of poetry, *Les Fleurs du Mal*, has always stirred much interest and caused considerable speculation concerning its meaning. The dedication to Théophile Gautier has likewise caused many critics to wonder why Baudelaire should dedicate his masterpiece to a poet whose work he had on occasion criticized. Perhaps some light can be thrown on Baudelaire's enigmatic title by a close analysis of this dedication in reference to the title.

One obvious factor which should not be overlooked is that opium comes from a flower.[31] Moreover, it has been shown that Baudelaire saw the "Esprit du Mal" as the vital force in the subjection of man to a life of drug taking. Considering this possible relationship between the "excitants" opium and hashish and the title of the work, it is not surprising that the collection should be dedicated to Théophile Gautier, for it was he who was in large part responsible for the introduction of opium and hashish to the *literati* in France during the first half of the nineteenth century.

In addition to the meaning generally given to the word "Mal," it is worth noting that, in the dedication, Baudelaire refers to the flowers as "maladives," suggesting the association that opium has

---

[31] It should also be remembered that hashish is collected from a flowering plant. Baudelaire writes in the "Poème du haschisch": "... c'est quand il est en fleur qu'il possède sa plus grande énergie; les sommités fleuries sont, par conséquent, les seules parties employées dans les différentes préparations..." (*Œuvres*, p. 352.)

with sickness.[32] If the identification of *fleurs* with drugs is correct, the title expresses beautifully the major problem of the poet's life and the principal themes of his poetry. For it is from his contact with woman that he contracted the sickness which probably led to his use of opium. But the opium, taken in an effort to cure his illness, introduced him to a malady as pernicious as any disease. Because of his association with opium, he lost control of his most precious faculty, the will. Baudelaire's poems (it should be recalled that he frequently referred to a poem as a flower) portray the physical and spiritual torments of his tortured existence, and no title could express more poignantly the dominant factors which caused his suffering.

In the powerful introductory poem, "Au lecteur," Baudelaire introduces the principal themes which he will treat in the collection of poems to follow. In the first stanza he writes that man's body and mind are dominated by stupidity, error, sin, and stinginess, and that "... nous alimentons nos aimables remords, Comme les mendiants nourrissent leur vermine."[33] The reference to "aimables remords," which man nourishes involuntarily, reminds one of the passage in "Le poème du haschisch" where Baudelaire describes the drug-user's first step in sin toward the supreme blasphemy of believing that he is God:

> Avais-je tort de dire que le haschisch apparaissait, à un esprit vraiment philosophique, comme un parfait instrument satanique? Le remords, singulier ingrédient du plaisir, est bientôt noyé dans la délicieuse contemplation du remords, dans une espèce d'analyse voluptueuse; et cette analyse est si rapide, que l'homme, ce diable naturel, pour parler comme les Swedenborgiens, ne s'aperçoit pas combien elle est involontaire, et combien, de seconde en seconde, il se rapproche de la perfection

---

[32] Professor Engstrom's interesting article on the title, "Les Fleurs du Mal," shows that the dual association of "evil" and "sickness" in the meaning of *mal* is well supported by the subject-matter of the poems themselves. (Alfred G. Engstrom, "Baudelaire's Title for *Les Fleurs du Mal*," *Orbis Litterarum*, XII, Fasc. 3-4: Numéro spécial sur Flaubert et sur Baudelaire [1957], pp. 193-202.)

[33] Charles Baudelaire, *Les Fleurs du Mal*, éd. Jacques Crépet et Georges Blin (Paris, 1942), p. 1. Hereafter cited as *Les Fleurs*.

diabolique. Il *admire* son remords et il se glorifie, pendant qu'il est en train de perdre sa liberté. [34]

Thus the man who has taken the drug feeds involuntarily the remorse which he finds so admirable, and in doing so he commits a sin far more serious than the ordinary sins of daily existence. He is led into the supreme blasphemy of which Satan himself was guilty.

In the next line Baudelaire refers to the obstinacy of man's sin and to his cowardly repentances: "Nos péchés sont têtus, nos repentirs sont lâches." [35] There is no better description of the pitiful plight of the addict who has vowed to give up the drug. Baudelaire himself many times experienced the bitter reality of his broken resolutions. In a letter to Mme Aupick in December 1851, he complains bitterly of his artistic inactivity. He resolves to work regularly in the coming year:

> Mais il n'y a pas à reculer. Il faut que dans le courant de 1852, je sois relevé de mon incapacité, et *qu'avant le jour de l'an, j'aie déjà payé quelques dettes et publié mes vers.* Je finirai par apprendre cette phrase par coeur. [36]

In the last line of Baudelaire's statement, one senses the hopelessness in the words "repentirs lâches." [37]

Stanzas three and four introduce the "Esprit du Mal" which Baudelaire saw in the use of drugs:

> Sur l'oreiller du mal c'est Satan Trismégiste
> Qui berce longuement notre esprit enchanté,
> Et le riche métal de notre volonté
> Est tout vaporisé par ce savant chimiste.
>
> C'est le Diable qui tient les fils qui nous remuent!
> Aux objets répugnants nous trouvons des appas;

---

[34] *Œuvres*, p. 380.
[35] *Les Fleurs*, p. 1.
[36] *Correspondance générale*, XI, 143.
[37] The last line of the second stanza, "Croyant par de vils pleurs laver toutes nos taches" is also echoed in "Le poème du haschisch": after a night of haschisch one feels "les titillantes envies de pleurer."

Chaque jour vers l'Enfer nous descendons d'un pas,
Sans horreur, à travers des ténèbres qui puent. [38]

The certainty of Baudelaire's reference to drugs can be seen in the figure of Satan Trismegistus, [39] curious amalgamation of the "Esprit du Mal" [40] and the thrice powerful Hermes, god of alchemy and the occult sciences, frequently represented adorned with the poppy. This clever alchemist rocks for a long time the enchanted mind and, as is mentioned again and again by Baudelaire in reference to taking drugs, he vaporizes the rich metal of our will. [41] In "Le poème du haschisch" Baudelaire stresses that Satan's hold over man may come through the reduction of man's will from his use of hashish.

In the fourth stanza Baudelaire writes that we find charm in repugnant objects and each day, without horror, take a step

---

[38] *Les Fleurs*, p. 1.

[39] See p. 35 of this work for Hermes Trismegistus' association with drugs and medicine.

[40] For Satan's importance in relation to drugs, see the quotations on pages 129 ff. from "Le poème du haschisch." In both "Du vin et du hachish" and "Le poème du haschisch" Satan is the evil spirit which dwells in the enchantment of the drug.

[41] Again see the quotations cited above concerning the loss of will through the use of drugs and the premium which Baudelaire put on the will. He called it variously "l'organe le plus précieux" (*Œuvres*, p. 342), the faculty "la plus précieuse" (*Œuvres*, p. 383) and "cette précieuse *substance*" (*Œuvres*, p. 384.) The line, "est tout vaporisé par ce savant chimiste," is especially happy if one thinks of Satan Trismegistus as working his evil will as a result of man's *smoking* opium or hashish. The word *vaporisé* would surely indicate this in view of the line, "rêve d'échafauds en fumant son houka." One should also recall the interesting passage concerning smoking in "Le poème du haschisch," where Baudalaire relates that, while under the influence of the drug, he had the strange feeling that he was smoking himself: "Je vous suppose assis et fumant. Votre attention se reposera un peu trop longtemps sur les nuages bleuâtres qui s'exhalent de votre pipe. L'idée d'une évaporation, lente, successive, éternelle, s'emparera de votre esprit, et vous appliquerez bientôt cette idée à vos propres pensées, à votre matière pensante. Par une équivoque singulière, par une espèce de transposition ou de quiproquo intellectuel, vous vous sentirez vous évaporant, et vous attribuerez à votre pipe (dans laquelle vous vous sentez accroupi et ramassé comme le tabac) l'étrange faculté de vous fumer. (*Œuvres*, p. 365.)

toward Hell.[42] The poet, who gradually becomes addicted to use of the drug, comes more and more into Satan's power. Thus does he daily move toward eternal damnation. In "Le poème du haschisch" Baudelaire describes the use of hashish as a slow suicide:

> Il est vraiment superflu, après toutes ces considérations, d'insister sur le caractére immoral du haschisch. Que je le compare au suicide, à un suicide lent, à une arme toujours sanglante et toujours aiguisée...[43]

In our minds are "un peuple de Démons,/ Et, quand nous respirons, la Mort dans nos poumons/ Descend, fleuve invisible, avec de sourdes plaintes."[44] The mind of the opium or hashish smoker is frequently filled with nightmarish visions produced by the drug, and as he inhales the smoke from the pipe, he breathes in the smoke of death.[45]

But of all the vices *Ennui* is the ugliest, for it provides an atmosphere in which sin and vice flourish. Itself the mother of vices, it is also in large part responsible for the poet's use of the dreaded stimulants:

> Il ferait volontiers de la terre un débris
> Et dans un baillement avalerait le monde;[46]

---

[42] In the "Poème du haschisch" Baudelaire describes just such an individual who finds charm in his repulsive state and goes toward his hell without horror. He makes of opium his only joy, "jusqu'à l'ivrognerie la plus répugnante des faubourgs," and with his "cerveau plein de flamme et de gloire, se roule ridiculement dans les ordures de la route." (*Œuvres*, p. 349.)

[43] *Œuvres*, pp. 384-385.

[44] *Les Fleurs*, p. 2.

[45] The comparison of smoke and water ("fleuve invisible") is rather common. In Arabic, for example, the verb meaning to drink (shariba), is used to express the act of smoking. Hence one literally drinks in the smoke. Il should also be noted in reference to the "fleuve invisible" and the association of water and smoke that the "houka" is a water pipe. The smoke is first drawn through the water and into the lungs. For more details see page 29 above. In the phrase "avec de sourdes plaintes" Baudelaire may be recalling the strange sounds that the drug-taker often makes. In "Le poème du haschisch" he writes: "Des soupirs rauques et profonds s'échappent de votre poitrine, comme si votre *ancien* corps ne pouvait pas supporter les désirs et l'activité de votre âme *nouvelle*." (*Œuvres*, p. 362.)

[46] *Les Fleurs*, p. 2.

Note that in "Le poème du haschisch" Baudelaire describes the morning after a night of drugs in nearly the same terms:

> Mais le lendemain! le terrible lendemain! ... La hideuse nature, dépouillée de son illumination de la veille, ressemble aux mélancoliques débris d'une fête.[47]

In an effort to escape from his own bordeom, *Ennui* "rêve d'échafauds en fumant son houka." The houka is, of course, a water pipe and a means of smoking hashish. Here Baudelaire refers directly to the use of hashish, as *Ennui* attempts to escape from itself. The irony of the situation is doubly underscored. Not only is it hopeless for *Ennui* to escape from itself, but in trying to escape by means of the drug, *Ennui* is deceived. Instead of the hoped for visionary paradise, he sees himself caught by the dreadful gibbet.[48]

In the "Au lecteur" Baudelaire outlines the central problem treated in the collection and the central problem of his life symbolized by the majestic figure, Satan Trismegistus. It is he and his instrument of destruction, drugs, which play such an influential role in the development of the poems concerning spleen and those concerning the ideal. In the last line of "Au lecteur" one finds all the frustration and irony of the poet's existence as well as the irony of the title, "Les paradis artificiels." The poet seeks escape from the horrible *ennui* of his daily existence into the beautiful visions produced by the hashish pipe. However, in the vision he sees only the gibbet, grim reminder that he cannot escape reality by means of an "artificial paradise."

In reading the first six poems of *Les Fleurs du Mal* one is most impressed by the optimism which is evident in each one. In "Bénédiction," Baudelaire sees God reserving a place for the poet in heaven. "L'albatros" and "Élévation" show the poet as an unusual, gifted individual who sees more deeply into life as he soars above it like a great bird. And with his larger vision

---

[47] *Œuvres*, p. 383.
[48] In another poem of the collection, "Un voyage à Cythère," Baudelaire dreams that he sees himself hanging from the gibbet: "Dans ton île, ô Vénus! je n'ai trouvé debout/Qu'un gibet symbolique où pendait mon image."

he understands the hidden symbols, the greater meaning of life ("Correspondances"). At this point it should be noted that the ability of the poet to seize the correspondences does not depend upon his use of drugs. Baudelaire remarks on several occasions that gifted poets have always understood the hidden relationships in life, and thus visions and associations brought about by hashish or opium are not without precedent. In the "Poème du haschisch" Baudelaire describes the transformations caused by hashish and then explains how it has always been the poet's task to decipher such analogies:

> C'est alors que commencent les hallucinations. Les objets extérieurs prennent lentement, successivement, des apparences singulières; ils se déforment et se transforment. Puis arrivent les équivoques, les méprises et les transpositions d'idées. Les sons se revêtent de couleurs, et les couleurs contiennent une musique. Cela, dira-t-on, n'a rien que de fort naturel, et tout cerveau poétique, dans son état sain et normal, conçoit facilement ces analogies. [49]

But these are the good days, when the poet "s'éveille avec un génie jeune et vigoureux..." (for the entire quotation see page 129 above), when he feels poetically inspired to work. However, such days are rare and come at unexpected intervals. In his desire to increase the number of these days when he enjoys a condition which he calls "paradisiaque" (Œuvres, "Le poème du haschisch," p. 347), the poet turns to drugs. But the paradise brought by these drugs is artificial, and the muse is quickly destoyed by them. In the seventh poem, "La Muse malade," the poet asks his muse what is wrong this morning:

> Ma pauvre muse, hélas! qu'as-tu donc ce matin?
> Tes yeux creux sont peuplés de visions nocturnes,
> Et je vois tour à tour réfléchis sur ton teint

---

[49] Œuvres, pp. 364-365. In another famous passage from his essay, "Richard Wagner et 'Tannhäuser' à Paris," Baudelaire writes: "... ce qui serait vraiment surprenant, c'est que le son *ne pût pas* suggérer la couleur, que les couleurs *ne pussent pas* donner l'idée d'une mélodie, et que le son et la couleur fussent impropres à traduire des idées; les choses s'étant toujours exprimées par une analogie réciproque, depuis le jour où Dieu a proféré le monde comme une complexe et indivisible totalité." (Œuvres, p. 1213.)

La folie et l'horreur, froides et taciturnes.

Le succube verdâtre et le rose lutin
T'ont-ils versé la peur et l'amour de leurs urnes?
Le cauchemar, d'un poing despotique et mutin,
T'a-t-il noyée au fond d'un fabuleux Minturnes? [50]

The eyes of the muse are hollow from the night of debauchery and still peopled by the visions which the drug produced. [51] The "succube verdâtre" and the "rose lutin" may well refer to hashish and opium [52] which pour "la peur et l'amour de leurs urnes," perhaps a reference to the nightmares and the fabled erotic visions produced by these drugs. Nightmare, with a despotic hand, has drowned the poet in the depths of a marsh ("fabuleux Minturnes"). [53]

The sestet makes the plea which Baudelaire so often expressed in his letters and in "Le poème du haschisch":

Je voudrais qu'exhalant l'odeur de la santé
Ton sein de pensers forts fût toujours fréquenté... [54]

Through regular work and healthful habits one can maintain the poetic frame of mind without resorting to the artificial ecstasy of drugs.

The poems that follow stress the pessimism and torment in which Baudelaire daily lived, and review the past and present of man and his future aspirations. [55] Through his pride, symbolized

---

[50] *Les Fleurs*, p. 13.

[51] The sunken eyes are typical of the drug user and the slight "ivresse" which remains on the following morning is described in "Le poème du haschisch": "Mais vous êtes à peine debout, qu'un vieux reste d'ivresse vous suit et vous retarde..." (*Œuvres*, p. 371.)

[52] Note that the famous hashish preparation is frequently referred to as "la pâte verdâtre" and that laudanum often had a reddish color.

[53] The third line of the second stanza of "Au lecteur" bears an interesting correlation with this line: "Et nous rentrons gaiement dans le chemin bourbeux." Having weakly vowed to break with the drugs *(repentirs lâches)*, man quickly breaks his vow and returns to the muddy road ("chemin bourbeux").

[54] *Les Fleurs*, p. 13.

[55] For the relationship between the poem, "La vie antérieure" and the opium vision of Franz d'Épinay in *Le Comte de Monte-Cristo*, see the interesting article by Dagens and Pichois, "Variétés: Baudelaire, Alexandre Dumas et le haschisch," *Mercure de France*, no. 331 (1957), pp. 357-364.

by Don Juan, man commits the supreme blasphemy of thinking that he has become equal to or greater than God. In the "Châtiment de l'orgueil" Baudelaire writes:

> Après avoir franchi vers les célestes gloires
> Des chemins singuliers à lui-même inconnus,
> Où les purs Esprits seuls peut-être étaient venus,
> Comme un homme monté trop haut, pris de panique,
> S'écria, transporté d'un orgueil satanique:
> 'Jésus, petit Jésus! je t'ai poussé bien haut!' [56]

Just as in the "Poème du haschisch," man is drawn by the drug into unknown regions where Satan deliberately discloses secrets to trick him into committing the supreme blasphemy.

> Immédiatement sa raison s'en alla.
> L'éclat de ce soleil d'un crêpe se voila;
> Tout le chaos roula dans cette intelligence,
> Temple autrefois vivant, plein d'ordre et d'opulence,
> Sous les plafonds duquel tant de pompe avait lui.
> Le silence et la nuit s'installèrent en lui,
> Comme dans un caveau dont la clef est perdue.
> Dès lors il fut semblable aux bêtes de la rue,
> Et, quand il s'en allait sans rien voir, à travers
> Les champs, sans distinguer les étés des hivers,
> Sale, inutile et laid comme une chose usée,
> Il faisait des enfants la joie et la risée. [57]

Because of his blasphemy man's mind is invaded by chaos. He is plunged into silence and darkness, just as the man who has become addicted to opium is unproductive, unable to force himself to work. The creative fertility of his mind is destroyed and, because of his inability to stop using the drugs, he is as if plunged into a "caveau dont la clef est perdue." Henceforth, he is like the animal in the street, [58] dirty, useless and ugly. [59]

---

[56] *Les Fleurs*, p. 20.

[57] Ibid., pp. 20-21.

[58] One should note the similarity in tone between this passage and the passage cited above (footnote 23) from the letter to Mme Aupick: "Je suis dans un état assez pitoyable, d'esprit et de corps, à ce point que j'envie le sort de tout le monde." (*Correspondance générale*, XII, 106.)

[59] It is a pitiful fact that the greatest harm from drug addiction comes from a complete disregard of hygiene by the user. He lives amidst filth and dirt and becomes emaciated and ugly as a result of improper diet and frequent sickness.

With the poem "La Beauté," the theme of the collection shifts to the various aspects of beauty. Even in this traditional, regular form of beauty one can see the influence of Baudelaire's experience with drugs. In the verse "Je hais le mouvement qui déplace les lignes," [60] Baudelaire expresses his distaste for anything which disrupts the harmony in art. The person under the influence of hashish feels this same emotion:

> L'harmonie, le balancement des lignes, l'eurythmie dans les mouvements, apparaissent au rêveur comme des nécessités, comme des *devoirs*, non-seulement pour tous les êtres de la création, mais pour lui-même, le rêveur, qui se trouve, à cette période de la crise, doué d'une merveilleuse aptitude pour comprendre le rythme immortel et universel. [61]

In the last stanza Beauty's eyes are mirrors which render everything more beautiful:

> Car j'ai, pour fasciner ces dociles amants,
> De purs miroirs qui font toutes choses plus belles:
> Mes yeux, mes larges yeux aux clartés éternelles! [62]

In describing the action of hashish, Baudelaire states that the beauties which one sees under the influence of the drug approximate reality, but that:

> ... le haschisch sera, pour les impressions et les pensées familières de l'homme, un miroir grossissant, mais un pur miroir. [63]

Another trait of the person influenced by hashish which Baudelaire mentions again and again is the largeness of the eyes:

> Vos yeux s'agrandissent; ils sont comme tirés dans tous les sens par une extase implacable. [64]

---

[60] *Les Fleurs*, p. 21.
[61] *Œuvres*, p. 377.
[62] *Les Fleurs*, p. 21.
[63] *Œuvres*, p. 355.
[64] Ibid., p. 361.

And in speaking of the beautiful nymphs which he sees on the decorated wall paper he remarks:

> Les nymphes aux chairs éclatantes nous regardent avec de grands yeux plus profonds et plus limpides que le ciel et l'eau... [65]

However, this is only the physical aspect of beauty which corresponds to the more superficial aspects of the drug experience, that part of the experience which causes the senses to become hypersensitive. In the "Hymne à la Beauté" a much more somber question is asked: Does beauty come from Heaven or from Hell? In practically every line of the poem one can apply the same attributes and questions to opium or hashish as are applied to Beauty. The fascinating aspects of woman, illustrated so beautifully in the poems to follow, have a direct parallel in the fascination of drugs for the poet. In the first stanza, the essential question, "Viens-tu du ciel profond ou sors-tu de l'abîme, O Beauté?" [66] is also asked concerning the apparition in "La chambre double."

> Sur ce lit est couchée l'Idole, la souveraine des rêves. Mais comment est-elle ici? Qui l'a amenée? quel pouvoir magique l'a installée sur ce trône de rêverie et de volupté? Qu'importe? la voilà! je la reconnais. [67]

Just as in the poem, the author dismisses the necessity of answering the question in his eagerness to enjoy his contemplation of the "Idole." In "Le poème du haschisch" the drug-user fails to answer this important question concerning the origin of the beautiful visions enjoyed through the use of hashish. In failing to look beyond the visions to their real source, the poet risks losing all for the enjoyment of the false creations of the "Esprit du Mal."

In the second stanza each line is meaningful in terms of the drug. Under its influence one sees the vast perspective of limitless horizons at dawn and in the setting sun: [68]

---

[65] Ibid., p. 375.
[66] *Les Fleurs*, p. 24.
[67] *Œuvres*, p. 234.
[68] The perspective of the setting sun is rather common to such visions. In the "Poème du haschisch" one finds: "En levant les yeux, je vis un

> Tu contiens dans ton oeil le couchant et l'aurore;
> Tu répands des parfums comme un soir orageux;
> Tes baisers sont un philtre et ta bouche une amphore
> Qui font le héros lâche et l'enfant courageux. [69]

The odor from hashish or opium, mixed with various perfumes such as musk or ambergris, filled the room in which the drug-user was indulging and must have been associated closely in the mind of the individual with the drug itself. The kisses of the "philtre" from its container, "la bouche," could cause the hero to be cowardly and the child courageous. [70]

In stanza three the question is repeated concerning Beauty's origin. Of whatever origin, she dominates all she surveys:

> Sors-tu du gouffre noir ou descends-tu des astres?
> Le Destin charmé suit tes jupons comme un chien;
> Tu sèmes au hasard la joie et les désastres,
> Et tu gouvernes tout et ne réponds de rien. [71]

Whether of satanic or divine origin, man's destiny, [72] once linked with opium or hashish, follows it like a faithful dog. From the

---

soleil couchant semblable à du métal en fusion qui se refroidit." (Œuvres, p. 368.)

[69] Les Fleurs, p. 24.

[70] In "Du vin et du hachish," "Baudelaire stresses the idea that a country could never survive if its citizens were hashish users: "Jamais un État raisonnable ne pourrait subsister avec l'usage du hachish. Cela ne fait ni des guerriers ni des citoyens." (Œuvres, p. 342.) There is also the consideration that man is made into a cowardly individual, for he is unable to stop using the drug. However, one must consider the traditional view that the drug gave man courage. Such is the famous story of the Assassins, taken at a young age and, by means of hashish, made into courageous, fearless followers of their leader.

[71] Les Fleurs, p. 25.

[72] In the "Poème du haschisch" Baudelaire mentions that the use of hashish is forbidden even in the Orient, where its use is so widespread, because of its power to derange man's normal life; and he continues: "En effet, il est défendu à l'homme, sous peine de déchéance et de mort intellectuelle, de déranger les conditions primordiales de son existence et de rompre l'équilibre de ses facultés avec les milieux où elles sont destinées à se mouvoir, en un mot, de déranger son destin pour y substituer une fatalité d'un nouveau genre." (Œuvres, p. 383.) Baudelaire was well aware that the use of drugs changed a man's destiny and made him follow blindly a new "fatalité."

drugs come moments of great joy but also terrible disaster, and man is completely governed by the edicts of this imperious mistress.

In stanza four the death and pride of the drug experience are stressed:

> Tu marches sur des morts, Beauté, dont tu te moques;
> De tes bijoux l'Horreur n'est pas le moins charmant,
> Et le Meurtre, parmi tes plus chères breloques,
> Sur ton ventre orgueilleux danse amoureusement. [73]

The drug walks scornfully upon its victims, yet fascinates them in all its horror. [74] And Murder, one of the drug's ornaments, dances amorously on its proud belly. The word "orgueilleux," recalling the part which pride plays in the drug experience, signifies murder of both the physical and spiritual self. Yet the drug-user remains in adoration of that which is killing him.

Stanza five develops the ephemeral pleasure of the experience and the adoration of the user:

> L'éphémère ébloui vole vers toi, chandelle,
> Crépite, flambe et dit: Bénissons ce flambeau!
> L'amoureux pantelant incliné sur sa belle
> A l'air d'un moribond caressant son tombeau. [75]

The dazzling, ephemeral visions flit before the eyes of the worshipping victim. [76] In a powerfully erotic image, the lover bends over his "belle" in an act of love, even though he is caressing, in reality, his own death ("tombeau"). The relationship between the erotic imagery associated with woman and the effects of the drug adds a dimension of irony to many of the poems in the collection. For, while woman and drugs were traditionally

---

[73] *Les Fleurs*, p. 25.
[74] One of the truly tragic aspects of drug addiction is the addict's stubborn adoration of his drug, even in full knowledge that it is leading him to destruction and death.
[75] *Les Fleurs*, p. 25.
[76] The drugs were frequently taken at night in a room lighted by candles. The flickering light was considered beneficial in stimulating the imagination. The shadowy figures produced by the candle light were a source for interesting hallucinations.

associated with erotic pleasures, each contributed to Baudelaire's inability to enjoy the sexual act. The disease which he contracted as a young man led to impotence, and it is well known today, as it was to Baudelaire, that prolonged use of opium or hashish decreases an individual's sexual desires and even makes difficult the climax of the sexual act.

Again in the sixth stanza it is a question of Beauty's two possible sources; but the poet now states that it does not matter whether Beauty is associated with good or evil, if only she introduces the poet to the infinite:

> Que tu viennes du ciel ou de l'enfer, qu'importe,
> Ô Beauté! monstre énorme, effrayant, ingénu!
> Si ton oeil, ton souris, ton pied, m'ouvrent la porte
> D'un Infini que j'aime et n'ai jamais connu? [77]

In the ecstasy brought on by the glimpse of the infinite the poet is enchanted into disregarding the important moral question which must be answered. [78] In the final two lines of the stanza Baudelaire mentions the various parts of the body which are capable of opening for him the door to the infinite. In the poems to follow, each of these members, the eye, the mouth (souris), and the foot will be used as devices to send the poet into the ecstasies of the infinite.

In the last stanza the association of Beauty with Satan or God is made definite. But what difference does it make where Beauty comes from, so long as it beautifies the universe and gives man pleasurable moments:

> De Satan ou de Dieu, qu'importe? Ange ou Sirène,
> Qu'importe, si tu rends, —fée aux yeux de velours,

---

[77] *Les Fleurs*, p. 25.

[78] Recall that this is the central point which Baudelaire tried to make in the "Poème du haschisch." The beauties disclosed by opium and hashish are important only to the "esprits enfantins." The truly important question concerning the use of drugs is a moral issue which is vital to man's destiny. Note that Beauty is described as a "monstre énorme." The natural beauties of life seen under the influence of hashish are as if seen in "un miroir grossissant." (*Œuvres*, p. 355.) Everything is seen more vividly and in a form grander than reality. This aspect of the drug experience should be kept in mind when one reads "La Géante."

> Rythme, parfum, lueur, ô mon unique reine!—
> L'univers moins hideux et les instants moins lourds? [79]

The last stanza is filled with the irony which seems to characterize man's situation in life. The question which is asked in the first line of the stanza is not simply academic, but a question which must be answered before one should espouse the so-called Beauty. Otherwise man will be lured to his destruction by the "Sirène," or by the "fée aux yeux de velours." By not answering this question first, man risks being lulled by "rythme," "parfum," and "lueur" into an artificial paradise where the universe is rendered less hideous, but only for moments. It is of interest that, after the parallels of Satan and God and Angel and Siren, Baudelaire refers to Beauty as the "fée," thus suggesting, along with the word Siren, the seductive, feminine powers leading to a seemingly blissful life, but which lead in reality to complete destruction. The last line stresses the irony in Baudelaire's title, *Les paradis artificiels;* for, if the Beauty which the poet contemplates is dominated by the "Esprit du Mal," he will be selling his soul and destroying his life for a few brief moments of bliss. [80]

---

[79] *Les Fleurs*, p. 25.

[80] Many other poems from the section "Spleen et Idéal" which concern the beauty of a woman have frequent possible identifications with opium or hashish. In "Semper Eadem" the poet laments a strange sadness which has come over him: "Quand notre coeur a fait une fois sa vendange, / Vivre est un mal..." He reproaches the woman for mocking him with her "bouche au rire enfantin," for "plus encore que la Vie, / La Mort nous tient souvent par des liens subtils." In the first stage of hashish intoxication the individual is characterized by his childish laughter at the least provocation. Such joy belies the dangerous game which he is playing. The ties with death are indeed subtle. In the last three lines of the sonnet the poet asks not to be reminded of the subtle ties to death:

> Laissez, laissez mon coeur s'enivrer d'un *mensonge*,
> Plonger dans vos yeux comme dans un beau songe,
> Et sommeiller longtemps à l'ombre de vos cils.

Baudelaire's use of the verb "s'enivrer" and the emphasis placed on *mensonge* suggest the desire for escape and yet with full realization that it is only an escape into an "artificial paradise." In the last line of the poem, Baudelaire may be recalling the strange sensation which Gautier experienced while under the influence of hashish: "... les cils de mes yeux s'allongeaient indéfiniment, s'enroulant comme des fils d'or sur de petits rouets d'ivoire..." (Pichois, "Le hachich," pp. 16-17.)

In the sonnet "Parfum exotique" the poet describes an exotic land which is suggested to his vivid imagination by the "odeur" of a woman's "sein chaleureux." Just as if he had taken opium or hashish, he sees "se dérouler des rivages heureux/Qu'éblouissent les feux d'un soleil monotone..." [81] In considering the many poems of Les Fleurs du Mal in which perfumes have an intoxicating, stimulating effect, it should be recalled that hashish, because of its rather sharp, nauseous odor and taste, was mixed with various ingredients such as musk to make it more agreeable. [82] It is only natural that an individual who was accustomed to taking hashish would associate the strong odors of these aromatics with the hallucinations produced by the drug. When one considers the hypersensitivity frequently produced by hashish, it is not difficult to imagine that Baudelaire was very conscious of the strongly aromatic atmosphere in which his visions unfolded. The natural association of perfumes with the Orient and the visions of faraway places produced by the drugs make a very natural association between perfumes and distant lands.

Baudelaire attributes the same stimulating effect to the woman's hair in "La chevelure." From the "parfum chargé de nonchaloir" the poet is carried into ecstasy. In the strong fragrance of Jeanne's hair there are "souvenirs dormants" which will fill the "alcôve obscure." Without leaving his room he can see "La langoureuse Asie et la brûlante Afrique,/Tout un monde lointain, absent..." [83]

The next three lines remind one of the sonnet "Correspondances" and the hypersensitivity of the drug experience. In the depths of the hair is a "forêt aromatique." Whereas many described how sensitive to music they became while under the influence of opium or hashish, [84] Baudelaire notes here his sensitivity to odor:

---

[81] Les Fleurs, p. 26.

[82] For the aromatic ingredients commonly mixed with hashish see p. 28 and footnote 24.

[83] Les Fleurs, p. 26.

[84] Gautier describes the intoxicating effect of music while under the influence of hashish: "... plus de cinq cents pendules me chantaient l'heure de leurs voix flûtées, cuivrées, argentines. Chaque objet effleuré rendait une note d'harmonica ou de harpe éolienne. Je nageais dans un océan de sonorité où flottaient comme des îlots de lumière quelques motifs de la Lucia ou du Barbier. Jamais béatitude pareille ne m'inonda de ses effluves..."

> Comme d'autres esprits voguent sur la musique,
> Le mien, ô mon amour! nage sur ton parfum. [85]

In Jeanne's hair, "mer d'ébène," is an "éblouissant rêve" — "Un port retentissant où mon âme peut boire/ A grands flots le parfum, le son et la couleur..." [86]

The poet's "tête amoureuse d'ivresse" from this "noir océan" is lulled by the "Infinis bercements du loisir embaumé" and he sees the "azur du ciel immense et rond." [87] Again he has been intoxicated by the fragrance of exotic perfumes:

> Je m'enivre ardemment des senteurs confondues
> De l'huile de coco, du musc et du goudron. [88]

In addition to the fact that the perfume from the woman's hair stimulates the poet's senses and imagination in a way reminiscent of opium and hashish, there are a number of phrases in the poem which recur again and again in literature describing the drug experience. The references in "La chevelure" to "ciel pur," "éternelle chaleur," "ciel immense et rond," "infinis bercements," and "féconde paresse" remind one of the most frequently mentioned aspects of the sensations and visions evoked by opium and hashish.

In the last two lines of the final stanza Baudelaire speaks of the woman's hair in terms which may be just as easily referring to opium:

> N'es-tu pas l'oasis où je rêve, et la gourde
> Où je hume à longs traits le vin du souvenir? [89]

(Pichois, "Le hachich," p. 18.) The unusual effect of music on those under the influence of hashish caused Moreau de Tours to consider it as a possible aid in curing those who were mentally deranged. The sensitivity of the person under the influence of opium or hashish to music is one of the most frequently described effects of these drugs.

[85] *Les Fleurs*, p. 26.
[86] Ibid.
[87] In "Du vin et du hachish" Baudelaire writes that under the influence of hashish "Vous planez dans l'azur du ciel immensément agrandi." (*Œuvres*, p. 339.)
[88] *Les Fleurs*, p. 27.
[89] Ibid.

The word "oasis" suggests a small, fertile area in the desert where one can get refreshment. Just so do the drugs offer a brief escape from the dreary desert of everyday life. And the poet drinks deeply from the liquid of the "gourde" (perhaps here meaning flask), which carries him into a land of dream and memory.

In the prose poem entitled "Un hémisphère dans une chevelure" (xvii), which follows the progress of the poem stanza by stanza, but in prose, Baudelaire mentions that the smell of opium and tobacco is mingled in the hair:

> Dans l'ardent foyer de ta chevelure, je respire l'odeur du tabac mêlée à l'opium et au sucre; dans la nuit de ta chevelure, je vois resplendir l'infini de l'azur tropical... [90]

The reference to opium in the prose counterpart of "La Chevelure" leaves little doubt that Baudelaire was aware of the relationship between the sensations and visions which he is describing and those produced by the drug.

Poem XXIV ("Je t'adore à l'égal de la voûte nocturne") should also be considered for its possible overtones concerning Baudelaire's use of opium. The erotic feminine image of the "vase de tristesse" may again be referring to Baudelaire's opium flask which, in "La chambre double," Baudelaire refers to as his "vieille amie." The phrase "ô grande taciturne" could easily have been suggested by the tendency of the person under the influence of opium to remain silent, to avoid all unnecessary movement and conversation. Baudelaire may well be referring to the fanciful visions produced by the drugs in the phrase "ornament de mes nuits," and the last two lines ("Et je chéris, ô bête implacable et cruelle!/Jusqu'à cette froideur par où tu m'es plus belle!") [91] perhaps refer to the experience some have while under the influence of hashish. In "Le poème du haschisch" Baudelaire describes the great joy derived by a certain "littérateur" from the intense cold that he experienced after having taken some hashish:

> Une légère fraîcheur s'était déjà manifestée au bout de mes doigts; bientôt elle se transforma en un froid très-vif, comme si j'avais les deux mains plongées dans un

---

[90] Œuvres, p. 253.
[91] Les Fleurs, p. 28.

seau d'eau glacée. Mais ce n'était pas une souffrance; cette sensation presque aiguë me pénétrait plutôt comme une volupté. [92]

The author continues to describe how he gained a feeling of superiority over the people around him who were unable to enjoy such a sensation of cold in midsummer:

> Enfin il vint à un tel point, il fut si complet, si général, que toutes mes idées se congelèrent, pour ainsi dire; j'étais un morceau de glace pensant; je me considérais comme une statue taillée dans un bloc de glace; et cette folle hallucination me causait une fierté, excitait en moi un bien-être moral que je ne saurais vous définir. [93]

If Baudelaire ever experienced the extreme feeling of cold which accompanies withdrawal pains, the last line becomes especially meaningful. Nothing is more welcome to the addict suffering from the cramps and chills of the withdrawal syndrome than a sufficient dose of the drug to remove these pains.

Poem XXV emphasizes the power of woman to subjugate the individual. But it may also be suggesting the power of opium over all who come into contact with it. The bright, fascinating quality of the eyes is a trait frequently described by Gautier and others who have written of their drug experiences. [94] The drug is a "machine" fertile in cruelty and seems in its promise to be a "salutaire instrument," [95] though in reality it is an instrument of Satan

---

[92] *Œuvres*, p. 362.
[93] Ibid., p. 363.
[94] In considering the lines "Tes yeux, illuminés ainsi que des boutiques / Et des ifs flamboyants dans les fêtes publiques," one should recall Baudelaire's description of the day after an evening of hashish: "La hideuse nature, dépouillée de son illumination de la veille, ressemble aux mélancoliques débris d'une fête." (*Œuvres*, p. 383.)
[95] The four lines beginning the second stanza:
   "Machine aveugle et sourde, en cruautés féconde!
   Salutaire instrument, buveur du sang du monde,
   Comment n'as-tu pas honte et comment n'as-tu pas
   Devant tous les miroirs vu pâlir tes appas?" (*Les Fleurs*, p. 28.)
recall Baudelaire's question in "Le poème du haschisch": "Si encore, au prix de sa dignité, de son honnêteté et de son libre arbitre, l'homme pouvait tirer du haschisch de grands bénéfices spirituels, en faire une espèce de ma-

in subjecting man to his will. With it Satan can subvert man's will and mould him into whatever shape he desires ("pétrir un génie"). The last line ("O fangeuse grandeur! sublime ignominie!") stresses the irony of drug-taking in the contradictory terms which are used. Man takes the drugs to escape his "habitacle de fange... d'emporter le Paradis d'un seul coup!" [96] But the grandeur brought by opium or hashish is only a chimaera, an illusion leading to an existence which is even filthier than that from which one sought escape. The illusion seems at first sublime, but it leads one in reality into degradation.

The next poem, "Sed non satiata," takes its title directly from Juvenal.

> Bizarre déité, brune comme les nuits,
> Au parfum mélangé de musc et de havane,
> Œuvre de quelque obi, le Faust de la savane,
> Sorcière au flanc d'ébène, enfant des noirs minuits,
>
> Je préfère au constance, à l'opium, au nuits,
> L'élixir de ta bouche où l'amour se pavane;

---

chine à penser, un instrument fécond?" (*Œuvres*, p. 385.) Baudelaire answers his own question emphatically in the negative. The seeming benefits are bought at the expense of man's will and even at the expense of his imagination. For, once accustomed to the use of the drug, one is unable to think without it. In spite of its length, the passage is worth quoting because of its relevancy to the entire second stanza of the poem: "Ensuite cette espérance est un cercle vicieux: admettons un instant que le haschisch donne, ou du moins augmente le génie, ils oublient qu'il est de la nature du haschisch de diminuer la volonté, et qu'ainsi il accorde d'un côté ce qu'il retire de l'autre, c'est-à-dire l'imagination sans la faculté d'en profiter. Enfin il faut songer, en supposant un homme assez adroit et assez vigoureux pour se soustraire à cette alternative, à un autre danger, fatal, terrible, qui est celui de toutes les accoutumances. Toutes se transforment bientôt en nécessités. Celui qui aura recours à un poison *pour* penser ne pourra bientôt plus penser *sans* poison. Se figure-t-on le sort affreux d'un homme dont l'imagination paralysée ne saurait plus fonctionner sans le secours du haschisch ou de l'opium?" (*Œuvres*, p. 386.) With the frightful prospect of such servitude, "la nature" should draw back in horror from employing this artificial means and from the horror of destroying the creative initiative of "le génie." In considering Baudelaire's ironic "salutaire instrument," one should recall his insistence that hashish is the perfect instrument of Satan: "Avais-je tort de dire que le haschisch apparaissait... comme un parfait instrument satanique?" (*Œuvres*, p. 380.)

[96] *Œuvres*, p. 348.

> Quand vers toi mes désirs partent en caravane,
> Tes yeux sont la citerne où boivent mes ennuis.
>
> Par ces deux grands yeux noirs, soupiraux de ton âme,
> O démon sans pitié! verse-moi moins de flamme;
> Je ne suis pas le Styx pour t'embrasser neuf fois,
>
> Hélas, et je ne puis, Mégère libertine,
> Pour briser ton courage et te mettre aux abois,
> Dans l'enfer de ton lit devenir Proserpine! [97]

Here Baudelaire compares the woman directly to the opium:

> Je préfère au constance, à l'opium, au nuits,
> L'élixir de ta bouche où l'amour se pavane...

The title itself suggests the insatiable quality of the woman and the frustration of his own impotency, to which both his syphilis and his addiction contributed. The drug is also insatiable in that the addict must continue his worship of it and continually increase the dose which his need requires.

The first quatrain lends itself nicely to the dual interpretation of drug and woman. The "bizarre déité" which is described as being "brune" could easily apply to the dark brown color of opium prepared for smoking. And the "bizarre déité" is mixed with "musc" (musk was frequently added to both opium and hashish preparations) and with "havane" (hashish was frequently mixed with tobacco for smoking). Note that it is the "œuvre de quelque obi," a "sorcière," thus suggesting the drug's frequent association with alchemy and the black arts.

In the second line of the first tercet ("O démon sans pitié!"), Baudelaire suggests the demonic nature of the "bizarre déité," thus linking it with the dreadful alchemist, Satan Trismegistus, and the "Esprit du Mal."

In the final tercet of the sonnet, Baudelaire may well be referring specifically to hashish when he uses the phrase "Mégère libertine." Megaera is one of the Erinyes or Furies, linked here with Proserpina, the Queen of Hades, who alone is seen as able to control her. In "Le poème du haschisch" Baudelaire distin-

---

[97] *Les Fleurs*, p. 29.

guishes between opium and hashish by saying that hashish is more violent and vehement, whereas opium is peacefully seductive:

> C'est dire, je crois, d'une manière suffisamment claire, que le haschisch est, dans son effet présent, beaucoup plus véhément que l'opium... beaucoup plus troublant... je dis que, pour l'heure présente et pour le lendemain, le haschisch a des résultats plus funestes; l'un est un séducteur paisible, l'autre un démon désordonné. [98]

In another passage from "Du vin et du haschish," Baudelaire writes that, under the influence of hashish, "Un libertinage effréné peut se mêler à un sentiment de paternité ardente et affectueuse." [99] It should be noticed that these passages not only refer to the violent nature of hashish, but also to it as a "démon désordonné," thus making a link with the word "Mégère."

If Baudelaire did have hashish in mind, another dimension of meaning is added to the second quatrain. He is not only referring to "constance" and "nuits" as wines, but he is saying that he prefers the violence of hashish to constancy, to the peaceful seduction of opium, and to the nights, a meaning which cannot fail to strike one's ear in spite of the singular contraction "au." Baudelaire allays his "ennui" by drinking in the intoxicating liquid (suggested by "tes yeux") of the "citerne."

The intoxicating effect of the saliva from the woman's mouth and its association with opium were suggested in the phrase "l'élixir de ta bouche" of "Sed non satiata." Again in "Le serpent qui danse" Baudelaire refers to the intoxicating effect of the woman's mouth:

> Quand l'eau de ta bouche remonte
> Au bord de tes dents,
>
> Je crois boire un vin de Bohême,
> Amer et vainqueur,
> Un ciel liquide qui parsème
> D'étoiles mon coeur! [100]

---

[98] Œuvres, p. 374.
[99] Ibid., p. 340.
[100] Les Fleurs, p. 31.

Here the comparison of the woman's saliva to the intoxicating opium is unmistakable. Although Baudelaire does not refer directly to opium, he is recalling lines from the poem "Gazhel" of Théophile Gautier in which opium is mentioned:

> L'opium, ciel liquide,
> Poison doux et perfide,
> Qui remplit l'âme vide
> D'un bonheur étoilé. [101]

Baudelaire's indirect reference to opium in the last lines of the poem is in keeping with the beautiful, lulling motion of the preceding stanzas and adds an aura of hallucination to the strange, swaying rhythm.

Is Baudelaire imploring God or opium in his famous sonnet, "De profundis clamavi?" It is difficult to say, but the sonnet is an excellent example of the deep despair caused by addiction. The poet lives in an "univers morne à l'horizon plombé,/Où nagent dans la nuit l'horreur et le blasphème," [102] a world filled with the nightmares of opium dreams. The word "blasphème" recalls what Baudelaire refers to as the supreme blasphemy committed frequently by those under the influence of the drug who come to believe that they are God. Baudelaire emphasizes the insidious effect of this extravagant pride in "Le poème du haschisch."

In this dreary existence, the poet spends half his time in darkness and the other half under a sun which gives off no heat:

> Un soleil sans chaleur plane au-dessus six mois,
> Et les six autres mois la nuit couvre la terre... [103]

Half the poet's existence is spent under the black sky of melancholy, of *ennui*. Only his use of drugs can give him an escape to a brighter land. But it is a land where the sun gives no heat; for

---

[101] Théophile Gautier, *Poésies complètes*, II (Paris, 1932), 235. The adjectives "amer" and "vainqueur" certainly apply to opium. Unless properly sweetened, opium has a particularly bitter taste.

[102] *Les Fleurs*, p. 33.

[103] Ibid., p. 34.

it is an artificially created sun which cannot furnish the life-giving warmth of a healthy life.[104]

> Or il n'est pas d'horreur au monde qui surpasse
> La froide cruauté de ce soleil de glace
> Et cette immense nuit semblable au vieux Chaos;
>
> Je jalouse le sort des plus vils animaux
> Qui peuvent se plonger dans un sommeil stupide,
> Tant l'écheveau du temps lentement se dévide![105]

The horror of life is magnified by the seemingly interminable nights of chaotic nightmare produced by the opium. The poet envies the lowly animal which escapes the boredom of passing time by means of a deep sleep, whereas the escape offered by opium is brief. Although great spans of time seem to pass under the influence of the drug, one finds upon awakening that in reality the time has been very short. Thus is the passing of time made even more painful by the fiction which the drug has created.

Poem XXXI, "Le vampire," is generally believed to be addressed to Jeanne Duval; but it expresses in poignant terms Baudelaire's unbreakable tie with the drug. The title suggests the unrelenting hold of drug addiction upon its victim and the horrible way in which it saps his strength.

> Toi qui, comme un coup de couteau,
> Dans mon coeur plaintif es entrée;
> Toi qui, forte comme un troupeau
> De démons, vins, folle et parée,
>
> De mon esprit humilié
> Faire ton lit et ton domaine...[106]

The entry of the drug into his life is as deadly to the poet as the blow of a knife in his heart. The vice makes of his body its bed and its dwelling where it parades its haunting visions ("forte comme un troupeau/ De démons, vins, folle et parée").

---

[104] One should recall here Baudelaire's statement that the drug-user gradually makes of opium "son unique hygiène et comme le soleil de sa vie spirituelle." (*Œuvres*, p. 349.)
[105] *Les Fleurs*, p. 34.
[106] Ibid.

> —Infâme à qui je suis lié
> Comme le forçat à la chaîne,
>
> Comme au jeu le joueur têtu,
> Comme à la bouteille l'ivrogne,
> Comme aux vermines la charogne,
> —Maudite, maudite sois-tu! [107]

Baudelaire's tie to the "Vampire" is here compared with several well known vices. Once again he refers to the unbreakable chain [108] and his frequent parallels between hashish and wine come to mind in his comparison with the alcoholic. The attachment of the "charogne" to the "vermines" is especially striking when one recalls the lines from "Au lecteur" and their possible interpretation (see page 139): "Et nous alimentons nos aimables remords,/Comme les mendiants nourrissent leur vermine." [109]

> J'ai prié le glaive rapide
> De conquérir ma liberté,
> Et j'ai dit au poison perfide
> De secourir ma lâcheté.
>
> Hélas! le poison et le glaive
> M'ont pris en dédain et m'ont dit:
> "Tu n'es pas digne qu'on t'enlève
> A ton esclavage maudit,
>
> Imbécile! — de son empire
> Si nos efforts te délivraient,
> Tes baisers ressusciteraient
> Le cadavre de ton vampire!" [110]

The poet's plight is such that he has looked to death for freedom from his enslavement. [111] But he finds no help, for his

---

[107] Ibid.

[108] Compare Baudelaire's reference here ("je suis lié / Comme le forçat à la chaîne") with the passage quoted above on page 128 concerning enslavement to opium.

[109] *Les Fleurs*, p. 1.

[110] Ibid., p. 35.

[111] Note that the word "lâcheté" is used by Baudelaire in his correspondence to describe his condition of weakened will and his inability to work creatively. The scornful term is often used to describe the addict's inability to keep from using the drug.

adoration of the drug is so great that not even death appears strong enough to break the habit. The last two lines of "Le Vampire" are especially vivid when one considers the almost hopeless situation of the addict who tries to break the habit again and again, only to resuscitate "le cadavre" of the "vampire."

In the sonnet, "Le Possédé," Baudelaire again emphasizes his relationship with the drug and its association with the "Esprit du Mal":

> Le soleil s'est couvert d'un crêpe. Comme lui,
> O Lune de ma vie! emmitoufle-toi d'ombre;
> Dors ou fume à ton gré; sois muette, sois sombre,
> Et plonge tout entière au gouffre de l'Ennui... [112]

For Baudelaire, the sun of life has been covered. It has been replaced by another ("O Lune de ma vie") to which he is devoted. It is fascinating that a variant for the phrase "O Lune de ma vie" is the phrase "O Soleil de mon âme," [113] immediately reminding one of the passage in *Les paradis artificiels* where Baudelaire writes that the "littérateur... obligé de chercher dans l'opium un soulagement à une douleur physique, et ayant ainsi découvert une source de jouissances morbides, en a fait peu à peu son unique hygiène et comme le soleil de sa vie spirituelle." [114] The phrase, "jouissances morbides," is also apropos in that the poet delights in plunging into the gulf of "Ennui." Lines three and four of the first quatrain recall Baudelaire's association of ennui and hashish in the final stanza of "Au lecteur": "C'est l'Ennui! — l'œil chargé d'un pleur involontaire,/Il rêve d'échafauds en fumant son houka." [115]

But there is another aspect of the drug experience which is the opposite of depression and *ennui*:

> Je t'aime ainsi! Pourtant, si tu veux aujourd'hui,
> Comme un astre éclipsé qui sort de la pénombre,

---

[112] *Les Fleurs*, p. 39.
[113] Charles Baudelaire, *Les Fleurs du Mal*, ed. Antoine Adam (Paris, 1961), p. 41. Hereafter cited as Adam.
[114] *Œuvres*, p. 349.
[115] *Les Fleurs*, p. 2.

> Te pavaner aux lieux que la Folie encombre,
> C'est bien! Charmant poignard, jaillis de ton étui! [116]

The poet is entirely willing to witness the fanciful visions so frequently described ("te pavaner aux lieux que la Folie encombre") and to enjoy the frequent erotic sensations associated with the drug experience ("Charmant poignard, jaillis de ton étui!"): [117]

> Allume ta prunelle à la flamme des lustres!
> Allume le désir dans les regards des rustres!
> Tout de toi m'est plaisir, morbide ou pétulant;
>
> Sois ce que tu voudras, nuit noire, rouge aurore;
> Il n'est pas une fibre en tout mon corps tremblant
> Qui ne crie: *O mon cher Belzébuth, je t'adore!* [118]

In a moment of ecstasy ("Il n'est pas une fibre en tout mon corps tremblant") [119] the poet again affirms his adoration of the "Esprit du Mal," this time in the form of Beelzebub. Adam points out that the line was probably drawn from Cazotte's *Le Diable amoureux* and adds that Cazotte had also written: "D'obsédé qu'il était, Alvare, devenu possédé, n'était plus qu'un instrument du Diable." [120] Baudelaire had himself become "Le Possédé," the "instrument du Diable." His feelings concerning opium and hashish cited above are worth a second citation because of their relevancy to the poem and Baudelaire's life:

> ... j'avouerai que les poisons excitants me semblent non-seulement un des plus terribles et des plus sûrs moyens dont dispose l'Esprit des Ténèbres pour enrôler et asservir la déplorable humanité, mais même une de ses incorporations les plus parfaites. [121]

---

[116] Ibid., p. 39.

[117] For reference to the erotic sensations of both men and women experienced while under the influence of opium, see page 25.

[118] *Oeuvres*, p. 39.

[119] For the slight trembling frequently experienced by subjects who have taken hashish or opium and the waves of excitement which run through the body, see the descriptions cited in chapter I.

[120] Adam, p. 320, note 1.

[121] *Œuvres*, p. 374.

Baudelaire's sequence of four sonnets grouped under the title "Un Fantôme" develops poignantly a typical night of opium, its misery and depression, the appearance of the hallucination, the exhilaration of the drug's fragrant odor mixed with aromatics, and the bitter realization of the destruction which it has brought to his life:

> Dans les caveaux d'insondable tristesse
> Où le Destin m'a déjà relégué;
> Où jamais n'entre un rayon rose et gai;
> Où, seul avec la Nuit, maussade hôtesse,
>
> Je suis comme un peintre qu'un Dieu moqueur
> Condamne à peindre, hélas! sur les ténèbres;
> Où, cuisinier aux appétits funèbres,
> Je fais bouillir et je mange mon coeur... [122]

In the first two quatrains, Baudelaire describes the darkness and depression to which fate has seemed to consign him. In the shadows of the night he prepares the opium ("Où, cuisinier aux appétits funèbres,/Je fais bouillir...") [123] which conjures up the poet's "belle visiteuse."

In the second sonnet the two quatrains are devoted to an exhilarating description of the sensation experienced when inhaling the smoke of the drug:

> Lecteur, as-tu quelquefois respiré
> Avec ivresse et lente gourmandise
> Ce grain d'encens qui remplit une église,
> Ou d'un sachet le musc invétéré?
>
> Charme profond, magique, dont nous grise
> Dans le présent le passé restauré!
> Ainsi l'amant sur un corps adoré
> Du souvenir cueille la fleur exquise. [124]

---

[122] *Les Fleurs*, p. 40.

[123] It is significant that the second quatrain may have been taken from De Quincey: "Many children, perhaps most, have the power of painting, as it were upon the darkness, all sorts of phantoms." (Adam, p. 321.) In the "cooking" of opium, the ball of chandoo is placed over a flame until it begins to bubble. See pages 22-23 for details of opium preparation for smoking.

[124] *Les Fleurs*, pp. 40-41.

The poet inhales slowly ("lente gourmandise") and in ecstasy ("ivresse") the strong aroma of incense or musk, frequently used in opium preparations to mask the drug's nauseous odor.[125] Seemingly from the fragance of these aromatics comes the vision of the past.

In the two tercets Baudelaire transfers the magic aroma to the "belle visiteuse," whose fragrant hair is as intoxicating as the drug itself:

> De ses cheveux élastiques et lourds,
> Vivant sachet, encensoir de l'alcôve,
> Une senteur montait, sauvage et fauve,
>
> Et des habits, mousseline ou velours,
> Tout imprégnés de sa jeunesse pure,
> Se dégageait un parfum de fourrure.[126]

The third sonnet, "Le Cadre," is devoted entirely to the description of the "belle visiteuse," her beauty and grace.

In "Le Portrait" the poet is again faced with the reality of his own situation. Sickness and Death have destroyed the tender reality of earlier days and have left only the memory. The poet is conscious of his horrible isolation and solitude.[127] His anguish at the thought of passing time is expressed in a number of works which are among his best.[128] His temporary escape from reality by means of opium or hashish only served to magnify the aspect of passing time. In view of Baudelaire's many references to hashish as "une arme pour le suicide"[129] and as causing the death of a poet's creativity through subversion of his will, it would not

---

[125] See pages 21-22 above for some of the many preparations of opium, and page 23 for a description of the method of smoking opium and the necessity of deep, regular inhalation for maximum enjoyment.

[126] *Les Fleurs*, p. 41.

[127] In his development of the contrast between wine and hashish, the principal accusation which Baudelaire brings against hashish is that it isolates man: "Le hachish est isolant... Le hachish appartient à la classe des joies solitaires; il est fait pour les misérables oisifs." (*Œuvres*, p. 343.)

[128] See especially the poem, "L'Horloge," and the prose poem entitled "La chambre double." See also page 134 and note 23 above. These works will be considered later in the chapter.

[129] *Œuvres*, p. 343.

seem unreasonable to suggest that the line, "Noir assassin de la Vie et de l'Art," [130] may also refer to the drug itself. [131]

A somewhat different note sounds in "L'aube spirituelle":

> Quand chez les débauchés l'aube blanche et vermeille
> Entre en société de l'Idéal rongeur,
> Par l'opération d'un mystère vengeur
> Dans la brute assoupie un ange se réveille.
>
> Des Cieux Spirituels l'inaccessible azur,
> Pour l'homme terrassé qui rêve encore et souffre,
> S'ouvre et s'enfonce avec l'attirance du gouffre.
> Ainsi, chère Déesse, Être lucide et pur,
>
> Sur les débris fumeux des stupides orgies
> Ton souvenir plus clair, plus rose, plus charmant,
> A mes yeux agrandis voltige incessamment.
>
> Le soleil a noirci la flamme des bougies;
> Ainsi, toujours vainqueur, ton fantôme est pareil,
> Ame resplendissante, à l'immortel soleil! [132]

This poem contains many characteristics of the morning after a night of opium debauchery. In the second quatrain the poet writes that the "inaccessible azur" of the "Cieux Spirituels.../ S'ouvre et s'enfonce avec l'attirance du gouffre." The danger of this abyss to the "dreamer" is described in similar terms in "Le poème du haschisch":

> L'eau s'étale comme une véritable enchanteresse, et, ... je n'affirmerais pas que la contemplation d'un gouffre limpide fût tout à fait sans danger pour un esprit amoureux de l'espace et du cristal... [133]

Baudelaire's use of the expression "s'enfoncer" perhaps suggests a comparison often drawn between the sky and the sea.

---

[130] *Les Fleurs*, p. 42.
[131] Not only does such an interpretation add to the force of the line, but may be further supported by the words "noir assassin." One should consider that prepared opium is very dark in color and that Baudelaire may well be thinking of the word assassin in terms of its etymology and connection with the Assassins of the Old Man of the Mountain, famed for their hashish-eating and startling assassinations.
[132] *Les Fleurs*, p. 50.
[133] *Œuvres*, p. 377.

In the first tercet the line "Sur les débris fumeux des stupides orgies" again indicates the debauchery of a hashish night and recalls Baudelaire's description of a morning after hashish in "Le poème du haschish":

> Mais le lendemain! le terrible lendemain! ... La hideuse nature, dépouillée de son illumination de la veille, ressemble aux mélancoliques débris d'une fête. [134]

And the second and third lines of the tercet describe the vision which the hashish-eater is witnessing. The phrase "à mes yeux agrandis" describes a common enough feature of the person under drug influence and was used by Baudelaire to describe an individual under the influence of hashish in "Le poème du haschisch":

> Je venais de me regarder, en passant, dans la glace d'une devanture, et mon visage m'avait étonné. Cette pâleur, ces lèvres rentrées, ces yeux agrandis! [135]

In the last three verses, Baudelaire compares the ever-conquering spectre to the "immortel soleil," reminding one of the addict, who makes of the drug "son unique hygiène et comme le soleil de sa vie spirituelle..." [136]

It has been suggested in the past that "Le Flacon" might be related to Baudelaire's experience with opium, but many would agree with Antoine Adam in declaring this hardly conceivable. [137]

---

[134] Œuvres, p. 383.

[135] Ibid., p. 360.

[136] Ibid., p. 349. The following poem, "L'harmonie du soir," although containing few direct reference which link it definitely with the poet's opium experience or the *Paradis artificiels*, should be considered carefully because of certain aspects that recall the drug experience. The atmosphere, pervaded by melodious sounds and the scent of perfume, is one of "langoureux vertige." The strong emotional effect of the violin is reminiscent of the passage in "Le poème du haschisch" (*Œuvres*, pp. 358-359) where the playing of a violin caused great emotion in an individual who was under the influence of hashish. Because of the great effect which it seemed to have on persons under such conditions, Moreau de Tours felt that music might be used therapeutically to calm those who were psychologically disturbed.

[137] "Les commentateurs ont tour à tour imaginé que ce flacon, c'était le recueil des *Fleurs du Mal*, ou l'âme corrompue de Baudelaire ou encore —chose à peine concevable— ils ont cru que le poète faisait allusion à sa prétendue passion pour l'opium et le haschich." (Adam, p. 332.)

However, there are a number of indications in the poem which leave little doubt that Baudelaire was not only making an allusion to his opium addiction, but was describing in vivid terms the destruction being wrought upon his soul by his addiction to the drug.

> Il est de forts parfums pour qui toute matière
> Est poreuse. On dirait qu'ils pénètrent le verre.
> En ouvrant un coffret venu de l'Orient
> Dont la serrure grince et rechigne en criant,
>
> Ou dans une maison déserte quelque armoire
> Pleine de l'âcre odeur des temps, poudreuse et noire,
> Parfois on trouve un vieux flacon qui se souvient,
> D'où jaillit toute vive une âme qui revient. [138]

In the first lines the poet writes of an oriental perfume whose odor is so strong all things seem porous to it. On many occasions Baudelaire praises the powerful fragrance of musk, incense, or ambergris,[139] used frequently, as we have seen earlier, in opium preparations to mask the drug's natural nauseous, acrid odor. In the dusty, acrid-smelling cupboard is a "vieux flacon qui se souvient." One is reminded of the prose poem, "La chambre double," where the beautiful spell of the artificial paradise has been broken and the poet is made frightfully aware of his "taudis, ce séjour de l'éternel ennui" with its "meubles sots, poudreux, écornés." [140]

> Et ce parfum d'un autre monde, dont je m'enivrais avec une sensibilité perfectionnée, hélas! il est remplacé par une fétide odeur de tabac mêlée à je ne sais quelle nauséabonde moisissure. On respire ici maintenant le ranci de la désolation. Dans ce monde étroit, mais si plein de dégoût, un seul objet connue me sourit: la fiole de laudanum; une vieille et terrible amie; comme toutes les amies, hélas! féconde en caresses et en traîtrises. [141]

---

[138] *Les Fleurs*, p. 51.
[139] See the first quatrain of the sonnet, "Le parfum," quoted on page 165 above.
[140] *Œuvres*, p. 235.
[141] Ibid.

Just as it is the "vieux flacon qui se souvient" in the poem, it is the "vieille amie" which reminds him of the bliss from which he has just been disturbed.

> Mille pensers dormaient, chrysalides funèbres,
> Frémissant doucement dans les lourdes ténèbres,
> Qui dégagent leur aile et prennent leur essor,
> Teintés d'azur, glacés de rose, lamés d'or.
>
> Voilà le souvenir enivrant qui voltige
> Dans l'air troublé; les yeux se ferment; le Vertige
> Saisit l'âme vaincue et la pousse à deux mains
> Vers un gouffre obscurci de miasmes humains;
>
> Il la terrasse au bord d'un gouffre séculaire,
> Où, Lazare odorant déchirant son suaire,
> Se meut dans son réveil le cadavre spectral
> D'un vieil amour ranci, charmant et sépulcral. [142]

From out of the "flacon" come the many thoughts and visions. A dizziness seizes the poet which nearly carries him into the dreadful "gouffre." [143] But here the idea of the poem changes. Now the poet compares himself to the "vieux flacon" which has been sitting in the cupboard forgotten:

> Ainsi, quand je serai perdu dans la mémoire
> Des hommes, dans le coin d'une sinistre armoire
> Quand on m'aura jeté, vieux flacon désolé,
> Décrépit, poudreux, sale, abject, visqueux, fêlé,
>
> Je serai ton cercueil, aimable pestilence!
> Le témoin de ta force et de ta virulence,
> Cher poison préparé par les anges! Liqueur
> Qui me ronge, ô la vie et la mort de mon coeur! [144]

Thus the poet, thinking of the time when he will be old and worn through use of the drug ("Décrépit, poudreux, sale, abject, visqueux, fêlé") sees himself as a hollow coffin, fitting container for the "aimable pestilence." This arresting transformation wherein the poet imagines that he, in his old age, will be like the "vieux

---

[142] *Les Fleurs*, p. 52.
[143] The danger of the "gouffre" to the drug-taker is underscored in "Le poème du haschisch."
[144] *Les Fleurs*, p. 52.

flacon" reminds one of the many descriptions of hashish experiments in which the drug-taker relates that he actually felt himself become the object which he was contemplating. This common experience while under the influence of hashish explains beautifully Baudelaire's complete identification with every detail of the "vieux flacon" and accounts for the ominous, horrible reality which the lines convey. The verses of the last two stanzas are vibrant with the horror of the transformation as if they described an experience from reality rather than an imagined comparison.[145]

The "cher poison" is both the life and death of his heart. It brings the beautiful reverie of the artificial paradise, and recalls memories of happier moments. Yet it is the death of his mental, spiritual, and physical being, and the phrase introduces the title of the following poem ("Le poison"):

>Le vin sait revêtir le plus sordide bouge
>   D'un luxe miraculeux,
>Et fait surgir plus d'un portique fabuleux
>   Dans l'or de sa vapeur rouge,
>Comme un soleil couchant dans un ciel nébuleux.
>
>L'opium agrandit ce qui n'a pas de bornes,
>   Allonge l'illimité,
>Approfondit le temps, creuse la volupté,
>   Et de plaisirs noirs et mornes
>Remplit l'âme au delà de sa capacité.
>
>Tout cela ne vaut pas le poison qui découle
>   De tes yeux, de tes yeux verts,
>Lacs où mon âme tremble et se voit à l'envers...
>   Mes songes viennent en foule
>Pour se désaltérer à ces gouffres amers.
>
>Tout cela ne vaut pas le terrible prodige
>   De ta salive qui mord,
>Qui plonge dans l'oubli mon âme sans remord,
>   Et, charriant le vertige,
>La roule défaillante aux rives de la mort![146]

---

[145] Baudelaire remarks in "Le poème du haschisch" that, while contemplating his pipe, he himself became the tobacco crouched in the bowl of the pipe and had the strange sensation of smoking himself. See footnote 41 for the quotation from "Le poème du haschisch."

[146] *Les Fleurs,* pp. 52-53.

In "Le Poison" Baudelaire thus compares the effects of wine, opium, and woman. In 1851 Baudelaire had contrasted the generally beneficent effect of wine with the malevolent action of hashish in his essay entitled "Du vin et du hachish." Here he continues that comparison in giving to woman the same harmful effect as opium, but to an even greater degree.

Just as opium is poisonous to his being and fills his soul beyond its capacity, so do the green eyes of his mistress have a poisonous, intoxicating effect. They too cause visions and draw the soul toward the terrible abyss of self contemplation mentioned in "Le poème du haschisch":

> L'eau s'étale comme une véritable enchanteresse, et... je n'affirmerais pas que la contemplation d'un gouffre limpide fût tout à fait sans danger pour un esprit amoureux de l'espace et du cristal, et que la vieille fable de l'Ondine ne pût devenir pour l'enthousiaste une tragique réalité. [147]

In a later passage Baudelaire writes that hashish pushes a man "jour à jour vers le gouffre lumineux où il admire sa face de Narcisse." [148]

Just as the poisonous, liquid opium plunges the remorseless soul into forgetfulness [149] and carries it to destruction, so does the woman's saliva have the same effect, carrying the poet to the "rives de la mort." [150]

The poet's direct comparison of the power of the woman's eyes and saliva with the power of opium again indicates clearly that Baudelaire associated woman with the drug. "Le Poison" helps clarify the many strange poems in *Les Fleurs du Mal* which seem to attribute to the perfume of a woman's hair, or the sensa-

---

[147] *Œuvres*, p. 377.

[148] Ibid., p. 385.

[149] In "Le poème du haschisch" the man under the influence of hashish "*admire* son remords et il se glorifie, pendant qu'il est en train de perdre sa liberté." (*Œuvres*, p. 380).

[150] Baudelaire mentions in "Le poème du haschisch" that he considers those who have used hashish and escaped its clutches to be "des Orphées vainqueurs de l'Enfer" (*Œuvres*, p. 374); that is, these persons have gone over the banks of the river of death and yet managed to return.

tion of touching a cat's fur, the same intoxicating charm which one would normally associate with opium or hashish. [151]

In "Le poème du haschisch" Baudelaire begins by stating that some days one awakens in a spirit of exhilaration conducive to creating. During these rare times he needs no artificial stimulus to taste the joys of the infinite. But since these days of inspiration are irregular and unpredictable, he seeks this exhilaration by an artificial means. Thus does Baudelaire in this passage and in others emphasize that the poet has the ability of experiencing naturally those sensations which he seeks in the use of opium or hashish.

Seen in this light the poem "L'invitation au voyage" is of great interest, for the poet here suggests a beautiful life of love in a faraway land of enchantment. This exotic paradise where beauty,

---

[151] In this regard, many poems from the collection should be considered. The first poem under the title "Le chat" praises the rich, beautiful quality of the cat's voice in a way that sounds as if the poet had drunk a potion of laudanum and had begun to feel its pleasurable effect:

> Cette voix, qui perle et qui filtre
> Dans mon fonds le plus ténébreux,
> Me remplit comme un vers nombreux
> Et me réjouit comme un philtre.
>
> Elle endort les plus cruels maux
> Et contient toutes les extases... (*Les Fleurs*, pp. 54-55)

One hardly need point out the liquid references suggested by the words "perle," "filtre," "remplit," and "philtre." Nor does it seem necessary to remark that, like opium, the voice soothes ("endort") the poet's hurts ("maux") and brings ecstasies to the shadowy depths of his soul. In the second poem under the title "Le chat" the scent from the cat's fur carries the poet into a kind of hypnotic trance. The eyes of the cat suddenly become strangely reminiscent of eyes described by those under the influence of opium or hashish:

> Je vois avec étonnement
> Le feu de ses prunelles pâles,
> Clairs fanaux, vivantes opales,
> Qui me contemplent fixement. (*Les Fleurs*, p. 55.)

Again in the wonderful poem, "Le beau navire," in an ambiance which borders on a hallucinatory description, Baudelaire praises the intoxicating charms of his mistress's beauty:

> Boucliers provoquants, armés de pointes roses!
> Armoire à doux secrets, pleine de bonnes choses,
> De vins, de parfums, de liqueurs
> Qui feraient délirer les cerveaux et les coeurs!
> (*Les Fleurs*, p. 56)

harmony, and peace reign supreme represents the experience which the individual seeks in taking opium or hashish.[152] And yet when one compares the poem with its counterpart in the prose poems, he sees that this beautiful vision can be the poet's without using artificial stimulants:

> Des rêves! toujours des rêves! et plus l'âme est ambitieuse et délicate, plus les rêves l'éloignent du possible. Chaque homme porte en lui sa dose d'opium naturel, incessamment sécrétée et renouvelée,...[153]

But, just as in the beginning of "Le poème du haschisch," it is indicated that these periods of exhilaration in life come far too infrequently:

> ...et, de la naissance à la mort, combien comptons-nous d'heures remplies par la jouissance positive, par l'action réussie et décidée? Vivrons-nous jamais, passerons-nous jamais dans ce tableau qu'a peint mon esprit, ce tableau qui te ressemble?[154]

Man's "goût de l'infini" (as Baudelaire writes in "Le poème du haschisch") causes him to seek a means of enjoying these ecstatic moments regularly. Thus does he turn to various stimulants in search of his ideal and as a means of escape from his spleen.

The theme of Baudelaire's "Alchimie de la douleur" illustrates well the despair which the poet felt in confronting life, where some poets find a joy and others only grief.

> L'un t'éclaire avec son ardeur,
> L'autre en toi met son deuil, Nature!
> Ce qui dit à l'un: Sépulture!
> Dit à l'autre: Vie et splendeur!

---

[152] For an excellent description of the transforming powers of hashish, the reader is referred to pages 377-378 of the "Poème du haschisch." There Baudelaire describes how the individual under the influence of hashish enters a world in which he experiences all the voluptuous pleasures of life.

[153] Œuvres, "L'invitation au voyage," p. 255.

[154] Ibid.

> Hermès inconnu qui m'assistes
> Et qui toujours m'intimidas,
> Tu me rends l'égal de Midas,
> Le plus triste des alchimistes;
>
> Par toi je change l'or en fer
> Et le paradis en enfer;
> Dans le suaire des nuages
>
> Je découvre un cadavre cher,
> Et sur les célestes rivages
> Je bâtis de grands sarcophages. [155]

Again there is the suggestion that Baudelaire's use of drugs is the principal reason for his bleak outlook on life. The cause of this twisted view is "Hermès inconnu," the thrice powerful. Is this "Hermès inconnu" not the "Satan Trismégiste" of "Au lecteur," who "tient les fils qui nous remuent" and who, "savant chimiste," vaporizes "le riche métal de notre volonté?" [156] It is the same "Esprit des Ténèbres" or "Esprit du Mal" from the "Poème du haschisch" who, with the aid of his "poisons excitants," enslaves man by destroying his will in offering him an easy means to a cheap paradise. Baudelaire writes that Hermes makes him equal to the unfortunate Midas, whose acquisition of the golden touch did not bring the happiness he expected, but only grief. Through the use of drugs Baudelaire hoped to experience frequently the creative sensations which it is the poet's pleasure to have on those rare days when he is inspired. But the paradise which he created by means of the drug turned out to be artificial. Each day, instead of gaining what he hoped, he became more enslaved to the "Esprit du Mal." Each day he took a step toward Hell. Baudelaire writes in "Le poème du haschisch":

> ...j'ai dit qu'aspirant sans cesse à réchauffer ses espérances et à s'élever vers l'infini, il montrait dans tous les pays et dans tous les temps, un goût frénétique pour toutes les substances, même dangereuses, qui, en exaltant sa personnalité, pouvaient susciter un instant à ses yeux ce paradis d'occasion, objet de tous ses désirs, et enfin que cet esprit

---

[155] *Les Fleurs*, pp. 83-84.
[156] Ibid., p. 5.

hasardeux, poussant, sans le savoir, jusqu'à l'enfer témoignait ainsi de sa grandeur originelle.[157]

Baudelaire is indeed comparable to Midas, for he too sought happiness from the gift of Hermes. But, as in the case of Midas, he was deceived by the results. Instead of turning the worthless into something valuable, he succeeded only in destroying the good in life: he changed the valuable into the worthless and the good into evil. In writing these lines filled with the anguish of his broken hope, Baudelaire was undoubtedly comparing his own situation with that of the opium-eater described by De Quincey in a passage which Baudelaire renders as follows:

> Midas changeait en or tout ce qu'il touchait, et se sentait martyrisé par cet ironique privilège. De même le mangeur d'opium transformait en réalités inévitables tous les objets de ses rêveries. Toute cette fantasmagorie, si belle et si poétique qu'elle fût en apparence, était accompagnée d'une angoisse profonde et d'une noire mélancolie. Il lui semblait, chaque nuit, qu'il descendait, indéfiniment dans les abîmes sans lumière, au delà de toute profondeur connue, sans espérance de pouvoir remonter.[158]

The despair which one finds expressed in "Alchimie de la douleur" is greatly heightened when one considers the implications of Baudelaire's own addiction, and his self-comparison with Midas, who has been trapped by his own "gift." And behind all is the "Esprit du Mal" in the figure of Hermes, who torments the poet and destroys his life.

Considering Baudelaire's association with opium and the generally hopeless plight of the addict who would break with the drug, one cannot help but notice the title of the following poem, "L'Irrémédiable," and its relevance to the addict's situation:

> Une Idée, une Forme, un Être
> Parti de l'azur et tombé
> Dans un Styx bourbeux et plombé
> Où nul oeil du Ciel ne pénètre;

---

[157] *Œuvres*, p. 386.
[158] Ibid., p. 426.

Un Ange, imprudent voyageur
Qu'a tenté l'amour du difforme,
Au fond d'un cauchemar énorme
Se débattant comme un nageur,

Et luttant, angoisses funèbres!
Contre un gigantesque remous
Qui va chantant comme les fous
Et pirouettant dans les ténèbres;

Un malheureux ensorcelé
Dans ses tâtonnements futiles,
Pour fuir d'un lieu plein de reptiles,
Cherchant la lumière et la clé;

Un damné descendant sans lampe,
Au bord d'un gouffre dont l'odeur
Trahit l'humide profondeur,
D'éternels escaliers sans rampe,

Où veillent des monstres visqueux
Dont les larges yeux de phosphore
Font une nuit plus noire encore
Et ne rendent visibles qu'eux;

Un navire pris dans le pôle,
Comme en un piège de cristal,
Cherchant par quel détroit fatal
Il est tombé dans cette geôle;

—Emblèmes nets, tableau parfait
D'une fortune irrémédiable,
Qui donne à penser que le Diable
Fait toujours bien tout ce qu'il fait!

II

Tête-à-tête sombre et limpide
Qu'un coeur devenu son miroir!
Puits de Vérité, clair et noir,
Où tremble une étoile livide,

Un phare ironique, infernal,
Flambeau des grâces sataniques,
Soulagement et gloire uniques,
—La conscience dans le Mal! [159]

---

[159] *Les Fleurs,* pp. 86-87.

The addict seems hopelessly attached to the drug, unable to free himself from bondage. And in Baudelaire's view that the drug is Satan's perfect means of enslaving man and of causing him to commit blasphemy one can see that both physically and morally the drug-user is irreparably lost.

Before he had read the sequel to De Quincey's *Confessions of an English Opium-Eater,* Baudelaire speculated on the outcome of De Quincey's condition. He decided that it was a condition from which there was no escape and for which there was no end. For although Robinson Crusoe might escape from his island and a lost ship strike upon land, "quel homme peut sortir de l'empire de l'opium?" [160] Baudelaire continues in "Un mangeur d'opium":

> Il y a des situations éternelles; et tout ce qui a rapport à l'irrémédiable, à l'irréparable, rentre dans cette catégorie. [161]

Other aspects of the poem also suggest that Baudelaire had the addict's problem in mind. In the last stanza of the first part, the poet specifies that the hopeless situations described above are the work of Satan. It is he, then, who is behind the "malheureux ensorcelé" of stanza four, whose futile gropings to flee from the reptile-infested place remind one of De Quincey's opium nightmares which Baudelaire found so attractive: [162]

> Sur chaque être, sur chaque forme, sur chaque menace, punition, incarcération ténébreuse, planait un sentiment d'éternité et d'infini qui me causait l'angoisse et l'oppression de la folie... les agents principaux étaient de hideux oiseaux, des serpents ou des crocodiles, principalement ces derniers. Le crocodile maudit devint pour moi l'objet de plus d'horreur que presque tous les autres... l'abominable tête du crocodile, avec ses petits yeux obliques, me regardait partout, de tous les côtés, multipliée par des répétitions innombrables; et je restais là, plein d'horreur

---

[160] *Œuvres,* p. 436.
[161] Ibid.
[162] Baudelaire writes that the pages of nightmarish visions which he is about to translate are "trop belles pour que je les abrège..." (*Œuvres,* p. 429.)

et fasciné. Et ce hideux reptile hantait si souvent mon sommeil... [163]

The fifth stanza is strikingly reminiscent of De Quincey's passage concerning the opium addict who, each night, descends into a deep abyss, "où veillent des monstres visqueux":

Il lui semblait, chaque nuit, qu'il descendait indéfiniment dans des abîmes sans lumière, au delà de toute profondeur connue, sans espérance de pouvoir remonter. [164]

But the horror of the situation is indicated in the two stanzas of part II, where the individual is completely conscious of the evil into which he has fallen. In the "Poème du haschisch," he is similarly aware of the prideful, blasphemous evolution of his thought. But the influence of the drug is such that he overcomes each objection and even converts self-criticism into prideful self-praise. Remorse becomes admirable,[165] and acts which he recognizes as vile are twisted by this evil influence until they seem worthy of praise. His critical self asks:

De combien d'actions sottes ou viles le passé n'est-il pas rempli, qui sont véritablement indignes de ce roi de la pensée et qui en souillent la dignité idéale? [166]

And the individual under the drug's influence responds:

Cette action ridicule, lâche ou vile, dont le souvenir m'a un moment agité, est en complète contradiction avec ma vraie nature, ma nature actuelle, et l'énergie même avec laquelle je la condamne, le soin inquisitorial avec lequel je l'analyse et je la juge, prouvent mes hautes et divines aptitudes pour la vertu. Combien trouverait-on

---

[163] Œuvres, pp. 431-432.
[164] Ibid., p. 426. In another passage De Quincey relates that in his opium dreams he was sometimes buried in the depths of great pyramids where he lay, "... confondu avec une foule de choses inexprimables et visqueuses, parmi les boues et les roseaux du Nil." (Œuvres, p. 431.)
[165] "Il admire son remords et il se glorifie, pendant qu'il est en train de perdre sa liberté." (Œuvres, p. 380.)
[166] Ibid.

dans le monde d'hommes aussi habiles pour se juger, aussi sévères pour se condamner? [167]

The "conscience dans le Mal," is indeed a "phare ironique, infernal," for, instead of leading the individual toward the good, it rather takes him deeper into the pit of evil. It is thus truly the "flambeau des grâces sataniques" and his "soulagement et gloire unique."

After "L'Irrémédiable," the next poem ("L'Horloge") terminates the section of *Les Fleurs du Mal* called "Spleen et Idéal."

> Horloge! dieu sinistre, effrayant, impassible,
> Dont le doigt nous menace et nous dit: '*Souviens-toi!*'
> Les vibrantes Douleurs dans ton coeur plein d'effroi
> Se planteront bientôt comme dans une cible;
>
> Le Plaisir vaporeux fuira vers l'horizon
> Ainsi qu'une sylphide au fond de la coulisse;
> Chaque instant te dévore un morceau du délice
> A chaque homme accordé pour toute sa saison.
>
> Trois mille six cents fois par heure, la Seconde
> Chuchote: *Souviens-toi!* —Rapide, avec sa voix
> D'insecte, Maintenant dit: Je suis Autrefois,
> Et j'ai pompé ta vie avec ma trompe immonde!
>
> *Remember! Souviens-toi*, prodigue! *Esto memor!*
> (Mon gosier de métal parle toutes les langues.)
> Des minutes, mortel folâtre, sont des gangues
> Qu'il ne faut pas lâcher sans en extraire l'or!
>
> Souviens-toi que le Temps est un joueur avide
> Qui gagne sans tricher, à tout coup! c'est la loi.
> Le jour décroît; la nuit augmente; *souviens-toi!*
> Le gouffre a toujours soif; la clepsydre se vide.
>
> Tantôt sonnera l'heure où le divin Hasard,
> Où l'auguste Vertu, ton épouse encor vierge,
> Où le Repentir même (oh! la dernière auberge!),
> Où tout te dira: 'Meurs, vieux lâche! il est trop tard!' [168]

"L'Horloge" is a fitting close to this section of *Les Fleurs du Mal*, for it stresses the slowness and the magnification of time caused by "Ennui" and "Spleen." Yet Baudelaire's feeling of

---

[167] Ibid., p. 381.
[168] *Les Fleurs*, pp. 87-88.

horror at the ticking seconds is expressed just as powerfully in an analogous passage from "La chambre double" of the *Petits poèmes en prose*.

Here the poet is at first in a state of revery, peace, and calm. He describes a room "véritablement *spirituelle*, où l'atmosphère stagnante est légèrement teintée de rose et de bleu. L'âme y prend un bain de paresse, aromatisé par le regret et le désir. — C'est quelque chose de crépusculaire, de bleuâtre et de rosâtre; un rêve de volupté pendant une éclipse." [169]

Just as in many reveries produced by opium or hashish the inanimate objects around the observer take on different shapes and bear singular significance:

> Les meubles ont des formes allongées, prostrées, alanguies. Les meubles ont l'air de rêver; on les dirait doués d'une vie somnambulique, comme le végétal et le minéral. Les étoffes parlent une langue muette, comme les fleurs, comme les ciels, comme les soleils couchants... Une senteur infinitésimale du choix le plus exquis, à laquelle se mêle une très-légère humidité, nage dans cette atmosphère, où l'esprit sommeillant est bercé par des sensations de serre-chaude. [170]

In his revery the poet is visited by his "Idole," who appears as if by magic. He wonders to what "démon" he owes the peace and mystery of these wonderful moments:

> A quel démon bienveillant dois-je d'être ainsi entouré de mystère, de silence, de paix et de parfums? O béatitude! ce que nous nommons généralement la vie, même dans son expansion la plus heureuse, n'a rien de commun avec cette vie suprême dont j'ai maintenant connaissance et que je savoure minute par minute, seconde par seconde! [171]

Suddenly he realizes that to speak of time in this state of revery is inaccurate. Time has ceased to exist. It is actually as if time had disappeared and his ecstasy were infinite:

---

[169] *Œuvres*, p. 233.
[170] Ibid., pp. 233-234. For similar experience under the influence of mescaline, see Aldous Huxley's *The Doors of Perception*.
[171] Ibid., p. 234.

> Non! il n'est plus de minutes, il n'est plus de secondes! Le temps a disparu; c'est l'Eternité qui règne, une éternité de délices! [172]

A knock at the door breaks the revery and brings the poet back to reality. The "Spectre" who enters is a reminder of the pressing obligations awaiting him in the world of time. [173] The knock at the door destroys abruptly the state of ecstasy which he was enjoying. By contrast, the world of reality and its demands are indeed horrible. The poet is made aware of his bleak surroundings and the terrible reality of the ticking clock:

> La chambre paradisiaque, l'idole, la souveraine des rêves, la *Sylphide,* comme disait le grand René, toute cette magie a disparu au coup brutal frappé par le Spectre.
> Horreur! je me souviens! je me souviens!...
> Et ce parfum d'un autre monde, dont je m'enivrais avec une sensibilité perfectionnée, hélas! il est remplacé par une fétide odeur de tabac mêlée à je ne sais quelle nauséabonde moisissure. On respire ici maintenant le ranci de la désolation...
> Oh! oui! le Temps a reparu; le Temps règne en souverain maintenant;...
> Je vous assure que les secondes maintenant sont fortement et solennellement accentuées, et chacune, en jaillissant de la pendule, dit: —'Je suis la Vie, l'insupportable, l'implacable Vie!'...

---

[172] Ibid.

[173] In the "Poème du haschisch" Baudelaire warns of the extreme discomfort entailed if, on the day one wishes to experience the wonderful ecstasy brought by hashish, he has failed to guard against the intrusion of pressing obligations. The burden of any obligation is greatly heightened in contrast with the peace of the revery: "Je présume que vous avez eu la précaution de bien choisir votre moment pour cette aventureuse expédition. Toute débauche parfaite a besoin d'un parfait loisir. Vous savez d'ailleurs que le haschisch crée l'exagération non seulement de l'individu, mais aussi de la circonstance et du milieu; vous n'avez pas de devoirs à accomplir exigeant de la ponctualité, de l'exactitude; point de chagrins de famille; point de douleurs d'amour. Il faut y prendre garde. Ce chagrin, cette inquiétude, ce souvenir d'un devoir qui réclame votre volonté et votre attention à une minute déterminée, viendraient sonner comme un glas à travers votre ivresse et empoisonneraient votre plaisir. L'inquiétude deviendrait angoisse; le chagrin, torture." (*Œuvres,* p. 356.)

> Oui! le Temps règne; il a repris sa brutale dictature. Et il me pousse, comme si j'étais un boeuf, avec son double aiguillon. —'Et hue donc! bourrique! Sue donc, esclave! Vis donc, damné!' [174]

Among the objects he sees, however, there is one that seems friendly — his faithful but terrible friend, opium, which created the timeless revery so brutally interrupted:

> Dans ce monde étroit, mais si plein de dégoût, un seul objet connu me sourit: la fiole de laudanum; une vieille et terrible amie; comme toutes les amies, hélas! féconde en caresses et en traîtrises. [175]

It is evident that the horror of time expressed in "L'Horloge" is the same as that expressed in "La chambre double." Indeed, "La chambre double" is the prose counterpart of "L'Horloge." In the latter, the clock reminds the poet that Time passes relentlessly, that Time is sovereign. In "La chambre double" the poet exclaims "je me souviens! je me souviens!..." and recognizes that "le Temps règne en souverain." [176] Baudelaire warns in "Le poème du haschisch" that any grief or worry which would require one's attention "viendraient sonner comme un glas à travers votre ivresse et empoisonneraient votre plaisir," [177] thus suggesting the lines from the poem:

> Les vibrantes Douleurs dans ton coeur plein d'effroi
> Se planteront bientôt comme dans une cible... [178]

Lines one and two of the second quatrain state that Pleasure will vanish like the "Sylphide." In "La chambre double" one sees the same reference:

> La chambre paradisiaque, l'idole, la souveraine des rêves, la Sylphide,... toute cette magie a disparu au coup brutal frappé par le Spectre. [179]

---

[174] *Œuvres*, pp. 234-235.
[175] Ibid., p. 235.
[176] Ibid.
[177] Ibid., p. 356.
[178] *Les Fleurs*, p. 87.
[179] *Œuvres*, pp. 234-235.

In the poem itself there are references which perhaps suggest opium independently of any reference to "La chambre double." In the second line of the fourth quatrain ("Mon gosier de métal parle toutes les langues") Baudelaire refers to a hallucinatory phenomenon which he attributed to the influence of hashish in "Le poème du haschisch": [180]

> ...j'attribuais aux oiseaux ce chant mystérieux du cuivre, et je croyais qu'ils chantaient avec un gosier de métal. [181]

And in the next to the last line of the poem, Baudelaire's reference to the refusal even of "Repentir" reminds one of the "repentirs lâches" of "Au lecteur" and the addict's numerous broken resolutions.

"La chambre double" and "L'Horloge" differ in their treatment of the passing of time. In "La chambre double" the emphasis is on time's interminable slowness and the necessity for the poet to live on in his damnable world. "L'Horloge," on the other hand, stresses the inexorable march of the second hand, threatening the poet with death before he can rectify his miserable existence.

The agony and horror of passing time expressed in "L'Horloge" is considerably more meaningful if considered in contrast with the revery and peace produced by opium or hashish and if considered in terms of Baudelaire's addiction. Baudelaire frequently expressed fear that he would die before he had the opportunity to complete his work. Certainly the many days spent in wasted revery and his lack of will to work regularly must have accentuated this recognition that time was growing short. The sharp contrast between the blissful revery in which time seemed to stand still and the dreadful ensuing reality and remorse accounts for the overwhelming sense of pervading despair in the poem. The poet could hardly have chosen a better poem to conclude the major section of the volume in which Spleen and the Ideal are placed in eternal conflict, for in "L'Horloge" the creator of the

---

[180] See page 100 above for the text in which Gautier mentions that one person spoke to him in Italian and that hashish transposed it into Spanish. Gautier also wrote of the voices of the "pendules," which he described as "flûtées, cuivrées, argentines." (Pichois, pp. 16-17.)

[181] *Œuvres*, p. 369.

Ideal, the poet, is threatened by an old enemy, time. The "thirsty abyss" threatens to gain an everlasting victory.

Among the poems found in the section called "Tableaux parisiens" there are few which seem to have been influenced by Baudelaire's experience with opium. One, however, which seems to be set in a mysterious atmosphere suggesting the hallucinatory state, is "Les Sept Vieillards."

> Fourmillante cité, cité pleine de rêves,
> Où le spectre en plein jour raccroche le passant!
> Les mystères partout coulent comme des sèves
> Dans les canaux étroits du colosse puissant.
>
> Un matin, cependant que dans la triste rue
> Les maisons, dont la brume allongeait la hauteur,
> Simulaient les deux quais d'une rivière accrue,
> Et que, décor semblable à l'âme de l'acteur,
>
> Un brouillard sale et jaune inondait tout l'espace,
> Je suivais, roidissant mes nerfs comme un héros
> Et discutant avec mon âme déjà lasse,
> Le faubourg secoué par les lourds tombereaux.
>
> Tout à coup, un vieillard dont les guenilles jaunes
> Imitaient la couleur de ce ciel pluvieux,
> Et dont l'aspect aurait fait pleuvoir les aumônes,
> Sans la méchanceté qui luisait dans ses yeux,
>
> M'apparut. On eût dit sa prunelle trempée
> Dans le fiel; son regard aiguisait les frimas,
> Et sa barbe à longs poils, roide comme une épée,
> Se projetait, pareille à celle de Judas.
>
> Il n'était pas voûté, mais cassé, son échine
> Faisant avec sa jambe un parfait angle droit,
> Si bien que son bâton, parachevant sa mine,
> Lui donnait la tournure et le pas maladroit
>
> D'un quadrupède infirme ou d'un juif à trois pattes.
> Dans la neige et la boue il allait s'empêtrant,
> Comme s'il écrasait des morts sous ses savates,
> Hostile à l'univers plutôt qu'indifférent.
>
> Son pareil le suivait: barbe, oeil, dos, bâton, loques,
> Nul trait ne distinguait, du même enfer venu,
> Ce jumeau centenaire, et ces spectres baroques
> Marchaient du même pas vers un but inconnu.

> A quel complot infâme étais-je donc en butte,
> Ou quel méchant hasard ainsi m'humiliait?
> Car je comptai sept fois, de minute en minute,
> Ce sinistre vieillard qui se multipliait!
>
> Que celui-là qui rit de mon inquiétude,
> Et qui n'est pas saisi d'un frisson fraternel,
> Songe bien que malgré tant de décrépitude
> Ces sept monstres hideux avaient l'air éternel!
>
> Aurais-je, sans mourir, contemplé le huitième,
> Sosie inexorable, ironique et fatal,
> Dégoûtant Phénix, fils et père de lui-même?
> —Mais je tournai le dos au cortège infernal.
>
> Exaspéré comme un ivrogne qui voit double,
> Je rentrai, je fermai ma porte, épouvanté,
> Malade et morfondu, l'esprit fiévreux et trouble,
> Blessé par le mystère et par l'absurdité!
>
> Vainement ma raison voulait prendre la barre;
> La tempête en jouant déroutait ses efforts,
> Et mon âme dansait, dansait, vieille gabarre
> Sans mâts, sur une mer monstrueuse et sans bords! [182]

In the opening stanzas Baudelaire describes the great city of Paris with its narrow streets covered by a heavy fog. It is a city swarming with life and dreams, a city in which the passer-by is confronted by spectres in broad daylight. Suddenly the poet sees an old man who, except for the evil look in his eye, might have stirred great pity. The hideous old man, clearly a spectre, is followed by others just as horrible. The poet is terrified, for, rather than being simply decrepit old men, "Ces sept monstres hideux avaient l'air éternel." [183] To avoid seeing another, which he did not feel he could endure, the poet turned his back on the "cortège infernal" and fled inside.

There are a number of indications in the poem that Baudelaire may be describing a hallucination experienced while under the influence of opium. The opening lines of the poem, "Fourmillante cité, cité pleine de rêves, / Où le spectre en plein jour raccroche le passant..." prepare the reader for the sudden appearance of the

---

[182] *Les Fleurs*, pp. 97-100.
[183] Ibid., p. 99.

sinister old man. The strange gleam in his eye and the "spectres baroques" which follow, all duplicates of the first old man, affirm the hallucinatory aspect of the encounter. Once inside the apartment the poet tries without success to bar the door. It is here that one sees most clearly that he is in a state of delirium. His "raison" wished to take the bar, but "la tempête ("délire" is a variant reading [Adam, p. 99]) en jouant déroutait ses efforts." [184] And his soul seemed to be dancing "sur une mer monstruese et sans bords!"

Various suggestions have been made concerning the allegorical meaning of the "Sept Vieillards," but evidence is lacking to ascertain any definite association. However, certain lines suggest that the hideous old man and his "cortège infernal" may be the spectre of Time which Baudelaire describes in a similar manner in "La chambre double":

> Oh! oui! le Temps a reparu; le Temps règne en souverain maintenant; et avec le hideux vieillard est revenu tout son démoniaque cortège de Souvenirs, de Regrets, de Spasmes, de Peurs, d'Angoisses, de Cauchemars, de Colères et de Névroses. [185]

In the ninth stanza the poet writes that he counted "sept fois, de minute en minute, Ce sinistre vieillard qui se multipliait!" And just like time, these "spectres baroques/Marchaient du même pas vers un but inconnu." In "La chambre double" the seconds which steadily tick away are "fortement et solennellement accentuées, et chacune, en jaillissant de la pendule, dit: — 'Je suis la Vie, l'insupportable, l'implacable Vie!' " [186]

Perhaps, then, the "vieillard" represents another of Baudelaire's horrible confrontations with the spectre of life in the implacable form of time, which seems to move on aimlessy yet relentlessly — the Enemy, "[qui] mange la vie, et... nous ronge le cœur." [187]

---

[184] In another version of the poem one finds the line: "Ma raison vainement réclamait son empire." (Ibid., p. 100.)
[185] Œuvres, p. 235.
[186] Ibid.
[187] Les Fleurs, p. 16.

A number of suggestions have been made concerning the poem, "Rêve parisien."

> De ce terrible paysage,
> Tel que jamais mortel n'en vit,
> Ce matin encore l'image,
> Vague et lointaine, me ravit.
>
> Le sommeil est plein de miracles!
> Par un caprice singulier,
> J'avais banni de ces spectacles
> Le végétal irrégulier,
>
> Et, peintre fier de mon génie,
> Je savourais dans mon tableau
> L'enivrante monotonie
> Du métal, du marbre et de l'eau.
>
> Babel d'escaliers et d'arcades,
> C'était un palais infini,
> Plein de bassins et de cascades
> Tombant dans l'or mat ou bruni;
>
> Et des cataractes pesantes,
> Comme des rideaux de cristal,
> Se suspendaient, éblouissantes,
> A des murailles de métal.
>
> Non d'arbres, mais de colonnades
> Les étangs dormants s'entouraient,
> Où de gigantesques naïades,
> Comme des femmes, se miraient.
>
> Des nappes d'eau s'épanchaient, bleues,
> Entre des quais roses et verts,
> Pendant des millions de lieues.
> Vers les confins de l'univers;
>
> C'étaient des pierres inouïes
> Et des flots magiques; c'étaient
> D'immenses glaces éblouies
> Par tout ce qu'elles reflétaient!
>
> Insouciants et taciturnes,
> Des Ganges, dans le firmament,
> Versaient le trésor de leurs urnes
> Dans des gouffres de diamant.
>
> Architecte de mes féeries,
> Je faisais, à ma volonté,

Sous un tunnel de pierreries
Passer un océan dompté;

Et tout, même la couleur noire,
Semblait fourbi, clair, irisé;
Le liquide enchâssait sa gloire
Dans le rayon cristallisé.

Nul astre d'ailleurs, nuls vestiges
De soleil, même au bas du ciel,
Pour illuminer ces prodiges,
Qui brillaient d'un feu personnel!

Et sur ces mouvantes merveilles
Planait (terrible nouveauté!
Tout pour l'oeil, rien pour les oreilles!)
Un silence d'éternité.

II

En rouvrant mes yeux pleins de flamme
J'ai vu l'horreur de mon taudis,
Et senti, rentrant dans mon âme,
La pointe des soucis maudits;

La pendule aux accents funèbres
Sonnait brutalement midi,
Et le ciel versait des ténèbres
Sur le triste monde engourdi. [188]

Some have suggested that there is a close relationship between this poem and Baudelaire's experience with opium and hashish, while others have denied explicitly any such connection; yet within the poem itself there are a number of indications which persuade one that the poem must be considered in the light of Baudelaire's drug experience.

In the second stanza Baudelaire marvels at the miracle of sleep in that he has been able to banish from his visions the "végétal irrégulier." That is, the visions created by the mind of the artist are superior in beauty because the harmony of art is superior to the disordered creations of nature. In writing of the experiences of the individual under the influence of hashish in

---

[188] Ibid., pp. 115-117.

"Le poème du haschisch" Baudelaire stresses that the "rêveur" is extremely sensitive to harmony and balance:

> L'idée de beauté doit naturellement s'emparer d'une place vaste dans un tempérament spirituel tel que je l'ai supposé. L'harmonie, le balancement des lignes, l'eurythmie dans les mouvements, apparaissent au rêveur comme des nécessités, comme des *devoirs*, non-seulement pour tous les êtres de la création, mais pour lui-même, le rêveur, qui se trouve, à cette période de la crise, doué d'une merveilleuse aptitude pour comprendre le rythme immortel et universel. [189]

The visions which one has while under the influence of hashish are not disordered, for the inner eye transforms them into artistic creations:

> Il ne faut pas croire que tous ces phénomènes se produisent dans l'esprit pêle-mêle, avec l'accent criard de la réalité et le désordre de la vie extérieure. L'oeil intérieur transforme tout et donne à chaque chose le complément de beauté qui lui manque pour qu'elle soit vraiment digne de plaire. C'est aussi à cette phase essentiellement voluptueuse et sensuelle qu'il faut rapporter l'amour des eaux limpides, courantes ou stagnantes, qui se développe si étonnamment dans l'ivresse cérébrale de quelques artistes. Les miroirs deviennent un prétexte à cette rêverie qui ressemble à une soif spirituelle, conjointe à la soif physique qui dessèche le gosier, et dont j'ai parlé précédemment; les eaux fuyantes, les *jeux* d'eau, les cascades harmonieuses, l'immensité bleue de la mer, roulent, chantent, dorment avec un charme inexprimable. [190]

Even in this passage concerning the ability of the inner eye to transform the disorder of the dreams into beauty, there are echoes which recall a number of the lines from the poem itself. In the fourth stanza there is reference to a "palais infini,/Plein de bassins et de cascades." In the fifth stanza there are "des cataractes pesantes,/Comme des rideaux de cristal," while the sixth and seventh stanzas refer to "Les étangs dormants" and "des nappes

---

[189] *Œuvres*, p. 377.
[190] Ibid.

d'eau." However, the similarity between this passage and the visions of the poem, though striking, is less than the similarity between the poem's images and those in a passage of "Un mangeur d'opium":

> D'étonnantes et monstrueuses architectures se dressaient dans son cerveau, semblables à ces constructions mouvantes que l'oeil du poète aperçoit dans les nuages colorés par le soleil couchant. Mais bientôt à ces rêves de terrasses, de tours, de remparts, montant à des hauteurs inconnues et s'enfonçant dans d'immenses profondeurs, succédèrent des lacs et de vastes étendues d'eau. L'eau devint l'élément obsédant... Les eaux changèrent bientôt de caractère, et les lacs transparents, brillants comme des miroirs, devinrent des mers et des océans.[191]

The entire architectural scene has echoes from De Quincey's *Confessions*, from whose opening passage Baudelaire translates as follows:

> ... tu [opium] bâtis sur le sein des ténèbres, avec les matériaux imaginaires du cerveau, avec un art plus profond que celui de Phidias et de Praxitèle, des cités et des temples qui dépassent en splendeur Babylone et Hékatompylos; et du chaos d'un sommeil plein de songes tu évoques à la lumière du soleil les visages des beautés depuis longtemps ensevelies...[192]

To the similarities between the imagery of the poem and certain passages from *Les paradis artificiels* should be added a marked similarity between certain aspects of the poem and the prose poem, "La chambre double." In the latter, just prior to the interruption of the revery by the knock at the door, Baudelaire wrote that Time had disappeared: "...c'est l'Eternité qui règne, une éternité de délices."[193] In the last stanza of the first part of "Rêve parisien," Baudelaire writes that "sur ces mouvantes merveilles/Planait.../Un silence d'éternité." The parallel continues in that each reference to the seeming eternity of the vision occurs

---
[191] Ibid., p. 428.
[192] Ibid., p. 388.
[193] Ibid., p. 234.

just before the dreamer returns to reality. In the last two stanzas of "Rêve parisien" (part II), there is again a striking similarity to the poet's description of the bleak reality seen by the dreamer in "La chambre double." In the poem the terrible contrast between the beautiful revery and bleak reality is again stressed. In opening his eyes still filled with the visions of the dream ("mes yeux pleins de flamme") the poet witnesses the miserable reality of his room: "J'ai vu l'horreur de mon taudis." In "La chambre double" the reaction is precisely the same:

> Horreur! je me souviens! je me souviens! Oui! ce taudis, ce séjour de l'éternel ennui, est bien le mien. [194]

In both works the poet is made fully aware of this reality by the ticking of the clock, horrible reminder of the relentless passage of time. In "Rêve parisien" the clock spreads a shadowy gloom:

> La pendule aux accents funèbres
> Sonnait brutalement midi,
> Et le ciel versait des ténèbres
> Sur le triste monde engourdi.

The poet writes in nearly the same terms in "La chambre double":

> Je vous assure que les secondes maintenant sont fortement et solennellement accentuées, et chacune, en jaillissant de la pendule, dit: 'Je suis la Vie, l'insupportable, l'implacable Vie.' [195]

From these many quotations taken from works which Baudelaire wrote in an attempt to illustrate the effects of opium and hashish on reality, there seems to be little doubt that the poet's descriptions of the elaborate vision in "Rêve parisien" and of the abrupt return to reality are likewise drawn from his rich but disastrous experience with opium.

For the most part the poems in the section called "Le Vin" do not concern the effects of any stimulant except wine, which Baudelaire considered rather beneficent in comparison with opium

---

[194] Ibid., p. 235.
[195] Ibid.

and hashish. If there is any influence in this section from the poet's experience with drugs it is in the last two poems, "Le vin du solitaire" and "Le vin des amants."

Although the tone of "Le vins du solitaire" is not sinister, there is perhaps a reference to hashish in the title of the poem itself. In his comparison of wine and hashish written in 1851, Baudelaire praises wine because it essentially causes one to be "bon et sociable." [196] He condemns hashish because it is "isolant" and because it belongs "à la classe des joies solitaires." [197]

Another indication that Baudelaire may be referring to hashish is in the last three lines of the poem. While giving to the poet "l'espoir, la jeunesse et la vie," [198] it also gives him "orgueil, ce trésor de toute gueuserie, / Qui nous rend triomphants et semblables aux Dieux!" [199] It has been shown previously that Baudelaire considered this pride to be the first step to the supreme blasphemy in the drug experience. Even in the earlier "Du vin et du hachish" there is evidence that he was aware of this danger. For, during the description of the hashish experience, Baudelaire remarks at one point:

> Dès lors, l'idée de supériorité pointe à l'horizon de votre intellect. Bientôt elle grandira démesurément. [200]

And later the dreamer reaches the supreme blasphemy in that he believes his superior intellect can easily solve all problems:

> Tous les problèmes philosophiques sont résolus. Toutes les questions ardues contre lesquelles s'escriment les théologiens et qui font le désespoir de l'humanité raisonnante, sont limpides et claires. Toute contradiction est devenue unité. L'homme est *passé* dieu. [201]

"Le vin des amants" bears no special indication to suggest that Baudelaire had in mind any stimulant other than wine. It is

---

[196] Ibid., p. 343.
[197] Ibid.
[198] *Les Fleurs*, p. 128.
[199] Ibid.
[200] *Œuvres*, p. 336.
[201] Ibid., p. 340.

the last poem of the section and leads directly into "La destruction," which begins the section called "Fleurs du Mal." On several occasions in the collection (as with "Elévation" and "Correspondances") Baudelaire ends a poem with lines leading directly into the one that follows. Considering the factors concerning Baudelaire's drug experience which have been developed above, it is not unlikely that such a relationship exists between the last tercet of "Le vin des amants" and the first lines of "La destruction." "Le vin des amants" is essentially an optimistic poem and the poet invites his "sœur" to share with him the "mirage lointain" of revery and ecstasy. Together they will flee to his paradise of dreams:

> Ma sœur, côte à côte nageant,
> Nous fuirons sans repos ni trêves
> Vers le paradis de mes rêves! [202]

However, this hope is short lived, for turning the page one reads the opening quatrain of "La destruction," where the "Démon" has once again tricked his prey:

> Sans cesse à mes côtés s'agite le Démon;
> Il nage autour de moi comme un air impalpable;
> Je l'avale et le sens qui brûle mon poumon
> Et l'emplit d'un désir éternel et coupable. [203]

Note that the same expressions are here used for the "Démon" as were used for the "sœur" of "Le vin des amants." In "Le vin des amants" he and the "sœur" are "côte à côte." So in "La destruction" is the "Démon" described as being "à mes côtés." Just as the verb "nager" is used to describe the action in "Le vin des amants" so is it used to describe the Demon's motion in "La destruction." Moreover Baudelaire writes in the next quatrain that the "Démon" often takes the form of a seductive woman:

> Parfois il prend, sachant mon grand amour de l'Art,
> La forme de la plus séduisante des femmes,
> Et, sous de spécieux prétextes de cafard,
> Accoutume ma lèvre à des philtres infâmes. [204]

---

[202] *Les Fleurs*, p. 129.
[203] Ibid., p. 133.
[204] Ibid.

Hidden in this disguise he gets the poet to drink the "philtres infâmes" which lead to his destruction. Once again the principal theme of "Le poème du haschich" can be seen. Because of Baudelaire's love for art, the vision-bringing stimulants are the perfect means by which Satan could wreak his destruction.

In the following poems there are no specific indications that Baudelaire had opium or hashish in mind as he wrote. However, the revolt which follows the destruction and perversion presented in the section called "Fleurs du Mal" is the result of the supreme blasphemy committed by Satan himself and which the drug-taker is led to commit. Following the physical destruction and spiritual revolt caused by Satan, there is nothing left for the poet but death.

At the beginning of "Le voyage," Baudelaire again takes the reader on the tragic voyage of life. Just as in the earlier poems of the book, the voyager departs with great expectancy, hoping to find fulfillment elsewhere. But the irony of man's destiny and the tragedy of his blindness are underscored in the second part of the poem. Seeking escape from the horrible desert of his life, piqued by curiosity, man hails each new island as the answer to his quest:

> Nous imitons, horreur! la toupie et la boule
> Dans leur valse et leurs bonds; même dans nos sommeils
> La Curiosité nous tourmente et nous roule,
> Comme un Ange cruel qui fouette des soleils.
>
> Singulière fortune où le but se déplace,
> Et, n'étant nulle part, peut être n'importe où!
> Où l'Homme, dont jamais l'espérance n'est lasse,
> Pour trouver le repos court toujours comme un fou!
>
> Notre âme est un trois-mâts cherchant son Icarie;
> Une voix retentit sur le pont: "Ouvre l'oeil!"
> Une voix de la hune, ardente et folle, crie:
> "Amour... gloire... bonheur!" Enfer! c'est un écueil!
>
> Chaque îlot signalé par l'homme de vigie
> Est un Eldorado promis par le Destin;
> L'Imagination qui dresse son orgie
> Ne trouve qu'un récif aux clartés du matin.
>
> O le pauvre amoureux des pays chimériques!
> Faut-il le mettre aux fers, le jeter à la mer,
> Ce matelot ivrogne, inventeur d'Amériques
> Dont le mirage rend le gouffre plus amer?

> Tel le vieux vagabond, piétinant dans la boue,
> Rêve, le nez en l'air, de brillants paradis;
> Son oeil ensorcelé découvre une Capoue
> Partout où la chandelle illumine un taudis. [205]

In each instance man's search has deceived him and his efforts at escape seem to end only in frustration. Man's efforts are as wasted as the motion of the spinning top ("la toupie"), and they are as foolish as those of the man who seeks rest in running "comme un fou." In the distance man believes that he sees "Amour... gloire... bonheur!" but, upon drawing near, he sees that the illusion was in reality "Enfer," a dangerous reef. Thus does each distant island appear to be an Eldorado to the "Imagination qui dresse son orgie," but the sobering rays of morning disclose only another reef. For the "matelot ivrogne... le mirage rend le gouffre plus amer." And the "vieux vagabond," stumbling in the mud "rêve... de brillants paradis." His bewitched eye finds charm even in a hovel.

The entire second part of "Le voyage" mirrors the drug experience which Baudelaire describes in *Les paradis artificiels*. Even the lines are reminiscent of those used to describe the illusions and pitfalls of the drug-taker. Just as the drug-addict seeks escape from the boredom of his daily existence by using opium or hashish, so does the voyager seek escape by his voyage. In each case the desired happiness, seemingly enjoyed for a time under the influence of the drugs and seemingly sighted by the voyager, turns out to be only an illusion. And in each case there is great danger in the illusion: the drug-taker gradually loses his freedom, and day by day moves toward Hell and subjection to the "Esprit du Mal," which was at the root of his illusion; the voyager, in like manner, believing he sees his Eldorado, finds it only a dangerous reef — and in one instance he calls it "Enfer."

In the last three stanzas of the second part of "Le voyage" there are lines which recall the experiences described in "Le poème du haschisch" and in other works related to the drug experience. In the fourth stanza of part two Baudelaire writes

---

[205] Ibid., pp. 160-161.

that "L'Imagination qui dresse son orgie/Ne trouve qu'un récif aux clartés du matin." One is reminded of the dreadful awakening of the hashish-eater described in "Le poème du haschich" ("Mais le lendemain! le terrible lendemain," etc. [Œuvres, p. 383.]) and the realization that the beautiful visions of the previous night were only an illusion. The lines concerning the "matelot ivrogne" remind one of "L'horloge" and "La chambre double," where the beautiful, timeless revery of the opium vision caused the brutal reality of time to seem worse than before. The "vieux vagabond, piétinant dans la boue," who is unconscious of the filth in which he walks, reminds one of the individual in "Le poème du haschisch" who was unaware of and even found joy in the repugnant filth in which he was mired. His "bewitched eye" sees beauty in the "taudis" lighted by candles, but would probably react to the hovel in the same way as the individual interrupted in his opium revery in "La chambre double" ("Horreur! je me souviens!... ce taudis, ce séjour de l'éternel ennui, est bien le mien," etc. [See Œuvres, p. 235 for entire passage]) if his eye were not bewitched.

In part three the voyager is asked to relate all the wonders that he has seen. Even the visions failed to bring the desired happiness: "Nous nous sommes souvent ennuyés, comme ici." [206] And when the questioners eagerly ask to hear more, the narrator disdainfully replies that "la chose capitale" was "le spectacle ennuyeux de l'immortel péché." [207] The sequence is here the same as in "Le poème du haschisch." As was pointed out earlier, Baudelaire first describes the various hallucinatory wonders evoked by hashish and then remarks that it is time to move on to the more important question.

> Il est temps de laisser de côté toute cette jonglerie et ces grandes marionnettes, nées de la fumée des cervaux enfantins. N'avons-nous pas à parler de choses plus graves... de la *morale* du haschisch. [208]

---

[206] Ibid., p. 161.
[207] Ibid.
[208] Œeuvres, p. 372.

Note that Baudelaire refers to "cerveaux enfantins" concerning these wonders just as he does ("O cerveaux enfantins") in his disdainful reply to those who have just heard of the many marvels that the voyager has seen. And, just as in "Le poème du haschisch," he moves to the more serious issue of sin.

The seventh part of the poem shows the bitter reality of the voyage and of life ("Amer savoir, celui qu'on tire du voyage!"). [209] Life is "une oasis d'horreur dans un désert d'ennui!" [210] The seemingly unimportant question is asked whether one should bother to depart ("Faut-il partir? rester?..."). [211] But whether one stays or leaves, Time is not to be tricked. Again the voyagers are beguiled by the call of an artificial paradise which seems to offer a refuge:

> Nous nous embarquerons sur la mer des Ténèbres
> Avec le coeur joyeux d'un jeune passager.
> Entendez-vous ces voix, charmantes et funèbres,
> Qui chantent: "Par ici! vous qui voulez manger
>
> Le Lotus parfumé! c'est ici qu'on vendange
> Les fruits miraculeux dont votre coeur a faim;
> Venez vous enivrer de la douceur étrange
> De cette après-midi qui n'a jamais de fin!"
>
> A l'accent familier nous devinons le spectre... [212]

For a moment, the "Lotus parfumé" seems to offer the needed refuge, an "après-midi qui n'a jamais de fin." But Time is not to be cheated. The "accent familier" (voices from the past) recalls the notion of time, and the voices call the dreamer to death. Yet death offers no rest, no consolation for man's plight. Again the voyager prepares for a voyage not unlike the previous voyage of life. Once again the question is posed: "Plonger au fond du gouffre, Enfer ou Ciel, qu'importe?" [213] And the answer is the same, thereby perpetuating the irony of man's existence: "Au fond de l'Inconnu

---

[209] *Les Fleurs*, p. 164.
[210] Ibid.
[211] Ibid.
[212] Ibid.
[213] Ibid., p. 165.

pour trouver du *nouveau!"* [214] The irony and perpetual frustration of human life can be seen in the poem which precedes "Le voyage" — the poem called "Le rêve d'un curieux."

Here the poet is about to die and feels mixed emotions of eager curiosity and fear:

> J'étais comme l'enfant avide du spectacle,
> Haïssant le rideau comme on hait un obstacle...
> Enfin la vérité froide se révéla:
>
> J'étais mort sans surprise, et la terrible aurore
> M'enveloppait. —Eh quoi! n'est-ce donc que cela?
> La toile était levée et j'attendais encore. [215]

Just when it seemed that man had found escape from *ennui* through the forgetfulness of death, the illusion is broken and he is again placed in a context of time ("et j'attendais encore"). Even in death man can be tricked and his ironic destiny perpetuated into an eternity of time and horror.

Thus in the last two stanzas of "Le voyage," although setting out with Death as the captain, man embarks on the same ironic, frustrating voyage. Even though a hopeful note is struck by emphasizing the expectancy of the quest, the destination remains in doubt ("Enfer ou Ciel"). Will not this voyage deceive man's expectations just like all the others?

* * *

From the foregoing analysis it is not difficult to see the importance of the opium experience in Baudelaire's life and works. Symbolically this experience represents the bitter reality of life itself. It symbolizes man's means of escape from his horrible existence and the eternal searching for the *nouveau,* which is his source of hope for a better life. The experience is also symbolic of man's quest. The drug experience seemingly provides the *nouveau* and the happiness which man is seeking; but in reality

---

[214] Ibid.
[215] Ibid., p. 159.

it, too, is only a voyage which must end. And because of the bliss of the illusion, the horrors of reality and of man's greatest enemy, Time, are greatly magnified. Moreover, because the "Esprit du Mal" is really the source of these illusions and enslaves man to them like a puppet on a string, man is no longer free to find true peace in life. He is condemned rather to a perpetual destiny of frustration, once the voyage into a blissful eternity, into the abyss of heaven, is denied.

BIBLIOGRAPHY

ADRIAN, E. D. *The Physical Background of Perception.* New York: Oxford University Press, 1947.
AFRICA, T. W. "The Opium Addiction of Marcus Aurelius," *Journal of the History of Ideas,* XXII (1961), 96-102.
ALIGHIERI, DANTE. *La Divina Commedia.* Éd. C. H. Grandgent. Boston: D. C. Heath and Company, 1933.
―――. *The Divine Comedy.* A new prose translation with an introduction by H. R. Huse. New York: Rinehart and Winston, 1954.
ALLAND, ROGER. *Baudelaire et l'esprit nouveau.* Paris, 1918.
ALLENDY, R. F. *L'alchimie et la médecine.* Paris, 1912.
ALLENTUCK, S., and BOWMAN, K. M. "The Psychiatric Aspects of Marihuana Intoxication," *American Journal of Psychiatry,* XCIX (1942), 248-251.
ARMAND. *Des fumeurs et des mangeurs d'opium dans l'Indo-Chine et de l'emploi thérapeutique de la fumée d'opium selon le mode exposé à l'Académie de Médecine de Paris le 8 décembre 1868.* Paris, 1872.
ARNOLD, PAUL. "Les paradis artificiels et Charles Baudelaire," *Les Cahiers de la Tour Saint-Jacques,* Paris, 1960.
AUBAN, B. DE ST. *Fragments pour servir à l'histoire médicale de l'opium.* Montpellier, 1864.
AUSTIN, LLOYD JAMES. *L'univers poétique de Baudelaire: Symbolisme et Symbolique.* Paris: Mercure de France, 1956.
AUSUBEL, DAVID P. *Drug Addiction.* New York: Random. House, 1958.
AYRES. "Des fumeurs d'opium" (trans.), *Archives de Médecine Navale,* LX (Paris, 1893), 357-366.
BALDICK, ROBERT. "The Bohemians," *Listener,* LXIV (1960), 977-979.
BALZAC, HONORÉ DE. *Œuvres complètes d'Honoré de Balzac.* Éd. M. Bouteron and H. Longnon. Paris: Louis Conard, 1938.
BARINE, ARVEDE. *Névrosés.* Paris: Librairie Hachette, 1936.
BAUDELAIRE, CHARLES. *Les Fleurs du Mal.* Éd. A. Adam. Paris: Garnier, 1961.
―――. *Les Fleurs du Mal.* Éd. J. Crépet et G. Blin. Paris: J. Corti, 1942.
―――. *Œuvres complètes.* Éd. J. Crépet. Paris: Conard, 19 vols. 1922-53.
―――. *Œuvres complètes.* Éd. Y.-G. Le Dantec, révisée par Claude Pichois. Paris: *Bibliothèque de la Pléiade,* 1961.
―――. *Les paradis artificiels.* Éd. C. Pichois. Paris: Le Club du Meilleur Livre, 1961.
BELEVITCH-STANKEVITCH, H. *Le goût chinois en France au temps de Louis XIV.* Paris: Jouve et Cie, 1910.

BENSUSSAN, I. J. *L'opium: considérations générales; histoire; géographie; chimie; fabrication et usage de l'opium et études économiques, sociales, et législatives*. Paris: Viget, 1946.
BÉRENGUIER, F. *De l'opium des fumeurs*. Montpellier, 1883.
BETT, W. R. *The Infirmities of Genius*. London: C. Johnson, 1952.
———. "Poppies, Dawamesk and the Green Goddess: An Exotic Study of Literary Genius," *British Journal of Addiction*, XLIV (1947), 5-9.
BLIN, GEORGES. *Baudelaire*. Paris: Gallimard, 1939.
———. *Le sadisme de Baudelaire*. Paris: Conti, 1948.
BONAPARTE, MARIE. "La structure psychique d'Edgar Poe," *Hygiène Mentale*, XXVIII (1933), 184-190 and 193-201.
BONAVENTURA, F. A. "Drug Addiction," *Journal of the American Medical Association*, CXLII (1950), 1252.
BOPP, LÉON. *Psychologie des Fleurs du Mal*. Genève: Droz, 1964.
BORNECQUE, JACQUES-HENRY. "Rêves et réalités du symbolisme," *Revue des Sciences Humaines*, LXXVII (1955), 5-23.
BOSC, EUGENE. *Traité théorique et pratique du haschich et autres substances psychiques*. Paris: Chamuel, 1895.
BOTTA, P. E. *De l'usage de fumer l'opium*. Paris, 1829.
BRAGMAN, LOUIS J. "The Weed of Insanity," *Medical Journal and Record*, CXXII (October, 1925), 416-418.
BROMBERG, W. "Marihuana Intoxication," *American Journal of Psychiatry*, XCI (September, 1934), 303-333.
BROGUET, LOUIS. *L'âme du vin, choeur à quatre voix*. Lausanne: Foetisch, 1937.
BROTTEAUX, P. *Hachich; herbe de folie et de rêve*. Paris: Vega, 1934.
BROUARDEL, P. *Opium, morphine et cocaïne*. Paris, 1906.
BROWN, THORVALD T. *The Enigma of Drug Addiction*. Springfield, Ill.: C. C. Thomas, 1961.
BRUNETIERE, F. "Charles Baudelaire," *RDM*, juin, 1887.
BUVAT-COTTIN, AMÉLIE. *Considérations cliniques et thérapeutiques sur les toxicomanies*. Paris, 1936.
CABANES, A. *Autour de la vie de bohème*. Paris: Michel, 1938.
———. *Balzac ignoré*. Paris: A. Charles, 1899.
———. *Grands névropathes*. Paris: Michel, 1930-35.
———. "La mort de Baudelaire," *La chronique Médicale* (1902), pp. 725-735.
CAHAGNET, A. *The Sanctuary of Spiritualism*. Trans. by M. Flinders Pearson. London, 1851.
CALKINS, A. *Opium and the Opium Appetite*. Philadelphia, 1871.
———. "The Psychological Action of Opium," *The Journal of Psychological Medicine*, IV (1870), 351-367.
CARLSON, E. T., and SIMPSON, M. M. "Opium as a Tranquilizer," *American Journal of Psychiatry*, CXX (July-September, 1963), 112-117.
CASTEX, PIERRE-GEORGES. *Le conte fantastique en France de Nodier à Maupassant*. Paris: Librairie José Corti, 1951.
CASTIGLIONE, ARTURO. *Adventures of the Mind*. Trans. from Italian by V. Gianturco. New York: A. A. Knopf, 1946.
CAUME, P. "Causerie sur Baudelaire. Décadence et modernité," *Nouvelle Revue*, August, 1899.
CAUZONS, THOMAS DE. *La magie et la sorcellerie en France*. Paris: Librairie Dorbon-Ainé, 1910-1911.

CHAMBERS, FRANK M. "The Troubadours and the Assassins," *MLN*, LXIV (1949), 245-251.
CHEIN, ISIDOR, JERARD, DONALD L., LEE, R. S., and ROSENFELD, EVA. *The Road to H: Narcotics, Delinquency, and Social Policy.* New York: Basic Books, 1964.
CHÉRIX, R. B. *Commentaire des Fleurs du Mal de Charles Baudelaire.* Genève: Cailler, 1949.
CHEVALLIER, J. B. A. *Notice historique sur l'opium indigène.* Paris, 1852.
―――. *Du café, son historique, son usage, son utilité, ses altérations, ses succédanés, et ses falsifications.* Paris, 1862.
CHIARI, JOSEPH. *Realism and Imagination.* London: Barrie and Rockliff, 1960.
CLAPTON, G. T. *Baudelaire et De Quincey.* Paris: Société d'Édition "Les Belles Lettres," 1931.
COCHUT, A. "De la colonisation de l'Algérie," *RDM*, n. s., XVIII (1847), 249-286.
COHEN, SIDNEY. *Drugs of Hallucination.* London, 1965.
COLENO, A. *Les portes d'ivoire. Nerval, Baudelaire, Rimbaud, Mallarmé.* Paris: Plon, 1948.
COLLUM, ARTHUR B. "Tears of the Poppy," *Journal of the Kansas Medical Society*, LVIII (1957), 614-626.
CREIGHTON, C. "On Indications of the Hachish-Vice in the Old Testament," *Janus*, VIII (Amsterdam, 1903), 241; 297.
CRÉPET, J. "Les derniers jours de Charles Baudelaire," *NRF*, Nov., 1932.
DAGENS, J., and PICHOIS, C. "Variétés: Baudelaire, Alexandre Dumas et le haschisch," *MF*, CCCXXXI (1957), 357-364.
DAUDET, LÉON. "L'homme et le poison," *Les Œuvres Libres*, XXXIX (1925), 5-90.
DEFRÉMERY, M. C. "Documents sur l'histoire des Ismaéliens ou Batiniens de la Perse," *Journal Asiatique*, fifth series, XV (1860), 130-210.
DEMONTPORCELET, C. *De l'usage quotidien de l'opium: les mangeurs d'opium.* Paris, 1874.
DE QUINCEY, THOMAS. *The Collected Writings of Thomas De Quincey*, edited by David Masson, Vol. VIII. London, 1897.
DESCHANEL, ÉMILE. *Physiologie des écrivains et des artistes.* Paris: Librairie de L. Hachette et Cie, 1864.
DESOILLE, HENRI. "Croyances et états mentaux des occultistes actuels," *Hygiène Mentale*, XXV (Paris, 1930), 121-145.
DIDEROT, D. *Encyclopédie, ou dictionnaire raisonné des sciences, des arts et des métiers*, t. XI. Neufchastel: Samuel Faulche & Compagnie, 1765.
DIMOFF, PAUL. "Autour d'un projet de roman de Flaubert: *La Spirale*," *RHL*, XLVIII (1948), 309-335.
DÖRING, M. *'Akróama medico-philosophicum de opii usu.* Jenae, 1620.
DUBOIS, J. A. *Description of the Character, Manners, and Customs of the People of India; and of Their Institutions, Religious and Civil.* Trans. from the French manuscript. Philadelphia: M. Carey & Son, 1818.
DUMAS, ALEXANDRE. *Le Comte de Monte-Cristo.* Éd. Jacques-Henry Bornecque. Paris: Garnier Frères, 1956.
DUPOUY, R. "Le poète de l'opium: Charles Baudelaire," *Aesculape*, mai, 1912.
―――. *Les opiomanes, mangeurs, buveurs et fumeurs d'opium.* Paris, 1912.
EBIN, D. *The Drug Experience.* New York: Orion Press, Inc., 1961.

ELLIS, E. S. *Ancient Anodynes.* London: W Heinemann Medical Books, Ltd., 1946.
Encyclopedia Americana, The. "Opium." New York, Chicago: 1962.
ESQUIROL, E. *Des maladies mentales.* Paris, 1838.
ESQUIROS, ALPHONSE. "Maladies de l'esprit: de l'hallucination et des hallucinés," *RDM,* n. s., XII (1845), 292-325.
———. "Maladies de l'esprit: des idiots et des travaux récens sur l'idiotie," *RDM,* n. s. XVIII (1847), 287-316.
FABRICE, D. *L'opium à Paris.* Préface de Rouzier-Dorcières. Paris, 1914.
FAIRLIE, ALISON. *Baudelaire: Les Fleurs du Mal.* London: E. Arnold, 1960.
———. "Some Remarks on Baudelaire's *Poème du haschisch,*" *The French Mind. Studies in Honour of Gustave Rudler.* Oxford: Clarendon Press, 1952, pp. 291-317.
FERRAN, ANDRÉ. *L'esthétique de Baudelaire.* Paris: Hachette, 1933.
FIELDS, ALBERT. "The Story of Opium," *The Merck Report* (April, 1949), pp. 4-8.
FINCH, BERNARD. *Passport to Paradise...?* New York: Philosophical Library, 1960.
FISER, EMERIC. *Le symbole littéraire.* Paris: Corti, 1941.
FLEISCHHAUER, W. "The Old Man of the Mountain: The Growth of a Legend," *Symposium,* IX (1955), 79-90.
FONDANE, BENJAMIN. *Baudelaire et l'expérience du gouffre.* Paris: Seghers, 1947.
FRAENKEL, S. *Das Opium, dessen Physiographie, Geschichte, Bestandtheile, Pharmakodynamik, Anwendungsweise und Präparate.* Breslau, 1837.
FUMET, S. "Préface aux Paradis artificiels de Baudelaire," *Age nouveau,* n.° 19, 1948.
GAIDE. "Du sortilège de l'opium dans la littérature," *Mémoires de l'Académie de Vaucluse,* III, 3ième série, 1938.
GAULAY, URBAIN. *Sur les effets de l'opium.* Paris, 1808.
GAUTIER, THÉOPHILE. *Nouvelles.* Paris: Bibliothèque-Charpentier, 1923.
———. *Poésies complètes de Théophile Gautier.* 3 vols. Paris: Firmin-Didot, 1932.
———. *Romans et Contes.* Paris: Bibliothèque-Charpentier, 1923.
———. *Spirite.* Paris: Charpentier, 1904.
———. *Théâtre.* Paris: Bibliothèque-Charpentier, 1905.
———. *Un Trio de Romans.* Paris: Charpentier, n. d.
GENDREAU, CECIL. "Baudelaire et la médecine," *Montréal Médicale,* IX (1957), 9-11.
GOODMAN, L. S., and GILMAN, A. *The Pharmacological Basis of Therapeutics.* New York: Macmillan, 1955.
HAMMER, J. VON. *Histoire de l'ordre des Assassins.* Paris, 1833.
HASSAN EL NOUTY. "Le calife Hakem et Gérard de Nerval," *Revue du Caire,* XXI (September, 1958), 191-195.
HODGSON, MARSHALL G. S. *The Order of the Assassins: The Struggle of the Early Ismâ'îlîs Against the Islamic World.* The Hague: 1955.
HOSKINS, R. G. *The Biology of Schizophrenia.* London: Chapman and Hall, 1946.
HUBBLE, DOUGLAS. "Opium Addiction and English Literature," *Medical History,* I (1957), 323-335.
HUGHES, RANDOLPH. "Vers la contrée du rêve," *Mercure de France,* CCXCIII (juillet à août, 1939), 545-593.

BIBLIOGRAPHY

HUXLEY, A. *The Doors of Perception.* New York: Harper and Brothers, 1954.
HUYGHE, RENÉ. *Baudelaire.* Paris: Hachette, 1964.
ISBELL, H. "Medical Aspects of Opiate Addiction," *Bulletin of the New York Academy of Medicine,* XXXI (1955), 886-902.
JOINVILLE, JEAN, SIRE DE. *Histoire de Saint Louis.* Éd. Natalis de Wailly. Paris, 1921, pp. 189 ff.
JONES, J. *The Mysteries of Opium Revealed.* London, 1700.
KANE, H. H. "The Chinese Opium-Pipe as a Therapeutic Agent," *Medical Record,* XX (1881), 511-515.
KARR, ALPHONSE. *En fumant.* Paris: Michel Lévy frères, 1861.
———. *Le livre de bord.* Paris: Calmann Lévy, 1879-1880.
KOPP, ROBERT, et PICHOIS, CLAUDE. "Baudelaire et le haschisch, expérience et documentation," *Revue des Sciences Humaines,* No. 127 (juillet-septembre, 1967), 467-76.
LA FORGUE, DR. RENÉ. "Charles Baudelaire ou le génie devant la barrière névrotique," *Hygiène Mentale,* XXV (1930), 242-256.
LARGUIER, LÉO. *Théophile Gautier.* Paris: Société des éditions Louis-Michaud, n. d.
LA ROQUE, JEAN DE. *Voyage de l'Arabie heureuse.* Amsterdam: Chez Steenhouwer et Uytwerf. MDCCXVI.
LECLERC, H. "Origine et histoire du laudanum," *Bulletin des Sciences Pharmacologiques,* XXV (Paris, 1918), 228-233.
LEDOUBLE, A. "Balzac et l'occultisme," *La Chronique Médicale,* VIII (1901), 270 ff.
LEMONNIER, LÉON. *Edgar Poe et les conteurs français.* Paris: Aubier ("Éditions montaigne"), 1947.
LEUBA, J. H. *The Psychology of Religious Mysticism.* New York: Harcourt, Brace & Company, 1925.
LEWIN, L. *Phantastica — Narcotic and Stimulating Drugs.* New York: E. P. Dutton & Co., 1931.
LEWIS, B. "The Sources and History of the Syrian Assassins," *Speculum,* XXVII (1952), 475-489.
LINDESMITH, A. R. *The Addict and the Law.* Bloomington: Indiana University Press, 1965.
LITTLEFIELD, W. "De Musset and the English Opium Eater," *The Bookman,* XV (1902), 437-440.
MACHT, D. I. "The History of Opium and Some of Its Preparations and Alkaloids," *Journal of the American Medical Association,* February 6, 1915.
MAIGRON, LOUIS. *Le romantisme et les moeurs.* Paris: Honoré Champion, 1910.
MARKS, JEANNETTE. *Genius and Disaster.* New York: Adelphi Company, 1925.
MARTIN, E. *L'opium: ses abus: mangeurs et fumeurs d'opium; morphinomanes.* Paris, 1893.
MARTINO, PIERRE. *L'Orient dans la littérature française.* Paris: Hachette, 1906.
MEUNIER, R. *Le hachich; essai sur la psychologie des paradis éphémères: avec 3 planches hors texte.* 3e éd. Paris: Blond et Cie, 1909.
MICHAUT. "Comment est mort Baudelaire," *La Chronique Médicale,* 1902, pp.186-189.

MICHELET, JULES. *La sorcière*. Édition originale publiée avec notes et variantes par Lucien Refort. 2 vols. Paris: Marcel Didier, 1952.

MILLER, EMMANUEL. "The Effects of Alcoholism on Literary Imagination," *The British Journal of Addiction*, LVI (January, 1959), 67-70.

MITCHELL, S. WEIR. "The Effects of Anhalonium Lewinii," *British Medical Journal*, II (1896), 1625.

MOREAU, J. *Du haschisch et de l'aliénation mentale; études psychologiques*. Paris, 1845.

MOSSOP, D. J. *Baudelaire's Tragic Hero: A Study in the Architecture of Les Fleurs du Mal*. London: Oxford University Press, 1961.

MOUAT, F. J. *The Ethics of Opium and Alcohol*. London: Lancet, 1892. I, 959; II, 1090, 1152.

MUSSET, ALFRED DE. *Œuvres complètes*. Paris: Éditions du Seuil, 1963.

NADAR, F. *Charles Baudelaire intime. Le poète vierge*. Paris, 1911.

NERVAL, GÉRARD DE. *Œuvres de Gérard de Nerval*. Texte établi, présenté et annoté par Albert Béguin et Jean Richer, Vol. II. Paris: Bibliothèque de la Pléiade, 1961.

NOWELL, C. E. "The Old Man of the Mountain," *Speculum*, XXII (1947), 497-519.

OLSCHKI, LEONARDO. *Marco Polo's Asia*. Trans. by John A. Scott. Berkeley and Los Angeles: University of California Press, 1960.

OPIUM CONFERENCE. *First Opium Conference, Geneva*. Minutes & annexes. Genève: Imprimerie de la "Tribune de Genève," 1925.

OWENS, DAVID EDWARD. *British Opium Policy in China and India*. New Haven: Yale University Press, 1934.

PARISH, E. *Hallucinations and Illusions*. London: Walter Scott, Ltd., 1897.

PASCAL, E. "Un révélateur du subconscient," *Revue Métapsychique*, No. 1, 1930, pp. 53-75.

PELTIER, PAUL. "Musset et Baudelaire, à propos des *Confessions d'un mangeur d'opium*," *MF*, 16 décembre 1918, pp. 637-647.

PEZZI, GIUSEPPE. "Patologia e psicologia di Carlo Baudelaire," *Riforma Medica*, 71 (1957), 449-451.

PICHOIS, C. et DAGENS, J. "Baudelaire, Alexandre Dumas et le haschisch," *MF*, 331 (1957), 357-364.

POMMIER, JEAN. *Dans les chemins de Baudelaire*. Paris: Corti, 1945.

———. *La Mystique de Baudelaire*. Paris: Les Belles Lettres, 1932.

POULET, GEORGES. "Nerval et le cercle onirique," *Cahiers du Sud*, XLII, No. 331 (October, 1955), 347-363.

PULLAR-STRECKER, H. "A Review on the 1949/1950 Literature of Addiction," *British Journal of Addiction*, XLVIII (January to July 1951), 3-119.

REES, LINFORD. "The Influence of Drugs on Literary Imagination," *The British Journal of Addiction*, LVII (January, 1961).

RÉVEIL, PIERRE O. *Recherches sur l'opium. Des opiophages et des fumeurs d'opium*. Paris, 1856.

ROBINSON, VICTOR. *An Essay on Hasheesh*. New York, 1912.

RUFF, MARCEL. *Baudelaire, l'homme et l'œuvre*. Paris: Hatier-Boivin, 1956.

———. *L'Esprit du mal et l'esthétique baudelairienne*. Paris: Armand Colin, 1955.

SAILLET, MAURICE. *Sur la route de Narcisse*. Paris: Mercure de France, 1958.

SCALES, DEREK P. *Alphonse Karr; sa vie et son œuvre*. Genève: Droz, 1959.

SCHUR, EDWIN M. *Narcotic Addiction in Britain and America.* Bloomington, 1962.
SCHWARTZ, W. L. *The Imaginative Interpretation of the Far East in Modern French Literature.* Paris: Honoré Champion, 1927.
SCOURAS, PHOTIS. "Baudelaire toxicomane," *Hygiène Mentale,* XXV (Paris, 1930), 231-241.
SILVESTRE DE SACY. "Mémoire sur la dynastie des Assassins," *Mémoires de l'Académie des Inscriptions et Belles-Lettres,* IV, part 2, Paris, 1818.
SONNEDECKER, GLENN. "Emergence of the Concept of Opiate Addiction," *American Institute of the History of Pharmacy.* Madison, Wisconsin, 1962.
SONNERAT, PIERRE. *Voyages aux Indes Orientales et à la Chine.* Paris: L'Auteur, 1782.
SPOELBERCH DE LOVENJOUL, CHARLES. *Histoire des oeuvres de Théophile Gautier.* 2 vols. Paris. Charpentier, 1887.
SPRONCK, MAURICE. *Les artistes littéraires.* Paris, 1889.
STARKIE, ENID. *Baudelaire.* London: Faber and Faber, 1957.
SUE, EUGENE. *Atar-Gull.* Paris, 1958.
SULLY, JAMES. *Illusions: A Psychological Study.* New York: D. Appleton and Company, 1891.
SULTZBERGER, HENRY. *All about Opium.* London: Wertheimer, Lea & Co., 1884.
TABARANT, ADOLPHE. *La vie artistique au temps de Baudelaire.* Paris: Mercure de France, 1924.
TANCOIGNE, M. *A Narrative of a Journey into Persia.* Taken from the French. London: William Wright, attc'd to Embassy of General Gardane, 1820.
TAVERNIER, JEAN-BAPTISTE. *Travels in India.* Trans. from the original French edition of 1676 by V. Ball. Ed. by William Crooke. London: Oxford University Press, 1925.
TAYLOR, N. *Flight from Reality.* New York: Duell, Sloan & Pearce, 1949.
TERRY, C. E., and PELLENS, M. *The Opium Problem.* New York: 1928.
THALE, T., GABRIO, BEVERLY W., and SALOMON, K. "Hallucination and Imagery Induced by Mescaline," *American Journal of Psychiatry,* CVI (1950), 686-691.
TONDRIAU, JULIEN. *L'occultisme.* Viviers, Belgique: Éditions Gérard & Co., 1964.
VALLERY-RADOT, PIERRE. "Baudelaire: (médecine et médecins)," *Presse Médicale,* LXIV (1956), 517-518.
———. "Gérard de Nerval et la maison de santé du docteur Esprit Blanche (1796-1852)." *Presse Médicale,* LXIV (1956), 1963-1964.
———. "Un névropathe de génie: le mal de Baudelaire par lui-même (1821-1867) d'après sa correspondance avec sa mère," *Presse Médicale,* LXIV (1956), 919-920.
VIATTE, A. *Les sources occultes du romantisme.* 2 vols. Paris: Champion, 1928.
VINCHON, J. *L'art et la folie.* Paris: Stock, 1924.
VIVIER, ROBERT. *L'originalité de Charles Baudelaire.* Paris: La Renaissance du Livre, 1926.
Voyages du Chevalier Chardin en Perse, et autres lieux de l'Orient. Éd. par L. Langlès. Paris: Le Normant, imprimeur-libraire, 1811.
WALTON, R. P. *Marihuana, America's New Drug Problem.* Philadelphia: J. B. Lippincott Company, 1938.

WIKLER, A. *Opiate Addiction.* Springfield, Ill.: Thomas, 1953.
———. *Opiates and Opiate Antagonists.* Washington, D. C.: U. S. Department of Health, Education, and Welfare, Public Health Service, 1958.
———. *The Relation of Psychiatry to Pharmacology.* Baltimore: William & Wilkins, 1957.
WILKINSON, P. B. "Cannabis Indica: An Historical and Pharmacological Study of the Drug," *British Journal of Inebriety,* XXVII (1929), 72-80.
WILKS, S. "On the Vicissitudes of Opium," *British Medical Journal,* I (1891), 1218.
WRIGHT, A. D. "The History of Opium," *Transactions of the College of Physicians of Philadelphia,* XXIX (1961), 22-27.
WRIGHT, M. G. *The Role of the Auditive Sense in Baudelaire's Works.* Philadelphia, 1929.

INDEX

Abu-Bakr, 49 n.
Adam, Antoine, 164, 168, 187.
Africa, T. W., 39.
Aimeric de Peguilhan, 54, 55.
Alamût, 49 + n.
Albuquerque, Don Alfonso de, 40.
'Alî, 49 + n.
Allendy, R. F., 71.
Alpinus, Prosper, 48.
Ancelle, 133, 134, 135.
Anesthetic, 41.
Arnold von Lübeck, 53.
Asia, 19.
Assassins, 48-57; Continuation of legend in 17th century and later, 56-57; Creation of legend, 52; Derivation of word, 50 n; Growth and spread of Ismâ'îlîs, 49-51; Legend in Boccaccio, 56; Legend in La Fontaine, 56; Legend in Provençal poetry, 54-55; Life at Alamût, 51; Marco Polo's version, 53-54; Proclamation of Hasan II, 51; Relation to Knights Templar, 56 + n; Two stories of the legend, 52-53.
Assyrians, 34; Herbal, 34.
Aubert-Roche, Dr., 77.
Aupick, Mme, 132, 133, 134 + n, 140, 146 n.
Aurelius, Marcus, 39.
Averroës, 39.
Avicenna, 39.

Bactriana, 47.
Baluba Tribe, 45.
Balzac, Honoré de, 58 n, 65, 70, 71, 82 + n, 83, 86; "Le Dôme des Invalides," 84-86; *Massimilla Doni*, 69; "L'opium," 83-84; *La peau de chagrin*, 69; "Voyage de Paris à Java," 65.
Bangertus, Henricus, 56.
Barbey d'Aurevilly, 58 n.
Baudelaire, Charles, 58 n, 64, 69 n, 70, 77-78, 82, 86, 90, 107 n, 108 n, 127 ff.; Association of woman and opium, 136-137; Baudelaire's use of drugs, 131-135; *Les Fleurs du Mal*, 136 ff.; "Alchimie de la douleur," 174-176; "L'aube spirituelle," 167-168; "Le beau navire," 173 n; "La Beauté," 147-148; "La chambre double," 148, 155, 166 n, 169-170, 181-184, 192; "Le chat," 173 n; "Châtiment de l'orgueil," 145-146; "La chevelure," 153-155; "La destruction," 194-195; "Un Fantôme," 165-167; First six poems, 143-144; "Le flacon," 168-171; "La géante," 151 n; "L'harmonie du soir," 168 n; "Un hémisphère dans une chevelure," 155; "L'Horloge," 180-185; "Hymne à la Beauté," 148-152; "L'invitation au voyage," 173-174; "L'Irrémédiable," 176-180; "Au Lecteur," 139-143; "La Muse malade," 144-145; "Parfum exotique," 153; Poem XXIV, 155-156; Poem XXV, 156-157; "Le poison," 171-173; "Le Possédé," 163-164; "De profundis clamavi," 160-161; "Le rêve d'un curieux," 199; "Rêve parisien", 188-192; "Sed non satiata", 157-159; "Semper Eadem," 152 n; "Les Sept Vieillards," 185-187; "Le ser-

pent qui danse," 159-160; "Le Vampire," 161-163; "Le vin des amants," 193-194; "Le vin du solitaire," 193; "Le Voyage," 195-199; "Un voyage à Cythère," 143 n; *Fusées*, 132 n; *Juvenilia*, 131-132; *Les Paradis artificiels*, 127 ff.; Destruction of the will, 131-133 + ff.; Importance of drug experience, 128-131; Interest in the drug, 127-129; Man's blasphemy, 130 ff.; Satan's role, 129 ff.; "Richard Wagner et Tannhäuser à Paris," 144 n; Title and Dedication, 138-139; "Du travail et de l'inspiration," 131; "Du vin et du hachish," 131, 133 n, 134 n, 149 n, 159.
Belevitch-Stankevitch, H., 64.
Bendj, 47 n.
Bensussan, 20, 21.
Bérenguier, F., 23.
Bernard de Clairvaux, 56.
Bernart de Bondeilhs, 55.
Boccaccio, 44, 56.
Boe, Sylvius de la, 42.
Boissard, François, 58 n, 77.
Borysthenes, 47.
Bosc, Eugène, 71.
Botta, P. E., 22, 67.
Brotteaux, P., 63.
Brouardel, P., 21.
Brown, 19 n.

Cahagnet, Alphonse, 73-75, 104, 110 + n.
Caliph Hakem, 63, 114-120.
Canton, 40.
Caspian Sea, 49.
Cazotte, 164.
Celsus, 39.
Ceres, 36.
Chardin, 60-61.
Chaucer, 43-44.
China, 40-41, 46, 60.
Club of Hashish Takers, 77-78, 82.
Coffee, 61, 82 n.
Colet, Louise, 87.
Compagnie des Indes Orientales, 59.
Conrad de Montferrat, 52.
Creighton, C., 47 + n.
Crépet, Jacques, 68.

Crete, 47.
Crumpe, Samuel, 43.
Cybèle, 36.

Dante, 52.
Deffand, Mme du, 59.
Democritus, 47.
De Quincey, Thomas, 67-69, 71, 86, 102, 128; *Confessions of an English Opium-Eater*, 67-69, 128, 165 n, 176-179, 191.
Desoille, Henri, 72.
Dimoff, Paul, 86-90.
Dioscorides, 20, 39.
Döring, Doctor, 42, 48.
Dozon, Auguste, 131.
Dubois, 61.
Dumas, Alexandre, 58 n, 64, 82, 92-94, 96; *Le Comte de Monte-Cristo*, 92-95, 96.
Duval, Jeanne, 153-154, 161.

East India Company, 41.
Ebers Papyrus, 35.
Egypt, 20 n, 32, 34, 35.
Engstrom, A. G., 139 n.
Esquirol, E., 75.
Esquiros, Alphonse, 75, 96, 97, 98, 112, 118.
Europe, 19.
Ezekiel, 48 n.

Fabrice, D., 71.
Falconet, M., 57.
Far East, See Orient.
Fâtimid dynasty, 50 ff.
Flaubert, Gustave, 65, 86-90; *La Spirale*, 86-90.
Frederick II, 52.

Galen, 35, 39, 47.
Galland, 61; *Mille et une nuits*, 61-63, 92, 108.
Gastinel, 86.
Gautier, Théophile, 28, 58 n, 64, 69, 70, 72, 77, 82, 95-114, 126, 128, 138, 152 n, 160; *Albertus*, 102; *Avatar*, 97-99; "Club des Hachichins," 95, 101; Club of hashish takers, 77-78; *Fortunio*, 103 n; "Le hachich," 95, 99-101; His interest in drugs, 95-96; Jettatura, 98 n; "La mille et deuxième nuit," 104,

INDEX

106-109; "La morte amoureuse," 99; "La négresse et le pacha," 103 n; "La Péri," 104-106 + n, 126; "Le pied de momie," 111-114; "La pipe d'opium," 95, 96-97, 99 + n, 100 n, 112, 118; *Poésies nouvelles*, 102-103; *Spirite*, 99, 109-111.
Gérard de Nerval, 58 n, 63, 64, 69, 70, 82, 90, 104, 105, 114-120; *Histoire du Calife Hakem*, 114-120.
Germany, 20.
Girardin, Mme de, 72.
Giraut de Bornelh, 55.
Grandville, 58 n.
Guillaume de Tyre, 50 n.

Haider, 46.
Hammer, J. von, 57.
Hanska, Mme, 83.
Hasan-i Sabbâh, 49 ff.
Hasan II, 51.
Hashish, 27 ff.; Aphrodisiac, 33; Artistic creation, 77-80; Bhang, 27-28; Cannabis, 27; Dawamesc, 28; Description of plant, 27; Etymology, 27 n; Euphoria, 30; Experiment with insanity, 76-79; Feeling of duality, 31; Ganja, 28; General use in literature, 80; Habituation, 29; Hallucinations, 32-33; History, 44 ff.; In medicine, 29; Middle Ages, 48-49 ff.; Names and preparations, 27-28; Physical effects, 30; Religious use, 45; Renaissance, 43 ff.; Synaesthesia, 79-80; Time and space perception, 31-32; Tolerance, 29; Use to reach the Beyond, 73-75; Water pipe, 29.
Helen, 36, 47 n.
Herbelot, 56.
Hermes Trismegistus, 35, 175.
Herodotus, 45.
Hippocrates, 38.
Homer, 36, 47 n.
Hôtel Pimodan, 75, 77, 78, 102, 114.
Hughes, Randolph, 69, 102.
Hulagu Kahn, 54 n.
Hul Gil, 34, 35.
Huysmans, J. K., 69 n.

India, 20, 60.
Isbell, Harris, 25.
Ismâ'îlîs, 49 ff.
Islâm, 49 ff.

Jarry, Alfred, 69 n.
Joinville, 64.
Jonathon, 48 n.
Jones, John, 23, 41 n, 43.

Karr, Alphonse, 58 n, 96, 101 n.
Kassai Tribe, 45.
Kermel, Amédée, 66.
Knights Templar, 55-56.

Labey de Batilly, Denis, 56.
La Fontaine, Jean de, 56.
Lamartine, Alphonse de, 58 n, 121.
Lane, E. W., 47 n.
Largus, Scribonius, 39.
La Roque, 61; *Voyage de l'Arabie heureuse*, 61.
Leclerc, 21 n.
Louis XIV, 59.
Lucca, Hugo de, 41.
Lucian, 37-38.

Magi, 47.
Maimonides, 39.
Marco Polo, 53-54, 94.
Marseille, 20.
Martino, P., 62.
Mezzrow, Mezz, 30-31.
Michelet, Jules, 71.
Midas, 175-176.
Mille et une nuits, 61-63, 92, 108.
Mohammed, 49 ff.
Moreau, Hégésippe, 58 n.
Moreau de Tours, Jean, 28, 64, 76-79, 114; Use of hashish in psychological experimentation, 76-79.
Mount Libanus, 47.
Muleete, 49 n.
Murger, H., 58 n.
Musset, Alfred, 58 n; *L'Anglais mangeur d'opium*, 67-69, 83.
Mysticism, 45-46.

Napoleon, 63.
Nepenthès, 36-37, 46 + n.
Nodier, C., 58 n.
Nowell, C. E., 56 n.

Odyssey, 36, 46 + n.
Old Man of the Mountain, 48-57, 92, 93 + n, 94, 120 n, 167 n.
Old Testament, 35, 48 n.
Oman, J. Campbell, 45.
Opium, 19 ff.; Abstinence syndrome, 24-25; Addiction, 23-25; Consumption, 20-22; English Blackdrop, 21; Euphoria, 26-27; European Middle Ages, 39 ff.; Extraction and preparation, 19-20; Greek mythology, 36-38; Greek medicine, 38-39; Habituation, 24; History, 34 ff.; Hygiene, 25-26; Mesopotamia, 34-35; Method of smoking, 22-23; Old Testament, 35; Pipe, 22-23; Poppy, 19 ff.; Reasons for taking drug, 26-27; Studies (1500-1850), 58; where grown, 19.
Opium wars, 41.
Orient, 40-41; As stimulus to 19th century interest in drugs, 58 ff.; Napoleon's campaign, 63; Travel literature, 60-61.
Ovid, 37.

Papaver, See Poppy under Opium.
Paracelsus, 20, 21, 42, 71.
Persia, 20 n, 47, 60.
Philip Augustus, 54 n.
Pliny, 39, 47.
Pluto, 36.
Polydamna, 46 n.
Poppy, See Opium.
Portuguese, 40.
Princess Nsykhounsu, 35.
Puycoussin, Edouard, 90; "La nuit du 31 décembre," 90-92.

Queen Tausrit, 35.

Rh-Yh, 45.
Richard Cœur de Lion, 52, 54 n.
Robinson, V., 27-28, 31, 33, 46.

Rousseau, Abbé, 21 + n.

Sabatier, Mme, 134.
Saillet, Maurice, 69 + n.
Sargon II, 34 n.
Satan, 129 ff.
Scarron, Paul, 64-65.
Scythians, 45.
Seljuk Turks, 50 ff.
Sertürner, 43.
Shakespeare, William, 44.
Shî'a, 49 ff.
Silvestre de Sacy, 57, 63.
Sind, 40.
Sonnerat, 63.
Soto, Charles, 68.
Stanislas de Guaita, 71.
Sue, Eugène, 58 n, 82, 104, 120-126; *Atar-Gull,* 121-126.
Sunnî, 49 ff.
Susa, 47.
Sydenham, Thomas, 21, 42.
Synaesthesia, 79-80, 100.
Syria, 47.

Tchaikovsky, P. I., 31.
Tea, 61, 66.
Telemachus, 36.
Theangelis, 47.
Theophrastus, 38.
Thompson, 34.
Thoth, 35.
True History, 37-38.
Turkey, 20 n.

Valéry, Paul, 31.
Van Helmont, 42.
Van Linschoten, 40.
Vergil, 37.
Vishnu, 61.

Wedelius, p. 22.
Wikler, A., 24.
World Health Organization, 23.

Zeus, 46 n.

www.ingramcontent.com/pod-product-compliance
Lightning Source LLC
Chambersburg PA
CBHW022020220426
43663CB00007B/1149